Black and Blue TV

Black and Blue TV

Industry Responses to the Black Lives Matter Movement

LAURENA BERNABO

Rutgers University Press
New Brunswick, Camden, and Newark, New Jersey
London

Rutgers University Press is a department of Rutgers, The State University of New Jersey, one of the leading public research universities in the nation. By publishing worldwide, it furthers the University's mission of dedication to excellence in teaching, scholarship, research, and clinical care.

Library of Congress Cataloging-in-Publication Data

Names: Bernabo, Laurena author
Title: Black and blue TV : industry responses to the Black Lives Matter movement / Laurena Bernabo.
Description: New Brunswick, New Jersey : Rutgers University Press, 2026. | Includes bibliographical references and index.
Identifiers: LCCN 2025026472 | ISBN 9781978844117 paperback | ISBN 9781978844124 hardcover
Subjects: LCSH: Police on television | Television broadcasting—Social aspects | Black lives matter movement | Race relations on television | Television cop shows—History and criticism | Violence on television | LCGFT: Television criticism and reviews
Classification: LCC PN1992.8.P583 B47 2026 | DDC 791.45/6556—dc23/eng/20250624
LC record available at https://lccn.loc.gov/2025026472

A British Cataloging-in-Publication record for this book is available from the British Library.

∞ The paper used in this publication meets the requirements of the American National Standard for Information Sciences—Permanence of Paper for Printed Library Materials, ANSI Z39.48-1992.

rutgersuniversitypress.org

For everyone who deserved better

Contents

Black and Blue TV

Introduction

When seventeen-year-old Trayvon Martin was killed by an armed civilian in 2012, it was not the first time an innocent Black life had been taken. However, the acquittal of his killer, George Zimmerman, lit a spark that turned into the Black Lives Matter (BLM) movement when activist Alicia Garza responded to this news by posting "#BlackLivesMatter" on Facebook. Garza, along with Patrisse Cullors and Opal Tometi, then started the organization Black Lives Matter with a mission "to eradicate white supremacy and build local power to intervene in violence inflicted on Black communities by the state and vigilantes."[1] Black Lives Matter quickly grew into a movement, fueled in large part by the viral #BlackLivesMatter hashtag on Twitter as well as continued police violence against Black communities and killings of unarmed Black people. One prominent example is Eric Garner, a forty-three-year-old man who was killed in 2014 by an illegal chokehold by NYPD officer Daniel Pantaleo and whose slow death was recorded, capturing eleven separate utterances of "I can't breathe." Then, after eighteen-year-old Michael Brown was killed by officer Darren Wilson in 2014, civil unrest erupted in Ferguson, Missouri. In the following years, hundreds of other Black men and women were killed by police, and the Black Lives Matter movement became part of the cultural tapestry of the United States.

Then came 2020. On March 13, 2020, Breonna Taylor was shot eight times after police entered her apartment using a no-knock warrant. Two months later, in the midst of a global pandemic, two viral videos were recorded on May 25, 2020. One showed a white woman named Amy Cooper calling 911 to falsely claim that a Black man was threatening her, and the other showed Minneapolis police officer Derek Chauvin calmly killing George Floyd by kneeling on the unarmed man's neck for eight minutes and forty-six seconds while three fellow officers stood nearby.[2] These videos drew attention to the ways that whiteness is weaponized, as well as the nonchalance with which some police officers are able to operate, even when taking a life. Protests erupted not just in Minnesota but in every state and in over sixty countries around the world, spanning all seven continents. In the three months following Mr. Floyd's death, roughly eight thousand #BlackLivesMatter protests were documented throughout the United States, nearly 95 percent of them peaceful.[3] Peaceful protests were not always met with a peaceful police response, however. While some officers joined marches, took a knee, or attended community meetings on reform, others were recorded violently assaulting protestors, and data shows they "disproportionately used force in demonstrations associated with the BLM movement, relative to other types of demonstrations."[4] Police demonstrations of force ranged from tear gas and pepper spray to rubber bullets and beatings with batons, and such demonstrations were present in more than half of the protests at which authorities were present. In New York City, one officer drove his patrol car into a crowd of protestors while another removed a protester's COVID-19 mask to pepper spray his face.[5] Amid protests against police brutality and the subsequent displays of more of the same, police procedurals came under fire for their role in the valorization of police—especially those who break the rules. While the Black Lives Matter movement is not solely about how police treat Black people in America, police certainly play a key role in contemporary discourses surrounding systemic racism, and the 2020 protests led to more scathing criticisms of police representations in media than ever before.

Police, detectives, and other crime fighters have been staples of U.S. entertainment since the birth of television. A prominent early example is *Dragnet*, a show about an LAPD detective that first aired on the NBC radio network from 1949 and shifted to NBC's television network in 1951. Though there were ebbs and flows in police procedurals' popularity, crime drama franchises started to develop in earnest in the 1990s with Dick Wolf's *Law & Order*, which went on to spur a large and successful franchise. *CSI*, *NCIS*, and *Chicago* franchises followed in the wake. From 2010 to 2020, there were anywhere from eighteen to twenty-nine crime shows on television, comprising between 19 percent and 28.7 percent of all scripted shows.[6] Nielsen ratings consistently show crime dramas to be highly rated, making up between three and eight of the top ten most popular scripted series during this same time frame.[7] Many scholars have found evidence that mass media texts like police procedurals play a key role in how most people develop their knowledge and perceptions of the police.[8]

Cop shows have demonstrated varying degrees of interest in engaging issues of systemic racism and police violence, including racist policing practices. Some programs, such as *NYPD Blue*, depicted officers who held racist views and used excessive force, but those perspectives and behaviors were often held up as problematic. In other cases, problematic policing practices were left unchallenged; in a report on representations of policing, activist group Color of Change found that police programs rarely show police being held accountable for violating civil liberties or using excessive force.[9] In a country where Black people are 2.9 times more likely to be killed by police than white people, this lack of accountability for officers across police dramas raises red flags.[10] Because television can influence how audiences perceive the world around them, this pattern of police series avoiding topics like systemic racism and police brutality and condoning civil rights violations proved difficult, if not impossible, with the rise of the Black Lives Matter movement. Within this cultural context, certain slayings, including Michael Brown and George Floyd, have become pressure points that encourage television's cultural forum foray into social activism.

Though police misconduct and racism might have occasionally served as plot points in prime-time programs, such themes took on a different flavor after Trayvon Martin's death. *Law & Order: SVU*'s October 2013 episode "American Tragedy," in the classic "ripped from the headlines" approach so popular among Dick Wolf productions, integrated elements of Trayvon's death with news reports of celebrity chef Paula Deen's racism. In January 2015, *The Good Wife* aired "The Debate," an episode with strong ties to Eric Garner's death, and *Scandal*'s March 2015 episode "The Lawn Chair" was inspired by the death of Michael Brown. Other shows, including *Chicago P.D.* and *black-ish*, engaged these themes in more general terms by having characters—a main character with a guest character in the former, the entire cast in the latter—discuss race and policing in the United States in a "very special episode." Against this new baseline, entertainment television's engagement with the growing Black Lives Matter movement escalated considerably after the pressure point of 2020 protests and allegations that police shows had contributed to "copaganda."

American police procedurals have long participated in a practice of "copaganda," wherein stories promote supportive images of police and undermine efforts at systemic reform.[11] This tendency toward "police fetishism" produces a media imaginary in which police protagonists are a "necessary evil," however admirably or unflatteringly they are depicted.[12] Notably, law enforcement characters have presented a broad spectrum of representations, good and bad, but they are consistently "burdened with the responsibilities of ever-watching guardianship, the bearers of legitimate force."[13] Like policing itself, the status quo of American police procedurals overlooking or even glorifying bad cops came under scrutiny in 2020.[14] Journalists note that the "tenor of the current conversation around racism and police brutality has undergone a tectonic shift" in how television addresses these issues.[15] Amid growing concerns about the ideological implications of how police are represented, the popular and long-running series *COPS* was canceled after 33 seasons,[16] as was A&E's recent hit *Live PD*.[17] Preparing for its final season, the producers of police comedy *Brooklyn Nine-Nine* scrapped scripts for four upcoming episodes to focus on racist policing, a topic it had rarely examined in its first seven seasons. American police procedurals, a genre known for highlighting police practices and endeavoring to accurately reflect law-enforcement agencies for better or worse,[18] were all but forced to grapple with the current state of U.S. policing.

Set against this backdrop of evolving industrial discourses, *Black and Blue TV* explores a broadcast television production culture that preceded, faced criticism from, and changed with the Black Lives Matter movement. I do not simply examine the cultural forum of scripted television shows that engaged issues of systemic racism and policing but contextualize this forum within the particular production cultures and contexts that formed and shaped it. My interest is in the production culture of scripted prime-time broadcast programming and the ways showrunners, writers, producers, actors, and other media professionals understand their roles and civic obligations in relation to the BLM movement and activism. Drawing on conversations I had with more than thirty media professionals and activists, I illustrate production as a site of struggle in which individuals grapple with issues of power, privilege, and equality under increasingly intense public scrutiny. This tension becomes clear in the ways different kinds of showrunners oversee different kinds of writers' rooms, which in turn incorporate different degrees and flavors of activist engagement. I account for factors that might influence production choices, including employment data, activist efforts, and police consultants, though I emphasize the above-the-line creatives who set and execute a plan for mediating the BLM movement and its numerous concerns about race in America.

As I demonstrate, broadcast television production cultures both mediate and are mediated by the national crises that occur around them. In the context of the Black Lives Matter movement, my focus on the intersection of activists and creatives—some of whom double as activists—illustrates the complex, contested, and material ways that the television industry negotiates cultural shifts. Growing concerns about representations of police and policing on television suggest that there are numerous social and pragmatic benefits to reforming television representations, but such reform is neither simple nor easy. *Black and Blue TV* argues that the BLM movement has fueled real conversations about and changes in representations of policing, but that television's function as a cultural forum continues to constrain entertainment programming's ability to embrace and promote social justice; comedies and dramas, particularly cop shows, are willing (to varying degrees) to raise questions and host conversations about police brutality and racial justice, but on the whole, entertainment television pulls its punches when it comes to its activist potential. This book sheds light on some of the dynamics that impede progress, including reticent showrunners, overwhelmingly white writers' rooms, and networks and studios that are eager to avoid bad PR but ultimately fail to make good on their promises.

My analysis includes scripted programs and media professionals from a range of genres, but my emphasis tends toward police procedurals; though television's engagement with the BLM movement is not limited to police shows, the genre's focus on people working in law enforcement inherently creates more opportunity to engage in BLM's central themes, and their use of police as protagonists inherently creates narrative tension when U.S. policing comes under fire. While other dramatic subgenres—crime shows, law shows, medical shows, and firefighter shows—tend to feature police, their focus is not on the police but on the criminals, lawyers, doctors, and firefighters, and any police involved are perhaps less likely to be presented favorably. Other genres, including sitcoms, have also incorporated the BLM movement into their narratives, though less frequently by virtue of their generic focus on lighthearted fare. Regardless of genre, my analysis is limited to scripted, live-action U.S. programs that present a fictionalized representation of police and policing through realistic interactions in the current era; unscripted and animated content, as well as programs with supernatural elements and caped crusaders, and programs set in previous decades, are outside the scope of my study.

Additionally, I limit my study to prime-time broadcast programming, which, even as streaming networks have grown in both number and size, continues to draw the largest audiences. This is not to say that streaming and cable content do not participate in BLM's cultural forum, and future scholarship can pursue this area of investigation, but my focus on broadcast content emphasizes the most widely available content. In the post–network television landscape of niche audiences, broadcast series often attract larger and broader audiences than cable or streaming series, and their audience is often expanded when they are made available on streamers subsequent to their original airing. Moreover, broadcast series are subject to Federal Communications Commission (FCC) oversight, which places some constraints on writers' creative freedom and has historically been understood to consider the wishes of their broadcast networks' advertisers; advertisers may have opinions on if and how a series addresses Black Lives Matter and typically do not want to be caught on the wrong side of history.

By weaving together critical analysis of televisual texts with insights gathered from interviews with the creatives, executives, and other individuals who make decisions about content, I'm able to chart how television writers and producers, as well as activists, mediated civil unrest for the public. I ask, what motivated writers and producers to engage issues of systemic racism and police misconduct in the ways they did? Why, and how, were some series able to limit or altogether avoid these topics? How did development and production practices change with the increased scrutiny faced by crime dramas, and what responses did network executives offer? This book pulls from interviews with television writers, producers, and others, as well as activist groups, the television shows themselves, and reports on television's representations.

Systemic Racism and/in Television

It is not terribly difficult to draw connections between systemic racism and television programs, particularly police procedurals. Numerous scholars have explored this connection, though the focus has tended toward explorations of how police racism is depicted or condoned, and arguments about the relationship between police representations and public perceptions of policing, with implications for public perceptions of Black people and Black communities. Little has been done to go behind the camera and shed light on the production of such images and the people involved. As Aoun notes, traditional media are historically "disinclined to acknowledge their own roles in maintaining structural racism through their representations of reality."[19] Aoun uses this to explain why news organizations, many of which promoted and legitimized BLM protestors and their cause, grew less sympathetic over time and reverted to their biased status quo. There are certainly some cases of crime dramas and other television programs for which this holds true, but for others, the 2020 protests marked a notable shift and a redirecting of creative energies.

While it is not the job of television writers and producers to solve cultural crises, crime dramas function within a televisual landscape that invites viewers to consider the role of policing in a democratic society, and their engagement with such crises provides valuable insight into the role of television in society. Historically, social research into U.S. attitudes toward crime fighting has revealed that Americans prefer that the government endorse police freedom and tough crime-fighting measures rather than pouring money into the social causes of crimes, which might prevent such crimes from occurring in the first place.[20] This approach—solving crimes rather than preventing them—has been a staple of police procedurals. Shows like *Hill Street Blues* and others that followed have strongly suggested that the police are incapable of repairing social ills and are instead relegated to maintaining social order at best.[21] Bowling, Reiner, and Sheptycki (2019) note that "American fictional police heroes have often been consciously modelled on 'real life' people, their careful crafting suggesting some behind the scenes awareness concerning the ideological importance of the police imaginary beyond merely making commercially successful shows."[22] Additionally, Reiner finds some evidence that "the media's representation of policing feeds back into policing practice."[23] Thus, though television writers and producers do not necessarily intend to affect policing practices, they may occasionally have some form of impact, and so an understanding of how writers, producers, and other executives view their roles and obligations is a central conceit of this project.

FROM HASHTAG TO MOVEMENT: BLACK LIVES MATTER

Though Black Lives Matter is just one organization dedicated to protecting racial minorities from violence, the Twitter hashtag #BlackLivesMatter helped to give a name to, and coalesce energy around, a movement. Twitter's #BlackLivesMatter offered Twitter users a succinct way to signal to each other their shared concern, serving as a metadiscoursal convention.[24] In turn, Twitter's trending records gave elevated visibility to the amount of conversation surrounding such concerns, amplifying both individual voices and collective opinions.[25] #BlackLivesMatter was first tweeted on July 13, 2013, and was slow to gain momentum: Nearly a year later the hashtag appeared in just 48 publicly available tweets in June of 2014 and 398 the following month, but Michael Brown's death and the subsequent protests—and the police's violent response to those protests—led to 52,288 tweets featuring the hashtag in August.[26] #BlackLivesMatter thus became a rallying cry that transcended Twitter to be used in offline conversations and throughout news programming, often referred to as the #BlackLivesMatter movement. I therefore use the term Black Lives Matter as a concise umbrella term to articulate a movement that recognizes the unique forms of violence committed against Black communities and the need to fight against that violence, particularly when committed by the state, often through policing.

Elizabeth Day provides a concise summary of how Alicia Garza, Patrisse Cullors, and Opal Tometi (see Figure 0.1) came to create first the hashtag

FIG. 0.1. The Black Lives Matter creators Alicia Garza, Patrisse Cullors, and Opal Tometi discuss the movement in a TED talk (2016).

#BlackLivesMatter and then the official organization.[27] According to Day, Garza had a young brother who resembled Trayvon Martin, and she could easily imagine him becoming a victim of a hate crime. George Zimmerman's 2013 acquittal struck a chord with her; she realized that day that Black people carried with them every day the twin burdens of racism and white supremacy, and that the Zimmerman verdict spoke to how dangerous it is for Black people in America. Garza took to Facebook with a post stating "Our lives matter," and Cullors, her friend, reposted Garza's words on Twitter with the hashtag #BlackLivesMatter, leading the two to discuss organizing a campaign around these sentiments. Garza and Cullors then reached out to Tometi, an activist with whom they were acquainted, and what started as a hashtag became an organization with dozens of chapters across the United States, the United Kingdom, and Canada. When Michael Brown was killed in 2014, Garza felt reinvigorated and organized a "freedom ride" to Ferguson. Garza's activism snowballed into a movement mobilized through the force of social media, linking disparate events to show a pattern of violence against Black people in America. Day writes, "It was a perfect example of new civil rights activism: online pressure brought to bear on a single potent issue with high visibility."

The killings of unarmed Black people in the twenty-first century and the subsequent protests that ignited around the world were not altogether new but rather a progression of the United States' policing system, one that faces increasing scrutiny and calls for change. What was in fact new was what was possible with the proliferation of smartphones and social media. These two technological developments facilitated citizens' ability to document and distribute evidence of police misconduct.[28] Footage from 2020 protests showed evidence that "citizens exercising their lawful right to assemble and protest police brutality were themselves being subjected to widespread instances of police brutality."[29] The ability to document and disseminate evidence of police brutality has contributed to more continuous public outrage and calls for reform.[30] The 2020 protests swept the world, reaching even Antarctica.

Prior to the Black Lives Matter movement, information about police brutality was novel and uninformed. As Zimring explains, the Bureau of Justice Statistics did not begin to gather data on police killings until the 2000s, and their findings were imprecise due in large part to limited cooperation from the roughly eighteen thousand U.S. law enforcement agencies.[31] As for consequences for officers who kill civilians, the Bureau of Justice Statistics estimates that just one in two hundred police officers is indicted for killing a civilian, and only one in one thousand is convicted. Zimring attributes this to district attorneys' hesitance to prosecute the police officers with whom they often work, and jurors' and judges' tendency to believe officers over civilian survivors.[32] The Black Lives Matter movement has been key in increased reporting of police-related civilian deaths (PRCD) and thus more reliable data, including the finding that "departments preventing homicide also tend to minimize the use of deadly force against civilians."[33]

While the hashtag #BlackLivesMatter began as a call to action, it became one of many tributaries in a river promoting change. As the movement grew, others found ways to shine a light on problems with police brutality. Samual Sinyangwe, a Stanford-educated data scientist and policy analyst, recognized the absence of—and need for—comprehensive data on police shootings that would allow for solution-driven conversations.[34] Sinyangwe worked with others to create the organization Mapping Police Violence, the purpose of which was to present comprehensive statistical data on police killings across the United States, particularly where the victims were Black. By sourcing data from three large crowdsourced databases and comparing that data with social media, newspapers, and police reports, Mapping Police Violence was able to determine the race of 91 percent of all victims. For the year 2014, in which Eric Garner, Michael Brown, and Tamir Rice were all killed, Mapping Police Violence determined that 26 percent of the more than 1,149 people killed by police were Black, more than a hundred of them unarmed when they were killed.

A central thrust of the Black Lives Matter movement has been to change policing practices that result in the deaths of Black people, and various studies propose particular changes. In their study of police departments in major U.S. cities, Bearfield, Maranto, and Wolf advocate for police professionalism, which they argue will reduce both homicides and PRCD, two areas in which African Americans are victims at disproportionately high rates.[35] In 2015 alone there were roughly 986 PRCD, and though Black people made up 13.2 percent of the U.S. population, they made up 26.2 percent of PRCD and 40.9 percent of unarmed PRCD that year. High-profile examples of PRCD with Black victims, including Michael Brown, Eric Garner, George Floyd, and Breonna Taylor, have "shaped narratives regarding police-related deaths"[36] and led to protests as well as calls for police reform, all under the banner of the Black Lives Matter movement.[37] As Bearfield et al. explain, police professionalism correlates with training and restraint, and dramatic changes in the police departments in New York City and Miami have demonstrably improved police performance, leading to decreased crime rates and fewer avoidable deaths. After new rules limiting the use of force were implemented in New York City, the NYPD's rates of shooting and killing civilians dropped far below the national average, and crime rates decreased considerably. In addition to these new rules, many attribute these successes to more systemic deployment of officers, improved national recruitment, and stronger training, as well as holding precinct commanders accountable for crime in the areas they oversee.

THE RISE OF THE AMERICAN COP SHOW

Cop shows serve a valuable purpose in U.S. culture, functioning as morality plays in which police defend and protect the community they serve.[38] Arntfield describes cop shows as interactive public documents, serving up evidence of our collective values and mirroring public sentiments regarding various social issues.[39] Cop shows also "tell us about our attitudes to crime, and hence what we think about the 'social contract' that exists between state and citizen."[40] They do this by ingesting cultural elements and presenting them to viewers through narratives.[41] As a genre, police series continuously reestablish the need to eliminate wrongdoing in the name of protecting the social order,[42] but it is not a black-and-white issue of good cops and bad villains. Instead, the police genre creates a space to address the complexities of modern policing and explores how the genre constitutes a dialogue about crime.[43] Mediated images of policing are thus important for reasons of transparency and accountability, as they provide information to a public that must consent to being policed in order for the police institution to maintain its authority.[44]

Though television's police may not be perfect or flawless, they nevertheless stand as protectors and are generally sympathetic characters engaged in Sisyphean struggles to maintain social order and are thus the "good guys."[45] As early as the 1950s, television's police were found to be prevalent, making up 17 percent of television characters, although, notably, rarely portrayed by nonwhite actors.[46] One early radio-turned-television cop show was *Dragnet* (NBC, 1951–1959), created by and starring Jack Webb. In his desire to tell authentic stories about police, Webb befriended LAPD chief William Parker and accepted "stringent censorship from the police department in exchange for story ideas, logistical help and a patina of truth."[47] LAPD's Public Information Division was granted the right to approve scripts and cut storylines, and Webb was granted access to shooting locations, the use of police equipment, and ideas and stories for scripts. Of course, *Dragnet* was, "by design, misleading about the harshest realities of the law enforcement agencies" it portrayed,[48] as shootings were all "squeaky clean" and committed by remorseful officers who were often forgiven by the families of the people they had killed.[49] Alyssa Rosenberg identifies the early 1970s as a turning point in which popular culture "began taking its inspiration not from the heads of law enforcement agencies, but from individual cops—men who believed policing was important work but also recognized the toll it took on individual officers."[50] This coincided with a growing tendency to depict "officers emotionally debilitated by fatal shootings . . . not as principled, but as weak," and the law as "an obstacle to justice rather than the mechanism facilitating it."

By the time Dirty Harry was introduced to moviegoers in 1971, television viewers had already begun to see a darker side of policing. As early as 1967, rates of violence among police characters began to climb, with few instances of reprisal.[51] In a study of 1972 programming, Dominick found that 72 percent of criminals were shown to be the victims of violence at the hands of police, while also noting that law enforcement characters "were also pictured as being basically honest and law-abiding . . . and only 2 per cent were shown as villains."[52] Historical analyses of television's police demonstrate that they are often professional heroes,[53] but that negative representations of police are also ubiquitous.[54] Following on the heels of Dirty Harry, "an enduring motif [of] a dirty cop on the side of right,"[55] the 1970s presented the trope of the maverick cop who bucks the system, sacrificing procedure in the name of the greater good.[56] Cop shows might have depicted violence, but they legitimized it in different ways. One was the depiction of an increasingly rough environment in which policing occurred, thus warranting the massive increase in use of force by police.[57] Another way police brutality was narratively condoned was by virtue of who it was directed at, namely people perceived to be deviants or villains;[58] this was facilitated in the 1970s by the turn to more serious crimes,[59] making it easier to justify or condone police officers' abuse of a suspect.

As the years wore on, the cop genre positioned officers' deficiencies and personal demons against the backdrop of a case-of-the-week structure,[60] and in 1980 *Hill Street Blues* created a space for openly addressing "the agonies and frustrations of modern-day policing—the real human frailty beneath the guise of heroic toughness."[61] Nichols-Pethick marks *Hill Street Blues* as the beginning of a "cycle of 'quality' police dramas" that carried into the twenty-first century.[62] Programs in this cycle include *Homicide: Life on the Street*, *Cagney and Lacey*, *Law & Order*, *NYPD Blue*, *The Shield*, and *The Wire*. Such series feature ensemble casts, antihero cops, and gritty realism, and are marked by "complex characters who are often haunted by their pasts or by the ethical dilemmas of policing, and who have changed over time" (7). Programs including *NYPD Blue* and *The Shield* demonstrated the contradictory nature of policing through characters who ranged from problematic to reprehensible.[63] Such characters might be shown to have prejudices against Black citizens and/or a willingness to break laws, either to benefit themselves or as a form of vigilantism. Reiner attributes the increasing complexity of representations and ambiguity of officers' morality to "a demystification of authority and law" and a reconceptualization of policing from sacred to flawed.[64]

In later years, other series, including the *CSI* and *NCIS* franchises, took a more traditional approach to the crime drama genre than their "quality" counterparts. They did this by employing either the "swift justice" model of capturing a known villain or the "whodunit" model of identifying an unknown criminal.[65] While they shared quality programs' tendency toward multiracial casts, they also tended to avoid presenting race as a problem, and Chopra-Gant argues that this in turn tended to result in the erasure of racial difference and thus the near-total absence of attempts to address racial problems, including systemic racism.[66] This may explain why the more traditional series "are often dismissed as trite and predictable escapism, sensationalist exploitation or, in the worst cases, politically reactionary dogma not to be taken seriously,"[67] despite the high ratings such programs often draw.

The result of evolutions within the crime drama genre and different approaches to televisual storytelling is an incoherent televisual landscape in which officers might be heroic or repressive, reliable or corrupt, effective or incompetent. For example, *NYPD Blue*'s Andy Sipowicz is an alcoholic who struggles to overcome his racist beliefs,[68] and *The Shield*'s Vic Mackey has been characterized as a dirty cop who nevertheless operates under an innate sense of the greater good.[69] Notably, David Simon, creator of HBO's *The Wire*, called out broadcast television for pulling punches in cop series by presenting an alternate reality of crime fighting, one that did not interrogate the amoral, dysfunctional, and criminal elements of police bureaucracy.[70] Indeed, many American police procedurals emphasize individual officers and detectives rather than the very foundation of police institutions.

The recent spotlight on representations of police and policing parallels national attention to the killing of unarmed Black people.[71] After years of police representations that paint officers in a primarily sympathetic-if-not-positive light, complete with godlike intelligence, skill, and intuition,[72] the term "copaganda" emerged to recognize how skewed these collective representations are. Even when police officers are depicted using unwarranted violence, scholars suggest that rule-bending is typically portrayed as essential to effective policing.[73] Indeed, a Color of Change study of American crime shows airing 2017–2018 found that criminal justice professionals constructed as "good guys" committed far more wrongful actions than those constructed as "bad guys," and that procedural violations were rarely acknowledged or regretted; this same study found that wrongful actions were almost entirely depicted as unrelated to racial bias.[74] Furthermore, Bowling et al. find evidence that watching cop shows reinforces public attitudes that favor freedom for the police over funding to combat social ailments that lead to crime,[75] two factors that are central critiques of the police reform movement.[76] Prior to 2020, crime shows bolstered antireform sentiments by largely ignoring these positions; Color of Change found just six discussions of reform across twenty-six crime series, each of them instigated by a person of color who receives a defensive or dismissive response from white officers and lawyers.[77] In the wake of the Black Lives Matter protests of 2020, cop shows' aversion to addressing larger systemic issues including implicit bias was called into question.[78]

Critical attention to the cop genre has not only challenged copaganda and its tendency to valorize police but has sought to explain and understand its continued existence. Some suggest that explanations for copaganda can be found in the production process. For example, police procedurals often employ an officer as a technical consultant who might demonstrate how to properly hold a weapon and otherwise assist the program in avoiding procedural errors.[79] Officers also facilitate filming, as they issue permits and act as security.[80] This is potentially problematic to industry professionals and

Black Lives Matter activists who see this role as a symbiotic bond that may influence the way police are presented on television,[81] and the civil rights activist group Color of Change has called for increased transparency regarding the relationship between police and Hollywood productions.[82] Scholars similarly consider the relationship between media producers and police representations and how producers routinely reproduce "the performative and promotional character of police news releases."[83] Expectations surrounding the positive representation of police are also reinforced by those studio executives who actively enforce "a harmful and inaccurate narrative that police officers can *never* do wrong;"[84] for example, when writer Alan Jenkins pitched a series in which a police officer wrongly accuses another character of a traffic violation, Fox's Standards & Practices department told him, "We can't portray police officers in a negative light." Despite the increased scrutiny placed on copaganda, it is unlikely that this highly lucrative genre will ever disappear, but public pressure has pushed for, at minimum, the inclusion of more diverse perspectives, the rejection of stories that normalize police brutality, and the addition of stories that explore police reform.

When cop shows came under fire amid the 2020 protests, those responsible for cop shows reacted differently. Dick Wolf, producer of multiple crime drama franchises and thus the "undisputed king of the police procedural," defended the *Law & Order* series as "equal opportunity offenders" that do not "operate from a position of blind allegiance to cops, lawyers or judges."[85] Advocates, however, saw things differently and argued that "the lack of diversity in the writer's rooms contributes to dangerous mischaracterizations by making heroes out of people who violate others' rights, portraying the powerless as skillful manipulators of the system, and depicting racism as a 'joke' or ploy for the guilty to hide behind." In response, Wolf indicated that the number of Black writers would be increased on his shows. CBS Studios met with criminal justice experts, including 21CP, an organization that typically works to remake police departments, to get input on their police shows.[86] CBS's *S.W.A.T.* and ABC's *The Rookie*, both of which had the exploration of policing practices as central premises when they were created, returned that fall with a directed indictment of bad policing and discussions of reform. Police workplace comedy *Brooklyn Nine-Nine* went on a year-long hiatus and returned with an overhauled narrative that overtly confronted contemporary problems in policing. Other programs said and did little or nothing to engage with the sociocultural crisis.

Television Production, Representation, and "Reality"

Contemporary television is rife with representations referencing the Black Lives Matter movement, and it is worth recognizing the ways that television has continued to act as a cultural forum,[87] even in the post-network era.[88] The cultural forum model brough attention to the collective view of reality as a social construction by addressing and explaining how commercial media contains numerous ideological valences. Newcomb and Hirsch's argument is that cultures use the art they create as a metalanguage through which they examine themselves, and consequently television "does not present firm ideological conclusions—despite its formal conclusions—so much as it comments on ideological problems."[89] Television thus presents a multiplicity of meanings rather than a monolithic point of view, and audiences reflect on their own positions in relation to social and political issues. Though developed for the network era with its scant broadcasting options, scholars like Amanda Lotz and Jonathan Nichols-Pethick have applied the cultural forum model in the post-network era. As Lotz points out, television remains our most mass-oriented medium and TV shows still contribute to the construction, circulation, and negotiation of ideas and values; therefore, the cultural forum model continues to serve as a framework for analyzing texts. Scholarship in the post-network era has applied the cultural forum model to topical forums like post-9/11 content and genres like cop shows,[90] and my own work has explored the topical forum of the Black Lives Matter movement in cop shows.[91] *Black and Blue TV* goes further, expanding the cultural forum model beyond textual analysis of the cop genre to emphasize the production cultures that create BLM's cultural forum on television. The cultural forum has historically been rooted in the idea of the circulation of culture across multiple sites, without as much attention to issues of production, and analyzing representations alone does not produce a complete understanding of this era of television. Julie D'Acci instead advocates an integrated approach to media studies that considers production, texts, reception, and sociohistorical context—four "porous and analytical rather than self-contained and fully constituted domains."[92] It is not the case that any given media study must go into depth in all four elements, but D'Acci's model "makes clear that cultural artifacts, reception, and sociohistorical context cannot truly be conceived or understood apart from the specific conditions of television production" in which they operate.[93] Therefore, while a cultural forum has developed around the Black Lives Matter movement in television, primarily but not exclusively in police procedurals, examining these programs requires that we also examine television's producorial and industry practices with respect to representing hot-button topics.

In *Black and Blue TV*, I endeavor to determine how television production has changed in the first decade of the Black Lives Matter movement. Production practices mark an important area of study that scholars have willingly explored, but few studies have been able to penetrate the Hollywood bubble and access writers, producers, and other television professionals directly, instead relying on secondhand reports and textual analysis. The reasons why television creatives and other executives make the choices they do is thus obscured by the difficulty of accessing these figures directly, as is deeper insight into how shifting industry practices are imbricated in the ideological dynamics of representation. Elana Levine calls for cultural studies of media production that fulfill Stuart Hall's and Richard Johnson's models of cultural circulation;[94] production-oriented scholarship has focused on the circulation of money more than meaning, often failing to consider the roles of discourse, knowledge, and daily practice in cultural production. Levine therefore proposes that scholars explore the avenues of production constraints, production environment, production routines and practices, and production of characters and stories. "If media researchers seek to understand the paths through which media products come to exist, if they seek to understand the constraints that shape the products available to us," she concludes, "then this sort of rigorous, layered attention to production processes is vital."[95]

Jason Mittell asserts that "commercial television rarely offers representations contrary to consensus ideologies for fear of offending sponsors, typically following social change rather than leading it,"[96] but this begs the question—what is the "consensus ideology" when it comes to U.S. policing practices? Moreover, commercial television is not a monolith but rather a complex organism in which thousands of individuals with alternatingly complementary and competing goals operate. In a similar vein, Turow characterizes cultural production systems as "a constant and pervasive tension between innovation and control."[97] Within this dynamic, innovation is necessary, but control works to minimize risk so that, for example, producers pursuing radical social objectives through their programs will not threaten the relationship between the television network and advertisers. Again, what constitutes a radical social objective when foundational principals of American democracy are being debated and when the status quo of televisual storytelling—especially in crime dramas—is destabilized?

The Black Lives Matter movement does not mark U.S. television's first foray into engaging issues of systemic racism and police violence. American television has always engaged, albeit to varying degrees, the social issues within which it is produced. Aniko Bodroghkozy explored "the crucial role American network television played during the civil rights revolution in reconfiguring a new 'common sense' about race relations."[98] Bodroghkozy noted how networks used different strategies to "narrate a new world of race relations,"[99] with prime-time entertainment programming self-consciously dialoging with societal changes in the wake of the civil rights movement. These representations "negotiated the trope of the 'worthy' black civil rights subjects" and "attempted to give white viewers black protagonists they presumably could be comfortable with." Years later, Sasha Torres wrote about television's response to Rodney King, coining the term "King TV" to address the cycle of programming that engaged issues of racism and police brutality in the early 1990s.[100] Considering the Black Lives Matter movement, Petermon and Spencer articulate how "BLM has reached a level of cultural familiarity such that drama television series on networks like ABC devote entire episodes to the movement" and argue that "drama series' representations of BLM matter in the ways they narrate the movement's politics and its history."[101] At the same time, Monk-Payton notes that "the stories that these popular programs tell about BLM in particular have been criticized in their appropriation and exploitation of the cause,"[102] and Morgan C. Blue recognizes how important it is "to acknowledge the complicated identity politics at work in [a crime drama] as it struggles to offer realistic depictions in a commercial medium like network television that often requires adherence to hegemonic, normative ideologies and representations."[103]

Methodology

The goal of this project is to explore how contemporary television has responded to and developed alongside the Black Lives Matter movement. My research primarily consists of analysis of television production as a site of cultural production through conversations with writers, directors, producers, actors, casting directors, and other industry professionals, as well as organizations focused on improving conditions for people of color in and on television. To complete this analysis, I conducted more than thirty interviews with television professionals and activists between 2021 and 2024. This methodological approach bridges industry and textual analysis to expose the off-screen complexities that shape on-screen representations. My goal is not to contribute to the pool of content analyses that track patterns of representation of criminals, crime, and officers, which previous scholars have done at length.[104] Likewise, my primary interest is not in exploring the effects of representations in police procedurals on the public's perception of policing.

Instead, I am concerned with the mechanics of what decisions are made, by whom, and for what reasons. Implicit in this is the additional consideration of how some shows were able to, in essence, opt out of engagement with BLM themes.

As advocated by Caldwell's cultural-industrial analysis framework and Havens, Lotz, and Tinic's (2009) critical media industry studies approach, *Black and Blue TV* pulls from various sites in which knowledge is produced and discourses are circulated.[105] Critical media industry studies conceives of power not "as a form of economic control over media organizations and laborers" but rather "as 'productive' in the sense that it produces specific ways of conceptualizing audiences, texts, and economics" and "as a form of leadership constructed through discourse that privileges specific ways of understanding the media and their place in people's lives."[106] This multimethodological approach encourages readers "to think more holistically not just about the results of institutional activities in the *corporations*, or film/television production forms *onscreen*," as is typical for industry scholars and critics, "but about *off-screen* media production *work worlds*" that "don't just 'produce' popular culture" but "are important cultural expressions and sociological activities in their own right."[107] This method of analysis synthesizes data from various modes of analysis, including trade articles, interviews, and employment studies. By incorporating this breadth of materials, I blend microlevel insight into workers' experiences during the BLM era with macrolevel shifts in broadcast television production practices. Herbert, Lotz, and Punathambekar articulate this kind of production culture approach as demonstrating an "anthropological interest in workers' meaning-making activities" through an examination of "the cultural values and logics that orient these people as industrial workers."[108] This book thus shows how individuals and activities in broadcast television production reflect the shifting dynamics in how issues surrounding race, both on- and off-screen, are understood and valued over time and across various contexts.

While my analysis emphasizes crime dramas in which police feature prominently, I also explore what Brandy Monk-Payton calls "BLM TV": the cycle of programming tied to the BLM movement that works "to construct ideas about TV's mediation of the racial politics of law and order," either implicitly or explicitly.[109] Some programs produced a "very special episode" on police brutality while others weave BLM themes throughout the series. BLM TV is not limited to police procedurals and crime dramas but rather includes dramas like *Scandal, This Is Us, Station 19* and *The Good Wife*, as well as comedies like *black-ish* and *The Neighborhood.* Similarly, BLM TV exists on broadcast and cable channels as well as premium networks and streamers.

While it would be impossible to comprehensively analyze the entirety of BLM TV, inclusive of crime dramas, I pull from diverse examples to more fully demonstrate the breadth of ways the BLM movement has left a mark on U.S. broadcast television production practices.

Understanding the inner workings of television production processes can shed light on how discourses surrounding racism and policing are negotiated by and mediated through the television industry. I propose that learning how showrunners, writers, directors, producers, casting directors, and activists collectively respond and adapt to civic unrest will produce a more nuanced understanding of the role of television as a cultural forum. This multimethodological approach will bridge production studies and representational analysis, adding behind-the-scenes insight into onscreen representations throughout the first decade of the Black Lives Matter movement. Critical examination of television programs as texts remains crucial, but I argue that first-hand accounts from the people who make decisions about what stories to tell (or not tell), how, and why are key to empowering media scholars to encourage much-needed changes in television production practices.

In chapter 1, "BLM and DEI: On- and Off-Screen Diversity Initiatives," I address the numerous ways, be they flimsy or substantive, that different bodies pushed for increased diversity in television in the past decade. The Writers Guild of America has long promoted increased representation of women; Black, Indigenous, and People of Color; and other underrepresented groups in writers' rooms, publishing a deluge of data in the twenty-first century to illustrate both the gains that have been made and the ongoing gaps in equity. Scholars at UCLA led by Dr. Darnell Hunt have published annual reports since 2014, reporting not just on diversity issues among writers but also showrunners, directors, and casts. Media activists, including the Geena Davis Institute on Gender in Media and Color of Change, have published increasingly detailed analyses of on- and off-screen representation. Similarly, the 2010s saw the development of Think Tank for Inclusion and Equity, an organization of writers from historically underrepresented communities that works to foster accurate and authentic storytelling. Networks and studios during this time were quick to champion their prodiversity stances and initiatives, especially after May 2020, but many of their promises proved empty or short-lived. This chapter provides data to illustrate trends in employment figures and brings together reports and interviews with activists, writers, and other broadcasting professionals to illuminate the battles being fought for diversity, equity, and inclusion behind the scenes.

Chapter 2, "Early BLM Cop Shows (2013–2020): Adjusting to a New Normal," bridges the status quo of the police procedural genre with early BLM (i.e., pre-Floyd) programs to outline the growing cultural forum of cop shows. Following on the heels of successful and critically acclaimed cop shows like *Homicide: Life on the Steet* and *NYPD: Blue*, numerous franchises abounded during this time—*Law & Order*, *Chicago*, *NCIS*, and so forth—alongside more independent procedurals like *Blue Bloods* and *The Rookie*, and their engagement with BLM's themes of systemic racism and police brutality varied widely in both frequency and tenor. Some shows took a defensive stance against the idea of police fallibility, while others considered it a reality worth exploring. Some gave BLM ongoing attention, while others moved on after a "very special episode." Some had already been on the air for years when #BlackLivesMatter was first tweeted, whereas others were developed amid the BLM movement and had these themes baked into their DNA. Interviews with creators of three such shows—*Chicago P.D.*'s Michael Brandt, *S.W.A.T.*'s Aaron Rahsaan Thomas and Shawn Ryan, and *The Rookie*'s Alexi Hawley—illustrate different degrees to which showrunners felt an interest and an obligation to be informed by BLM in their approach to telling stories about policing and criminal justice. This chapter explores the conversations among showrunners, writers, directors, actors, and executives, and how police were depicted in the years leading up to Floyd's death to articulate shifts in the consensus ideology of cop shows. After exploring the role of police consultants and mapping the ways "accuracy" is embedded and limited in police programs, I provide a brief background of the cop genre's successes at the turn of the century. I then pair analyses of police shows during this time (2013–2020) with industry interviews to highlight the ways television professionals saw their role in an increasingly commonplace conversation about race in America.

In chapter 3, "Post-Floyd TVPD: How Policing Is Broken and Why It Will Never Be Fixed," I focus specifically on how cop shows and their networks reckoned with the fever pitch of the Black Lives Matter movement in the television season immediately following the pressure point of George Floyd's murder. As with television in the aftermath of 9/11, cop shows in the fall of 2020 reacted to "an eruption of cultural sentiment," specifically one that threatened the very foundation of their genre; as Americans called for police reform and defunding the police, cop shows faced their own vociferous critiques. In this context, many writers felt compelled to self-reflexively examine their complicity in the failings of the justice system. Returning to interviews with industry insiders, I explore the ways many writers and producers felt compelled to participate in a national discussion of policing while others did not, as well as the ways networks promoted new approaches to making television. In the process, this chapter exposes various blind spots and moments of cultural awakening among television professionals, often informed by a damning report from the activist organization Color of Change that implicated police procedurals in contemporary problems in policing.

Chapter 4, "Beyond the Police Procedural: Black Lives Matter in Comedies and Dramas, Too," turns the focus to BLM TV outside of cop shows. While police procedurals are arguably the most obvious platform for addressing America's tendency toward racist policing practices, other genres have tackled this topic as well. Indeed, genres where police are not the de facto heroes are perhaps better suited to offer critiques of policing. In this chapter, I offer insight into the contributions of other genres to conversations around systemic racism and police brutality. Examples of sitcoms include *New Girl*, *Superstore*, *The Neighborhood*, *The Carmichael Show*, and *black-ish*, which engaged these topics to different extents over the course of the past decade while operating under—or sometimes pushing back against—the generic mandate of lighthearted humor. I give particular attention to *Brooklyn Nine-Nine*, a workplace comedy about NYPD detectives that drew some criticism for copaganda in 2020. I then turn to programs like *The Good Wife*, *Scandal*, and *This Is Us*, and offer a survey of the ways broadcast television dramas tackled these themes within the contexts of their varied storyworlds. For many programs, BLM served as the basis of a "very special episode" or received a smattering of attention as background to a larger central narrative. As a point of contrast, I offer as a case study a closer investigation into *Station 19*, a series about Seattle firefighters that launched an incisive multiseason critique of race and policing.

I close this book by considering the aftermath of the post-Floyd 2020–2021 season. In chapter 5, "Beyond 2020: Or, Back to Business as Usual?" I offer insight into the apparent lasting effects of the BLM movement for the television industry, as well as the ways in which steps towards progress have faded. Interviews with the creators of *Will Trent* and *East New York*, two police shows that premiered post-Floyd, demonstrate a cautious return of a temporarily maligned and culturally suspect genre. By reinforcing how television professionals and production practices operate within and throughout moments of civil unrest and under the directed gaze of critical activists, I aim to demonstrate the possibilities and constraints inherent in destabilizing the status quo.

Through these chapters I trace the development of a proreform movement in a cultural art form that has long relied on somewhat limited, often conservative, and frequently concerning representations of law enforcement, while also recognizing that hegemonic ideologies have historically tended to domesticate nondominant ideologies.[110] I unpack the ways television is narratively (re)shaped in an era of increasing racial consciousness and the messages scripted entertainment programming contributes to public discourses surrounding racism in policing and the justice system, as well as the industrial and production factors that constrain these narratives. Despite the well-intentioned actions of numerous writers, producers, actors, showrunners, and others working in broadcast entertainment television, television's tendency to fold negotiated and oppositional ideologies into dominant discourses makes clear the limits of these individuals' ability to utilize the broadcast medium as a site for cultural change. The stories presented across prime-time programming constitute a cultural forum inextricably interwoven with television production structures of power, including overwhelmingly white writers and producers and a history of copaganda.

1

BLM and DEI

On- and Off-Screen Diversity Initiatives

With the election of Barack Obama in 2008, many Americans considered racism a thing of the past, seeing a Black man in the White House as incontrovertible proof that systemic racism had been eradicated. However, these progressive sentiments often serve as a thin facade over a slog marked by two steps forward and one, two, or three steps back. A 2015 study from the Writers Guild of America (WGA) notes that "writers' rooms simply do not reflect the America of today or the America that is steadily emerging" as the United States becomes increasingly racially diverse; this is problematic because whitewashed writers' rooms "typically fail to include the diversity of voices and perspectives necessary for breathing life into characters and imagining situations that diverse audiences are likely to relate to."[1] The historical dearth of Black, Indigenous, and People of Color (BIPOC) television professionals across all roles has resulted in "a truncating of the domain of media images available for circulation in contemporary society."[2] For example, a predominantly white television industry could easily minimize its acknowledgment and inclusion of issues surrounding civil liberties and state-sanctioned violence that directly affects Black Americans. By contrast, showrunner Aaron Rahsaan Thomas acknowledges that as a Black man, "leaning into Black Lives Matter, that was never really a choice for me, that's just who I am. . . . It was never a luxury where I could turn it on, turn it off."[3] The premise of studies highlighting the underrepresentation of BIPOC people in media is that "when marginalized groups in society are absent from the stories a nation tells about itself, or when media images are rooted primarily in stereotype, inequality is normalized and is more likely to be reinforced through our prejudices and practices."[4] The WGA's 2015 study concludes by pointing out that diverse writers' rooms create content that is more appealing to diverse audiences in an increasingly diverse country, which means failure to improve diversity in television will negatively affect the bottom line.

That "diversity is good for business" is commonly accepted in Hollywood, yet Rebecca Sun proposes that the phrase be retired because it tokenizes and minimizes the presence of BIPOC people as well as women and other minoritized groups.[5] The idea that diversity sells does not posit diversity in media as socially responsible but instead relies on corporate self-interest; the sentiment is utilized to encourage gatekeepers to effect change. Data supports the financial benefits of diversity in studies that consistently show viewers increasingly consuming content with diverse casts and created by a diverse writers' room.[6] Shows that are "written from diverse perspectives result in more plausible characters, make for more interesting television, and boost a show's overall appeal."[7] Sun therefore proposes a more nuanced understanding of the ways diversity brings "fresh perspectives and original studies . . . that can enliven the palates of frequent consumers while also enticing underserved ones."[8] Diverse media are successful when helmed by creatives who understand the themes they engage in and are empowered to execute their vision. Like so many of the studies I explore in this chapter, the proclamation that "diversity is good for business" has helped to bring attention to issues of equity in television, but it has proved insufficient for effecting meaningful change across broadcast television professions. Ample data illustrates the social and financial benefits of a diverse employment pool, but efforts to turn this ideal into a reality have met with numerous roadblocks.

With increases in the numbers of BIPOC writers, producers, and actors, among others, came increased interest and investment in telling a broader and more nuanced range of stories on broadcast airwaves and the ability to do so. These increases did not come about quickly, nor has it been a steady progression over time; rather, racist backlash and other setbacks have rendered a rocky road to progress, and equity remains elusive. Still, a growing movement has fought for gains and made inroads in chipping away at a disproportionately white industry by highlighting concerning statistics and proposing changes to production practices. Organizations such as the Geena Davis Institute on Gender in Media (GDI) and Color of Change have challenged post-race assertions with detailed studies of diversity in television. These studies demonstrate the underrepresentation of BIPOC people and highlight concerns regarding how BIPOC communities are represented. In addition to these studies, other groups, foremost the WGA, have turned attention to writers' rooms and the industry that develops and creates content, publishing a wealth of data on diversity behind the screen. Studies that highlight ongoing under- and misrepresentation of BIPOC people, both on and off screen, have served as resources for activists, including people within the industry, who work to improve diversity in all facets of development and production. For example, writers banded together to form the Think Tank for Inclusion & Equity (TTIE, pronounced "tie"), which works to promote BIPOC writers and representations. Alongside this, the twenty-first century has seen the championing of diversity initiatives on behalf of major networks, including diversity, equity, and inclusion (DEI) offices and incentives for diverse hiring practices. Still, a closer examination of the landscape reveals that many of these measures have proven toothless, amounting to little more than PR stunts.

This chapter offers a survey of studies and initiatives, informed by representatives from activist organizations as well as writers, showrunners, and actors, to illustrate the televisual landscape throughout the first decade of the Black Lives Matter movement. The wealth of data that scholars and activists have compiled in their numerous studies does more than simply identify the myriad ways BIPOC people have been marginalized across broadcast television production processes. Rather, it also reflects a desire to promote and effect industrial and institutional change. A history of racialized employment gaps throughout the television industry has been well documented in annual studies from the WGA and UCLA, among others, and these studies are often cited in trade articles that bring attention to the underemployment of BIPOC people in television.[9] However, as Courtney Brannon Donoghue points out, "this macrolevel approach assumes that pressuring industry gatekeepers with the dismal realities of employment numbers . . . will result in structural changes"; scholarship that utilizes quantitative analysis, she concludes, "works best when contextualized and used in conversation with qualitative research methods" that shed light on the experiences of marginalized people and the discourses that hinder their career advancement.[10]

Black Lives Matter (BLM) brought increased scrutiny to industrial employment practices, compelling networks to account for their behaviors and in some cases make changes, many of which were short-lived failures that further demonstrate the ongoing nature of systemic racism in the United States. This background on racial and ethnic diversity in scripted prime-time broadcast television gives context to the issues that various media activists have confronted and articulates different ways activists have tried to make inroads, offering a critique of these strategies and their varied efficacy. In her exploration of Asian American media activism, Lori Kido Lopez notes that if we can recognize problems in the lived experiences of a group of people, "it is incumbent upon those interested in representation to move beyond mere critique to consider sites for change, pathways towards demonstrating agency or empowerment within media structures, and courses of action that can realistically be taken up."[11] As with many attempts at police reform, these courses of action tend not to seek the wholesale dismantling of the industry (the equivalent of abolition), nor do media activists typically "challenge the system of media structures that uphold racial hierarchies and inequalities"; rather media activists are "simply fighting for access to greater participation and a recognized voice in the process that already exists."[12] However, disagreements persist regarding ideals of what change looks like and what strategies would prove most useful. Additionally, media activists—both within and external to media industries—must negotiate industrial constraints and legal interventions. By focusing on the discourses that circulate among these activists and the strategies they have implemented, I explore broadcast television as a site where issues of race and representation are "deliberately engaged, formed, and recreated through the body of the collective."[13]

(Getting) Inside the Writers' Room

The Writers Guild of America (WGA) has long tracked and reported employment data for television writers in WGA-covered projects. Early reports were published sporadically until a changing of the guard between the fourth report in 1987 and the fifth report in 2005; the sixth report in 2007 announced the WGA's intention to make this report annual and marked a shift in the report's release to the spring months, when hiring decisions would be made for the coming television season. Alternately dubbed writers reports, staffing briefs, and inclusion report cards, these reports emphasize the extent to which women, people of color, and people over forty are employed or excluded from employment as writers for film and television. The purpose of this data is to help bring attention to the underrepresentation of these communities within writers' rooms and encourage showrunners and other executives to hire more BIPOC, women, and older writers. This data also enables us to recognize trends in growth and stagnation over time.

The 2005 report compares findings with data from the previous report in 1998 and provides insight into the state of the television industry in the earliest years of the twenty-first century. Data from 2005 raises numerous concerns. It shows BIPOC writers comprising just under 10 percent of television writers, a slight improvement over the 7 percent reported in 1998, but facing a greater earnings gap with median earnings of $18,000 less than their white counterparts, as opposed to the $8,500 gap of 1998.[14] The 2005 report also points out that of the ten shows employing the highest number of Black writers for the 2004–2005 season, seven aired on UPN, making its parent company Viacom the second-largest employer of Black television writers (16.5%) after Carsey-Werner (18%). Also worth noting is that 39–47 percent of BIPOC television writers were employed on minority-themed sitcoms during this period, and that the shuttering of UPN to make room for the CW the following year would put many of these writers out of work as it cut down the number of series in production that would be more likely to employ Black writers.

The 2007 report is even more bleak, with BIPOC writers making up just 9 percent of writers' rooms and the median wage gap expanding to just under $20,000.[15] Additional data from 2009 shows that BIPOC writers' median earnings increased 8.8 percent between 2001 and 2007, topping at $87,652, but that white men's earnings increased 18.4 percent for the same period, topping at $112,500—a pay gap of nearly $25,000 for BIPOC writers.[16] The 2009 report adds insight into earnings among the ninety-fifth percentile, where white men's wages increased 40 percent to just over $795,000, while BIPOC writers' wages dropped 13.8 percent to approximately $395,000. Data from 2009 also begins to break down data among BIPOC writers to show that gains and losses are not consistent among Latine, Asian, and Black writers. The decline in earnings for BIPOC writers was greatest for Black writers, with a decline of 1.7 percent for a median of $67,000, versus the stagnant median for Asian writers at nearly $74,000 and the increase for Latine writers of 80.8 percent to nearly $89,000. Similarly, while BIPOC representation in television writers' rooms increased by 3 percent between 2001 and 2007, Asian writers more than doubled their numbers, and Latine writers gained 7.5 percent, but Black writers saw a 14.9 percent decline; much of this is attributed to UPN's demise and the cancellation of numerous Black-cast sitcoms, as the number of Black writers dropped by 33.9 percent after UPN merged with the WB to form the CW. The 2009 report also sheds light on employment shares at different positions. During the 2007–2008 season BIPOC writers reached 27.3 percent of lower-level staffing positions but at the higher-level positions made up just 6.4 percent of co–executive producers and 7.1 percent of executive producers. The 2011 report shows little or no change in rates of employment or compensation for BIPOC writers in television.[17] The 2012 Hollywood Writers Report shows a rebound to 11 percent for BIPOC writers employed in television, though the wage gap compared to white writers continued to grow.[18] The 2014 report shows the share of employed BIPOC television writers holding steady but notes Black writers' median income at roughly 72 percent of their white counterparts.[19]

The WGA'S 2013 staffing brief reports that the amount of BIPOC television writers in staff positions nearly doubled from 2000 (7.5%) to 2012 (15.6 %), but since the U.S. population also increased in diversity during this same period (from 30.9% to 36.3%), BIPOC writers continued to be far from proportionately represented in writers' rooms.[20] Moreover, a closer examination of BIPOC inclusion in writers' rooms in this study reveals higher gains for Asian (from 1% to 3.9%) and Latine (from 1.1% to 4%) writers. By contrast, Black writers gained just .7 percent during this same period, from 5.8 percent to 6.5 percent, far below the 12 percent of the U.S. population that were Black in 2012. Similar patterns were found among executive producers: The 2013 brief reports that the minority share of these positions doubled from the 2010–2011 season to the 2011–2012 season but were nevertheless drastically underrepresentative, rising from 3.9 percent of executive producers to 7.8 percent.[21] Notably, rates of BIPOC executive producers varied across broadcast networks, ranging from 2.3 percent at NBC to 13.3 percent at ABC. Though the overall average for BIPOC writers on broadcast and cable was 15.6 percent for the 2011–2012 season, most broadcasters were below this average—as low as 8.1 percent at CBS—with just Fox (19.2%) surpassing the overall average, but still far below the national share. Aside from Black-themed programs on cable networks, BIPOC representation in writers' rooms was highest on Shonda Rhimes's hit ABC series *Grey's Anatomy* (45.5%) (see Figure 1.1).

When the WGA published a follow-up study in 2015, they found another decline in BIPOC representation in television writers' rooms. The 2013 brief reported a peak of 15.6 percent BIPOC writers across broadcast and cable networks, but this dipped to 13.7 percent in the 2015 study, ranging from 11.3 percent to 16.1 percent on broadcast networks.[22] Similarly, in this two-year period the share of BIPOC executive producers dropped from 7.8 percent to 5.5 percent overall. Rates were higher at the CW (9.5%) and lower at the larger broadcast networks: 4.9 percent at CBS, 4.7 percent at Fox, 4.2 percent at ABC, and 0 percent at NBC.[23] The 2016 Hollywood Writers Report shed light on pay disparities and found that BIPOC television writers earned eighty cents for every dollar earned by their white men counterparts in 2014, down from ninety-seven cents in 2011.[24] Of the most highly paid writers in 2014, white men in the ninety-fifth percentile averaged upwards of $646,000, while BIPOC writers in that same echelon averaged just under $387,000, or sixty cents on the dollar to their white male counterparts in the ninety-fifth percentile.[25]

The WGA released its first Inclusion Report Card in 2018. These annual report cards highlight the pervasiveness of systemic discrimination against BIPOC television writers. For the 2017–2018 television staffing season, BIPOC

FIG. 1.1. Dr. Pierce, Dr. Fox, Dr. Bailey, and Dr. Grey discuss a case on the *Grey's Anatomy* episode "Sing It Again" (2020).

people made up 39 percent of the U.S. population but just 27 percent of television writers, increasing the BIPOC share considerably in the four years since the WGA's 2015 report of 15.6 percent but still not reaching proportionate representation.[26] BIPOC people were even more underrepresented at higher ranks, comprising just 12 percent of television showrunners and 12 percent of executive producers. This first report card brought attention not just to the low rates of hiring but also the high rates of bias, discrimination, and workplace harassment that BIPOC writers experience when they are hired, and it encouraged studios and showrunners to increase diversity hiring.

The 2019 report card reported an increase to 30 percent BIPOC representation in television staffing, and the 2020 report card showed another increase to 35 percent BIPOC writers, but by this point the BIPOC population of the United States had risen to 40 percent so that underrepresentation persisted.[27] In addition to employment shares at different ranks, the 2020 report card highlights the importance of script credits, noting that script credits are an important measure of equity and inclusion with powerful implications for a writer's career trajectory. For the 2019–2020 season, BIPOC people made up 35 percent of television writers but earned just 31 percent of script credits;[28] the disparity was more pronounced among Black writers, who comprised 15.9 percent of TV jobs but just 12.8 percent of TV script credits.[29] By correlating script credits with data on showrunners, the WGA demonstrates that underrepresented TV writers received 24 percent more credits when their showrunner was also underrepresented as opposed to a white man as showrunner. Beyond staffing, this pattern of racial inequity in script credits demonstrates an additional obstacle to employment and advancement for BIPOC television writers.

The cumulative data reveals substantive changes in the years following Michael Brown's death and the proliferation of BLM discourses. BIPOC people made up just 13.6 percent of employed television writers in 2010, climbing to 35.3 percent in 2019 and 37 percent in 2020.[30] However, despite gains in the share of BIPOC writers in 2020, the pandemic resulted in a sharp decline of overall employment for television writers, with forty-nine fewer series releases compared to 2019 because while their share increased from 2019 to 2020, the number of employed BIPOC writers dropped from 833 to 660.[31] This period also failed to produce high rates of BIPOC writers at the higher positions; the 17.9 percent BIPOC share of executive producers and showrunners in 2020 was a substantive improvement over the 7.8 percent share for these positions in 2011 but was still drastically underrepresentative compared to the U.S. BIPOC population.

Impediments to Progress in the Production Pipeline

Quantitative data tracking BIPOC employment in writers' rooms is important in articulating the extent of the problems in representation, but it does not provide a complete picture of BIPOC writers' experiences, nor does it address other important areas of production where BIPOC representation has been hindered. Beyond getting into the writers' room, writers face additional barriers to entry. In her time at Color of Change, Amity Paye has recognized "a slow creep" in terms of writers' room diversity, one woman or BIPOC writer at a time.[32] Paye attributes this in part to studios' recent diversity commitments, but she also recognizes systemic barriers. Some of these factors include the pilot pipeline, marketers and advertisers, the overrepresentation of white men among showrunners, the types of writers' rooms that showrunners cultivate, and roadblocks to career advancement.

The underrepresentation of BIPOC writers is due in part to the pilot pipeline, which constrains diversity. After examining the 566 projects in the TV pilot pipeline in 2013, the WGA found that only 9 percent had even one BIPOC writer. Echoing a similar study conducted in 2007, the 2013 brief suggests "that an important avenue to increasing the representation of . . .

minorities throughout the television production process probably involves finding ways to increase their participation at the very beginning."[33] The WGA's 2022 Inclusion & Equity Report found that BIPOC writers had increased to 23.3 percent of development and pilot writers, indicating that their inclusion in development had grown but was still lower than the 37 percent share of BIPOC writers staffed on television series.[34] Black writers specifically were proportionately represented in writers' rooms, making up 12.1 percent of the population and 15.5 percent of television writers, but they made up just 9.7 percent of development and pilot writers. As writer Niceole Levy notes, "There's a lot of developing shows from underrepresented writers [but] not a lot of greenlighting them."[35]

Even when a show survives the pipeline, it can be stymied by marketers. Writer/producer Amanda Green recounts her experience working in the mid-2010s on a pilot for CBS about which "everyone who ever saw it said 'This is what a cop show should be. This is how we should be talking and processing through the issues.'"[36] Green recalls that this pilot was "universally loved, even by the network," and had "a majority Black and Brown cast" containing just one white man, as well as a queer Black director. "But it got to the marketers, who are ultimately involved in what shows make it on the air and not. And they basically said, 'It's too Black, too Brown, too female. We don't know how to sell this.'" Green's story points to a reticence to support diverse content as though diversity were a niche and not a central feature of U.S. society. Similarly, writer/producer Niceole Levy, who has credits on *S.W.A.T.*, *Shades of Blue*, and *Found*, has dealt with nervous studio and network executives who are "a bit uncomfortable when you pitch an episode and have to explain why it's important to tell the story and get them on board," and has friends whose proposed episodes were killed by studios because "they've got advertisers to answer to." By contrast, Shondaland writer/producer Kiley Donovan points to the fact that select individuals earn sufficient "capital" through successful broadcasts in which they are able to tackle serious topics in unconventional ways, for example, by having an episode of a *Station 19* in which the firefighters spend the hour discussing racism with a therapist rather than fighting fires.[37]

While it is worth noting that by 2020 Black people make up 13.4 percent of the U.S. population and 15.9 percent of television writers, BIPOC writers continued to be underrepresented in the more powerful positions of showrunner (18%) and executive producer (19%) in the spring of 2020. Writer/producer Amanda Green attributes the overwhelming whiteness (and maleness) of showrunners, especially within the cop genre, to the truism that women and BIPOC people usually want a to tell a different kind of narrative that does not fit the established broadcast network model; from Green's perspective, the white savior trope is deeply entrenched in the psyche of white male creators, and cop shows are their fantasy of masculinity, violence, and aggression come to life. Green notes that she has only worked for white men in Hollywood, and that they generally have the same psychological backstory or profile, which she describes as "theater nerds or band kids" who spent high school socially isolated, "down in the basement . . . watching movies on repeat and quoting lines with their other two nerdy friends." These men then go to Hollywood, "the land of this projected American masculinity, and they really get a hard-on for cops and FBI agents and spies." In writing about cops, they get to hang out with and learn from cops, and "there's a fetishization of that world. . . . There's no interest in change because . . . it makes these guys feel more successfully masculine." Green connects this with other positions, noting that CBS has an abundance of cop shows but no Black executives in the television development pipeline and that it is hard selling old, white, wannabe cops on diverse and progressive content. "I don't think it's an accident that Shonda [Rhimes] has had the success that she has had at a network that, for most of her tenure when she was at ABC . . . was run by a Black woman," Green concludes.

Unsurprisingly, a showrunner sets the tone for the writers' room, leading to different kinds of environments. Activist group Color of Change's 2017 report titled *Race in the Writers' Room* addresses these variations as it explores the relationship between writer demographics, the experiences of Black television writers, and the storylines that result from different types of writers' rooms. Specifically, Color of Change articulates distinctions between different kinds of writers' rooms based on the ways Black writers operate in those spaces: isolated, included, and liberated.[38] In isolated writers' rooms, making up 91 percent of the rooms in the study, a white showrunner presides over a room with either no or only one Black writer. If a Black writer is present, they are tokenized by virtue of being the sole Black person in the room, as was the case for half of all series with any Black writers. Because they are alone, writers' room dynamics "make it difficult for Black writers to have genuine input into the creative process" due to colleagues who routinely shut down conversations about race.[39] Inclusive writers' rooms also have a white showrunner, but they include at least three BIPOC writers and do not tokenize Black writers. Instead, these rooms are more open so that Black writers are empowered and conversations about race are less likely to be shut down. As a result, inclusive rooms develop more complex Black characters and narratives. Liberated rooms are those with Black showrunners, making up just 5 percent of series in the study, and five or more Black writers who can feel comfortable in the writers' room. This critical mass of BIPOC writers allows for the freer exchange of ideas regarding the complexities of race, and the content they produce captures a wider range of Black characters and narratives, often centering these characters rather than using them as supports for white leads.

Though they did not use Color of Change's vocabulary, writers evoked this distinction in describing different kinds of rooms they had experienced. Speaking to isolated writing rooms, *NCIS: New Orleans* writer Talicia Raggs explains that networks seemed surprised that adding a single Black person to the writers' room did not fix everything, and that network executives did not seem to understand that staff writers feel powerless and stay quiet for fear of losing their job or earning a reputation as "difficult" or "not a team player."[40] As a result, isolated rooms produce content that emphasizes developed white characters and their storylines while BIPOC characters play limited stock supporting roles. Showrunner Alexi Hawley describes isolated writer rooms as something he deliberately avoids, noting how mostly white writers' rooms are all too common and frequently uncomfortable: "You can open the doors to your room to people from marginalized communities, but unless you sort of let them know what it's a safe place to express a point of view, to disagree on stuff, to have that conversation, then they're not going to speak up because . . . they don't know that it's safe."[41] Hawley suggests that isolated rooms have historically abounded in cop shows, and that in the aftermath of George Floyd's murder, many of these showrunners "seemed like they literally just discovered that diversity in the room was . . . a thing . . . and they were proud of it. And you're like—mm, that's a problem." By contrast, Hawley—a white man—runs inclusive rooms.

Like Color of Change, the Think Tank for Inclusion and Equity was motivated to highlight the experiences of BIPOC writers. TTIE was first developed when BIPOC writers started to gather and share stories in 2016 and was inspired by Color of Change's 2017 report. TTIE was officially founded in 2018 when it received a grant to conduct its first Behind the Scenes report, which uses surveys and focus groups to gather quantitative and qualitative data regarding inclusion and equity in television writing through a more intersectional lens that could trace similarities and differences across identities. Writer Angela Harvey describes how writers from historically excluded communities would share stories and recognize shared experiences but would be gaslit if they raised the subject of those experiences with executives or agents: "'I'm so sorry that happened to you, but it's just you' and blah, blah, blah."[42] Frustrated with this collective gaslighting, a group of writers gathered to launch a report and quantify issues like how frequently writers from historically excluded communities would have to repeat levels, especially early in their careers, while white male colleagues rose more quickly through the ranks.

First published in 2019, TTIE's annual Behind the Scenes report is presented as "a tool to help [effect] meaningful change in the TV industry by (1) identifying key areas where inclusion and equity are still challenged and (2) providing actionable recommendations to help remove barriers toward producing more authentic and diversified TV content."[43] The 2019 findings, which are based on survey results from roughly half of all BIPOC television writers, find that 82 percent of them had to repeat a title at least once, 65 percent have been the only BIPOC writer on staff, 64 percent experienced bias, discrimination, or harassment by other writers, and 42 percent entered the industry as "diversity hires." Though BIPOC writers are frequently hired on the basis of their diversity, they find resistance to diversity in story content to be pervasive: Sixty-one percent noted resistance from showrunners, 41 percent from the network, 37 percent from the writers' room, and 35 percent from the studio. The 58 percent who received pushback when pitching nonstereotyped BIPOC characters or storylines reported experiencing microaggressions and being excluded from the writers' room or not assigned a script. These writers would undoubtedly have more agency with greater power—for example, as showrunners—but only 37 percent of respondents who sold a pilot that went to series were appointed showrunners, and just 50 percent were made executive producers; agents and managers, they report, failed these writers by not fighting for them. Respondents overwhelmingly encouraged networks and studios to support equal treatment and promotion of diverse writers by hiring more diverse showrunners, encouraging current showrunners to hire and promote diverse writers, and mandating diverse representation across all levels of staff.[44]

Tracking the Importance of Off-Screen Diversity for Diverse Characters & Stories

As the previous sections indicate, diversity in writers' rooms is an important, albeit not the sole, factor in creating content for a diverse U.S. population. Other key roles include showrunners, directors, and cast, all of whom inform on-screen representation. In addition to the WGA, UCLA's Hollywood Diversity Report (HDR) series publishes reports that are intended to generate analysis of diversity throughout television, identify and promote best practices for increasing diversity, and consider the implications of media diversity for society, but pushes beyond data on writers. This series of annual studies originated with the Ralph J. Bunche Center for African American

Studies at UCLA and aimed "to explore the relationships between diversity and the bottom line in the Hollywood entertainment industry."[45] Starting with the 2014 report that tracked the 2011–2012 television season, the annual HDR tracks rates of BIPOC series creators, directors, leads, and casts. The first annual HDR was released in 2014, initially combining data from television and film until 2020, when they started to release two separate annual medium-specific reports. When reporting on television, the HDR accounts not just for writers' demographics but also the racial diversity of other key roles, including lead talents, overall casts, show creators, and directors. For example, the 2015 HDR found BIPOC people made up just 4 percent of television network and studio heads, 7 percent of senior management, and 14 percent of unit heads.[46]

The Hollywood Diversity Reports confirm that BIPOC people are consistently underrepresented among show creators, making up just 4.2 percent in its first report, with Shonda Rhimes serving as creator for the majority of these with *Grey's Anatomy*, *Private Practice*, and *Scandal*. The 2014 report suggests that by "successfully selling the concept for a television show, a show's creator sets the stage for a number of production choices that ultimately impact the degree of diversity in writing and casting."[47] More than 60 percent of scripted broadcast series in the 2011–2012 season had writers' rooms with 10 percent or fewer BIPOC writers, and just 2.1 percent, or one series—*Grey's Anatomy*—approximated the U.S. population with 31–40 percent BIPOC writers.[48] The only series to exceed *Grey's* in writers' room diversity was the Fox sketch comedy series *In the Flow with Affion Crockett*, which was produced by Jamie Foxx and lasted just one season. BIPOC people made small gains and occasional losses as show creators over the course of nine years, with no apparent response to the birth of the BLM movement, leading to 13.1 percent for the 2020 fall season, which would have been greenlit prior to George Floyd's murder; what is worth noting is that in the aftermath of Floyd's murder and the subsequent protests, as programs were greenlit to premiere in the 2021–2022 season, the proportion of BIPOC creators nearly doubled to 23.2 percent.[49]

When the first HDR was published, there was even less diversity in the director's chair, and just one series—the short-lived *Charlie's Angels* reboot on ABC—had 51 percent or more episodes helmed by BIPOC directors. However, as in other areas, BIPOC directors also made steady progress in the following decade, directing just 7.5 percent of episodes in the 2012–2013 season up to 30.9 percent of episodes in the 2021–2022 season. HDR data (Table 1) goes into detail, showing that at the beginning of this period, 73 percent of shows had 10 percent or fewer of their episodes helmed by

TABLE 1.1 Percentage of series by percentage of BIPOC directors, by television season

	2011–2012	2012–2013	2013–2014	2014–2015	2015–2016	2016–2017	2017–2018	2018–2019	2019–2020	2020–2021	2021–2022
0–10% episodes have BIPOC directors	73	64	68	50	52	41	38.1	35.6	25.9	29	22.4
11–20%	17	21	16	25	25	23	17.8	27.8	21.4	13.1	19.4
21–30%	6	11	10	14	8	18	21.2	17.8	22.3	15	14.3
31–40%	2	2	4	4	8	8	12.7	5.6	13.4	16.8	18.4
41–50%	0	2	2	4	4	5	5.1	0	8	12.2	7.1
>50%	2	0	0	3	3	5	5.1	13.3	8.9	14.4	18.4

SOURCES: Darnell Hunt, Ana-Christina Ramón, and Zachary Price, *2014 Hollywood Diversity Report: Making Sense of the Disconnect* (UCLA, 2014), 15; Darnell Hunt and Ana-Christina Ramón, *2015 Hollywood Diversity Report: Flipping the Script* (UCLA, 2015), 27; Darnell Hunt, Ana-Christina Ramón, and Michael Tran, *2016 Hollywood Diversity Report: Busine$$ as Usual?* (UCLA, 2016), 30; Darnell Hunt, Ana-Christina Ramón, Michael Tran, Amberia Sargent, and Vaness Díaz, *2017 Hollywood Diversity Report: Setting the Record Straight* (UCLA, 2017), 36; Darnell Hunt, Ana-Christina Ramón, Michael Tran, Amberia Sargent, and Debanjan Roychoudhury, *Hollywood Diversity Report 2018: Five Years of Progress and Missed Opportunities* (UCLA, 2018), 30; Darnell Hunt, Ana-Christina Ramón, and Michael Tran, *Hollywood Diversity Report 2019: Old Story, New Beginning* (UCLA, 2019), 30; Darnell Hunt and Ana-Christina Ramón, *Hollywood Diversity Report 2020: A Tale of Two Hollywoods* (UCLA, 2020), 47; Darnell Hunt and Ana-Christina Ramón, *Hollywood Diversity Report 2021: Pandemic in Progress* (UCLA, 2021), 41; Ana-Christina Ramón, Michael Tran, and Darnell Hunt, *Hollywood Diversity Report 2022: A New, Post-Pandemic Normal?* (UCLA, 2022), 41; Ana-Christina Ramón, Michael Tran, and Darnell Hunt, *Hollywood Diversity Report 2023: Exclusivity in Progress* (UCLA, 2023), 45.

BIPOC directors, down to just 22.4 percent of shows by the end of the 2021–2022 season. Over that same period, just 2 percent of shows had BIPOC directors for half their episodes at the beginning, up to 18.4 percent of shows by the end.

Perhaps the greatest improvements have been found among actors, as additional data shows increases in on-screen diversity. The HDR shows a general increase in the percentage of shows with a BIPOC lead, albeit with the occasional small backslide, from 5.1 percent in fall of 2011 to 32.6 percent in fall of 2021. Here, the biggest year-to-year increases come on the heels of the two largest protests; BIPOC leads increased by 7.3 percent in series greenlit for the 2015 season after the Ferguson protests, and 5.2 percent in series greenlit for the 2021 season after George Floyd's murder. The data provided by HDR is somewhat incomplete, as the reports only start to break down leads by race with the fall of 2017, but this data shows that Black leads specifically held steady at around 11 percent until the 2021 season, when it grew to 18.4 percent. HDR data from the 2011–2012 season reveals that just 15.2 percent of these series approximated the U.S. population of 36.3 percent diversity share, with 10.2 percent of shows' casts being more diverse than the

TABLE 1.2 Percentage of series by percentage of BIPOC cast members, by television season

	2011–2012	2012–2013	2013–2014	2014–2015	2015–2016	2016–2017	2017–2018	2018–2019	2019–2020	2020–2021	2021–2022
0–10% BIPOC actors	23.2	30.8	28.1	26.8	16.1	10.3	12.4	9.9	11.6	6.6	8.2
11–20%	35.4	28	24.8	27.6	17	16.5	13	15	8	11	13
21–30%	16.2	14	20.7	10.6	17	16.5	13	11	8	7.5	3
31–40%	15.2	16.8	17.4	22	22	18.1	22	10	19	14	14
41–50%	8.1	10.3	5.8	4.1	10	19	16	26	21	26	24
>50%	2	0	3.3	8.9	17.9	19.8	23.1	27.3	32.1	34.9	39.8

SOURCES: Hunt et al., 2014; Hunt and Ramón, 2015; Hunt et al., 2016; Hunt et al., 2017, Hunt et al., 2018, Hunt et al., 2019, Hunt and Ramón, 2020; Hunt and Ramón, 2021; Ramón et al., 2022; Ramón et al., 2023.

TABLE 1.3 Cumulative percentages of cast members by race, by television season

	2013–2014	2014–2015	2015–2016	2016–2017	2017–2018	2018–2019	2019–2020	2020–2021	2021–2022
White	80	76	66	63.6	61.4	58.7	56.6	53.2	50.4
Black	9	13	17	20.6	15.7	18.2	18.4	18.6	22.7
Latine	5	5	6	6.2	6.4	5.3	6.3	5.3	5.7
Asian	4	4	5	4.6	5.2	5.6	4.7	5.5	5.5
Indigenous	0	0	0	0.1	0.6	0.5	0.9	2	1
Multiracial	2	2	6	5.2	9.9	10	11.9	14	13.5
MENA	0	0	0	0	0.7	1.8	1.3	1.3	1.3

SOURCES: Hunt et al., 2014; Hunt and Ramón, 2015; Hunt et al., 2016; Hunt et al., 2017, Hunt et al., 2018, Hunt et al., 2019, Hunt and Ramón, 2020; Hunt and Ramón, 2021; Ramón et al., 2022; Ramón et al., 2023.

U.S. population and 74.8 percent of series' casts being less diverse than the United States. By contrast, 24 percent of series in the 2021–2022 season approximated the 43.1 percent BIPOC share of the U.S. population in 2022, and 39.8 percent were more diverse than the United States, leaving just 30 percent of series to underrepresent BIPOC people. More data is provided regarding the overall racial breakdown of casts (Tables 2 and 3).

Part of the reason for gains among actors is that diversity sells, even if marketers sometimes struggle to understand how, and networks, studios, and advertisers all benefit from developments in casting. Diverse content does well in terms of ratings, and the evidence suggests that diversity has a meaningful impact on scripted broadcast networks' bottom line. Median ratings for the 2011–2012 season were highest (5.84) for shows with 41–50 percent diverse actors, and lower (3.79) when the casts were 10 percent or less BIPOC actors. The 2023 HDR shows that of the top ten broadcast scripted series for the 2021–2022 season, four had casts with over 50 percent minority share, two had 41–50 percent, and one had 31–40 percent; just three had less than 20 percent BIPOC characters.[50] Additionally, one implication argued by the 2014 HDR is that diverse content also wins awards, which again translates into more money for the networks and studios behind diverse content. Of the sixteen broadcast comedies and dramas with 21–30 percent BIPOC casts, five (or 31.3%) won at least one Emmy, as opposed to 17.4 percent of series with 10 percent or less BIPOC casts and 20 percent of 11–20 percent BIPOC casts. Twenty percent of series with 31–40 percent diverse casts garnered awards, as did 35 percent of series with 41–50 percent diverse casts.[51]

Diversity in casting seems to be a given for many of the industry professionals I interviewed, but not all seem to place the same value on it, nor are they on the same page about what constitutes success where casting BIPOC actors is concerned. Echoing Hawley's comments about the importance of diversity in writers' rooms, *Chicago P.D.* creator Michael Brandt acknowledges the importance of on-screen diversity, but it is unclear to what extent he follows through. Brandt tells me, "Certainly you wanna be representative, you want to be authentic—Chicago is a very diverse city,"[52] and there are indeed BIPOC characters throughout the *Chicago* franchise (*Chicago Fire*; *Chicago P.D.*; *Chicago Med*), but the main ensemble of the law-enforcement series is predominantly white, with one Latino and one Black man serving as the primary splashes of color. Writer Niceole Levy mentions *Chicago P.D.* specifically when describing her issues with racial diversity, pointing out, "If you look at the demographics of the Chicago police department, it's 50 percent white and 50 percent Hispanic and Black, and you never see that really reflected in the show." Brandt's explanation—or justification—for premising the first Chicago series (*Chicago Fire*) on the antagonisms between two white men illustrates the complexity of dealing with race in the twenty-first century (see Figure 1.2). As Brandt shares, former NBC chairperson Bob Greenblatt thought one of the leads should be Black, "purely for representational purposes." Brandt's concern was that the antagonism between the heads of the firehouse and the elite rescue squad, which he observed at a Chicago fire station early in the development process, should be about jealousy and hierarchy and even ageism: "If one of them is Black, the conflict is about race, whether we ever say it or not—that changes the dynamic that lives in the firehouse." If both leads are white, then "it's purely about one's ability to be a firefighter, that's it, and it's about the things that go along with that," but if one of them is Black, then "there will be a perception that there

FIG. 1.2. Severide gets news from Chief Boden in the pilot episode of *Chicago Fire* (2012).

was a race element to this, and we don't want that." When I suggested that they could solve that problem by making both leads Black, Brandt responds that "that wouldn't be representative" because "the fire department isn't that Black," and he suggests that taking that route would be "pandering to a movement" and would be "not truthful. We're not telling a Chicago firefighter show at that point; we're telling a Hollywood version of a Chicago firefighter show, and nobody wanted to do that." Given that Chicago's firefighter population is 15 percent Black,[53] having two Black Chicago firefighters does not seem outlandish; rather, it speaks more to some white showrunners' reluctance to tell stories about Black characters and highlights their internalized beliefs about what constitutes "truthful" storytelling as well as what they expect will make for successful television. As a point of contrast, ABC's highly successful Shondaland series *Station 19* featured three Black men among its firefighters. Having established her frustration with the whitewashing of the Chicago Police Department in *Chicago P.D.*, Niceole Levy contrasts the Dick Wolf franchise with *S.W.A.T.*—created by a Black man, Aaron Rahsaan Thomas, and co-run by a white man, Shawn Ryan—and shares that one of her favorite things about writing for *S.W.A.T.* is that the cast reflects LA's diverse population: "Whether that's what a real SWAT team looks like or not, we're trying to show that. That's what it *should* look like, it *should* look like the city that it works."

What is clear from the dozens of published reports as well as hours of conversations with activists and content creators is that diversity behind the scenes has implications for what viewers see on their television screens. As TTIE program director Maha Chehlaoui puts it, "What is going into your food is going to influence the flavor."[54] For example, Color of Change rates *Chicago P.D.* among the worst offenders according to its Racial Integrity Index, which "assesses the relationship between writers' room diversity and series content in the crime genre, i.e., who is representing the lives of people of color."[55] The index shows *Chicago P.D.* averaged 7.18 BIPOC characters per episode in the 2017–2018 season and had no Black writers and only one nonwhite writer during this time. More broadly, the Color of Change report finds the crime genre to be the least representative for Black writers despite featuring high rates of Black characters in a way that "shapes public attitudes about issues that affect Black people so greatly."[56]

Writers' room diversity has important implications for what viewers ultimately see on screen. Actor Jason George (*Grey's Anatomy* and *Station 19*) notes that writers' rooms are increasingly diverse but that "it can always be more."[57] Though he has spent more than a decade on Shondaland series with diverse writers' rooms, George has also been on shows where the writers' room was entirely white. Recalling these whiter writer rooms, George notes, "When they chose to write some things that were culturally based for my character, it was largely coming out of what they'd read or their understanding and . . . very little out of personal experience." SAG-AFTRA's Diversity Advisory Committee, which George chairs and lovingly calls "the United Nations of underrepresented communities," has task forces for various racial and ethnic groups, women, seniors, performers with disabilities, and more. These groups trade best practices to help each other in dealing with issues like playing tropes and colorism in casting. However, with increased diversity, George feels BIPOC characters are no longer "extra credit" or "the token this, the token that"; rather, the current "business model requires diversity." In some cases, as in Shondaland shows, George is grateful to "work for people who have the humility to understand that they don't know everything" and are eager to correct blind spots when they realize certain groups do not feel seen or represented. Echoing this sentiment, casting director Jenny Jue shares, "When I see tokenism, it's just being lazy."[58] Such laziness, it seems, is easily avoided when creatives care.

While some writers and producers undoubtedly think and care about the relationship between media diversity and society, for others it is more about the bottom line. Because broadcast television's financial model is still built on the selling of audience eyeballs to advertisers who expect a return on their investment, advertisers have a vested interest in content that brings in a large audience, and the growing BIPOC population is increasingly appealing. White audiences have historically been the default mainstream, but market research and Nielsen ratings have exposed the value of BIPOC audiences.

For example, Nielsen shows that Black viewers spend 31.8 percent more time consuming media than the general population and that they are more likely to support brands with content featuring Black people.[59] Increased critical attention to and discussion about popular media has made it more difficult to get by with mere visibility alone; instead, public scrutiny has prodded more nuanced representation. In the following section, I turn to specific resources and programs that seek—if only on the surface—to improve representation.

Activist Interventions: Pushing for Progress

This section surveys programs, trainings, and other strategies that ostensibly aim to increase the quantity and improve the experiences of BIPOC people working in television. The 2007 Hollywood Writers Report echoes previous reports in arguing that "industry business as usual has been wholly insufficient for addressing the Hollywood diversity problem" and suggesting that the solution is likely "grounded in an appreciation for the connections between stories and society" that recognizes diversity "as both a public good and a sure bet for the bottom line."[60] Specifically, it calls for those in a position to change the landscape to push beyond token gestures to "establish clear goals, reasonable timetables and effective mechanisms for an industry truly committed to catching up with a changing America" in hopes that doing so would produce a new business-as-usual industrial discourse. The data provided by WGA and in the Hollywood Diversity Reports over the years, along with Color of Change's 2017 *Race in the Writers' Room* report, shows a rocky road to progress marked by increases in the inclusion of Black writers on the one hand and unequal pay and impediments to career advancement on the other. In pushing for change throughout the broadcast industry, activism can take many forms, including quantitative and qualitative reports detailing deficiencies as well as programs that promote progressive hiring practices and intervene in storytelling processes. While these many reports help to paint a detailed picture of the problem and articulate best practices for a path forward, other strategies are more hands-on in increasing and improving opportunities for Black television creatives. Lopez notes that "all activism begins with the identification of a social problem based on inequality, injustice, or harm to society" and that after identification, "activists engage in any number of activities designed to bring about social change."[61] The writers, producers, actors, and activists I interviewed are interested, albeit to varying degrees and through different lenses, in engaging the cause of racial injustice that was foregrounded on the national stage through the Black Lives Matter movement. Some interview subjects were enthusiastic about their activist intentions, while others came off as hesitant or even reluctant participants in the cultural forum.

One form of activism comes from the networks themselves through diversity programs and quotas. Writer Angela Harvey recounts that there have long been pipeline diversity programs in Hollywood, which she traces back to a 1999 NAACP report about "the abysmal representation of folks of color, specifically Black people in Hollywood." This report put a spotlight on studios, which in turn responded by launching exceedingly competitive pipeline programs. Because there are so many applicants and so few slots available, Harvey shares, it is statistically easier to get into Harvard than one of these programs. Those elite few who are accepted to the program are "placed in writers' rooms on the studio's dime, so the showrunners didn't have to pay for them," which means "there was no incentive to promote them—they would just get a new free writer every time that they could." As a result, these programs functionally brought in "historically excluded folks, chewing them up and spitting them back out" with a bit of experience under their belt but also the stigma of appearing to have been fired. Harvey points out that increases in writers' room diversity did not seem to have a clear effect on content "until we saw all those pledges from the studios in 2020," but also that the studios "now seem to be pretty actively backtracking" by getting rid of those hires and whitewashing development executives so that BIPOC people work in HR rather than content creation. As a result, there was an uptick in the number of projects from BIPOC writers that were picked up and put into development after the summer of 2020, but time has shown that very few ever made it to air. Most of these shows "have either died or are just stuck in the cycle of development. . . . So once again, it's a lip service thing where it's like, sure, we want folks of color present. We just want them to still promote white supremacy."

These diversity programs thus seem to largely function as political cover for studios seeking to avoid or mitigate public relations disasters. The WGA's 2019 *State of Career Advancement for Diverse Hollywood Writers* report interviewed BIPOC writers with a focus on their experiences with DEI programs. These programs commonly teach participants a variety of skills needed for television writers, including how to pitch story ideas, navigate the writers' room, interview, and interact with executives and showrunners. More than these skills, though, DEI programs provided participants with opportunities to meet and network with each other, but also executives to whom they might not otherwise have access. According to their survey, 46.3 percent of Black respondents believed their participation in a diversity program directly led to work, and their evidence suggests that these programs may help

BIPOC writers onto pathways to more sustained careers. Additionally, 70 percent reported being satisfied or very satisfied with their program.[62] In their own study, TTIE's 2019 Behind the Scenes report describes network and studio writing programs as "the holy grail of opportunities"; in surveying BIPOC graduates of these programs, TTIE found that 67 percent had staffing meetings, 60 percent were staffed, and 58 percent secured representation, with 19 percent reporting no immediate career advancement.[63] Despite the benefits that can come from participating in a DEI program, both reports also highlight a common pitfall. Networks and studios habitually subsidize entry-level staff writer positions for BIPOC writers—that is, "diversity slots"—that ostensibly allow BIPOC writers to prove themselves and be rehired by showrunners for additional seasons, but showrunners rarely do so. Instead, these programs are described as "little more than a revolving door of one-year stints in the writers' room for diverse talent—where one 'free' writer simply replaces another."[64] There is no system to support career advancement, and so it can take participants even longer to move up because they are stalled in diversity hire slots. In short, DEI programs for writers may gain them entrance into the industry but are also abused by a large number of showrunners who are willing to free labor from people of color but unwilling to integrate those writers into their staff long-term.

Like diversity programs, diversity quotas have also proven questionably useful. In July of 2020, the new president and chief executive of CBS Entertainment Group George Cheeks—a gay Black man—announced the network's goal of 40 percent or more BIPOC writers in writers' rooms for the 2021–2022 season, and 50 percent or more the following year.[65] Showrunner Shawn Ryan expressed pride that "when CBS put those diversity hiring requirements later, [*S.W.A.T.* was] already above the threshold for that, before they ever instituted that" and suspects that CBS "used [*S.W.A.T.*] as a model for what they wanted things to look like on screen and off screen."[66] Elsewhere on CBS, as numerous interview subjects noted, pushes to increase diversity have been met with backlash, as in the case of a straight white script coordinator on *SEAL Team* who sued CBS for "anti-white discrimination," claiming that he was passed over for promotion due to being a straight white man;[67] every person who mentioned this man while speaking with me rolled their eyes at the absurdity of his claims and chalked it up to his poor performance rather than discrimination. Accusations of "reverse racism" such as this are just one challenge that has come from attempts to level the playing field in Hollywood and to build diverse writers' rooms that can better write diverse characters. Showrunner Alexi Hawley thus articulates the importance of a diverse cast and crew, noting, "If we're writing for actors of color and stories of those people, we should have voices in the room," and sharing that his writers' room has "always been a more diverse staff than not." However, only seventeen of twenty-one shows met CBS's target in the 2021–2022 season, and writers' rooms on shows like *Blue Bloods* remain perniciously white.[68]

Fred Berner raises concerns about the way increases in BIPOC representation happened, having served as producer and director on numerous Dick Wolf series.[69] Berner suggests that after Black Lives Matter developed into a recognized movement, people began casting more Black and Latine characters without having real conversations about what they were doing and why: "I feel like once social awareness took hold, people hurdled into a slightly new form without ever having the real conversation about what it meant, what it felt like, who these people were," and why it was important to consider the world from someone else's perspective. *NCIS: Los Angeles* was a bit of a contradiction, one writer notes, because they "had a pretty diverse cast compared to a lot of the other shows that [Color of Change's *Normalizing Injustice* report] looked at, but the writers' room was not very diverse. It was mostly male, mostly white," until efforts to increase writers' room diversity after the summer of 2020. "We brought it up a lot, like I think most of the hires that we had from that point on were people of color and female writers," though white men were still the majority for the remainder of the series. Berner traces the challenges of increasing diversity beyond writers and actors to directors and believes that this reactionary approach produced a new problem. As he explains, "We would submit our roster of director to Wolf Films and to the network and they would go, 'No, not enough diversity.'" Berner's response was to insist that when bringing new voices "into the fold" they "position them for success" by bringing them in early, having them shadow more experienced directors and acclimating to the show "because every show has its own culture." In this way, Berner worked on the individual level to avoid the chewing-up situation that so many "diversity hire" writers were made to experience.

It is problematic that these programs and quotas fail to help get BIPOC writers past the lowest rungs of television writing, especially when they are outnumbered or tokenized and unable to contribute meaningfully. In order to even make it into these rooms, writers often have to participate in interviews, and TTIE's Shireen Razack points out that "a lot of hiring for historically excluded writers is about trading on your trauma."[70] TTIE thus offers an "Acing the Interview" consultation that helps writers develop skills for avoiding uncomfortable questions and retraumatization. TTIE also offers a training called "Navigating the Writers' Room," which helps BIPOC writers to deal with toxic environments and nudge potentially harmful stories into more authentic spaces without jeopardizing their careers. It is therefore not enough to be dropped into a writers' room because BIPOC writers must navigate a veritable minefield.

The ability of lower-level BIPOC writers to rise through the ranks depends on the perceived value they hold among their superiors. As *The Rookie* writer/producer Fredrick Kotto notes, "If you contribute something to the table, then you're valuable; if you don't contribute to the table, then you're not as valuable."[71] The problem, though, is that a "diversity hire" who is there simply for diversity purposes is not likely to be able to contribute substantively. Kotto says this is because unless a writer has some special expertise to bring to the table, "I don't know how most showrunners would look at writers of color and see their value if they don't already appreciate it." In other words, a showrunner who appreciates the value of a diverse writing staff likely has numerous BIPOC writers in their writers' room and creates an environment that welcomes nuanced discussions, while a showrunner who does not value diversity might merely tolerate a free BIPOC writer.

Speaking to this untenable position, *S.W.A.T.* creator Aaron Rahsaan Thomas describes the survival techniques required to navigate these lower-level positions and the minefields of people who almost speak a different language; he explains that Black industry professionals have to figure out "how to get [their] point across without going to a place where this could end relationships really quickly." This is frequently marked by concerns about being diplomatic and essentially protecting white fragility, which requires BIPOC creatives to "learn the skillset of being able to build bridges, of learning how to speak different languages." This adaptability, Thomas feels, allows Black writers to write white characters because they have learned this language, whereas white writers who have not had to accommodate a predominantly Black industry are less equipped to write Black characters well. Black creatives learn and develop these skills as they rise through the ranks, and "by the time you get to a point when you're in charge, you're probably a Jedi knight in that." In becoming a showrunner with *S.W.A.T.*, Thomas says he had "not just a freedom to . . . have a more candid and smart and more nuanced conversation, but . . . an obligation because you put in all of that work, that sacrifice to get to [that] point."[72]

In addition to increasing numbers of BIPOC individuals on- and off-screen, networks and studios can push to create a more productive environment for an increasingly diverse industry. For example, Shondaland's Krista Vernoff, who served as writer, producer, and showrunner for *Grey's Anatomy* and later *Station 19*, wanted to help address racial tensions in the production process, and so she created the position of Director of Diversity and Inclusion at her production company.[73] In this role, Kasha Foster worked with writers, actors, and producers to guide the storytelling process.[74] *Station 19* producer Kiley Donovan shares that Vernoff worked to normalize this position in television, as it provides a series with a staff member whose job it is to act as liaison and facilitate not just conversations with outside organizations like Color of Change but also almost all cast and crew; for example, if a cast member reads a line of dialogue that does not feel culturally authentic but they are afraid to speak up to their white showrunner, or a writer wants to include a mixed-race character that is informed by some specific matter, Foster moderates and helps conversations to take place that have historically been avoided. In this role, Foster describes herself as "hardconversations.com."

One popular network strategy seems to be implementing bias training seminars in which trained professionals educate writers and other television creatives on the relationship between their internalized perspectives, their professional behaviors, and the kinds of content they create. *NCIS: New Orleans* writer and co–executive producer Talicia Raggs recalls her showrunner arranging for a bias training seminar even before Color of Change's damning report was published. Facilitated by CBS, moderators took the writers through exercises that helped them to understand how their biases developed and who benefits from or is harmed by those biases. Raggs recalls learning that people who are disadvantaged due to their identities "contort themselves to be in a writers' room or be acceptable to their coworkers," calling this practice "colluding."[75] In this context, colluders "make nice by playing into the role everyone thinks they should be in." Raggs recognizes that this seminar was designed to help her as a Black woman by educating her white colleagues, but she reports feeling gutted by the realization that she colludes even when she intends to bring people together. The seminar revealed "how a dominant culture that's not actively trying to be inclusive lets things develop in biases and maintain the status quo," and Raggs shares that she and her fellow writers were all profoundly affected. TTIE offers similar trainings for historically excluded writers to help them thrive, as well as trainings specifically aimed at executives and showrunners that are geared toward creating an inclusive room that fosters truly open sharing and creativity.[76]

Studios and networks are not alone in developing programs to include and elevate BIPOC creatives; so too has the WGA, in addition to compiling data and publishing reports. In 2009, the WGA put forth an initiative called the Writers Access Project to enlist WGA members in identifying and spotlighting outstanding and underutilized BIPOC writers. This project invites showrunners and executive producers to review and judge spec scripts from BIPOC writers to identify experienced and qualified talent. This program would both endorse "showrunner-certified" writers for staffing and expose the showrunner judges to the breadth of talented BIPOC writers. After the first year of the Writers Access Project, fourteen BIPOC honorees were hired. The WGA's 2013 brief refers to the Writers Access Project and other interventions as "an important first step toward the goal of diversifying the contingent of storytellers whose work fuels the Hollywood industry."[77] As the brief concludes, subsequent steps toward progress "will require renewed commitment on the part of other industry players—the networks, studios, and agents—to go beyond what has been done in the past to address the status quo on the industry diversity front," because each step along the production pipeline entails potential barriers to increased diversity.

The Writers Guild Foundation (WGF), a nonprofit organization associated with the WGA, hosts numerous additional programs designed to help writers, including the Writers' Access Support Staff Training Program (WASSTP), which began in 2021. WGF director of community programs Kira VandenBrande explains how WASSTP was prompted by showrunners' concerns about the closed loop of hiring whereby people would recommend their friends and others with whom they had preexisting connections.[78] This often means that support staff who are hired for these positions are the ones to become staff writers, especially when showrunners tend to promote internally. Because they did not know where to find qualified support staff, showrunners defaulted to people within their network, and so the WASSTP works to develop that specific niche skill set among underrepresented communities and advocate for them to showrunners. Like network and studio fellowships, WASSTP is highly competitive, accepting just eighteen of their twenty-two hundred applicants in 2023. At the end of the program, partner networks like NBC get "the first pass at this lookbook—they get to reach out to folks first before they get scooped up," and executives and showrunners will be invited to mixers to connect with program graduates. VandenBrande is proud that they "get to give people that sort of first step or first rung on the ladder, to at least make their name established," and that their program participants have been successful in getting staffed. Because studios had already identified this as "a space that they were lacking," WASSTP functions to help both BIPOC aspiring writers and studio executives.

In addition to studios, networks, and labor groups, activist organizations like Color of Change and the Geena Davis Institute have also invested in promoting progress in the television industry and have by necessity taken a different approach, as they have little official power. Because they have no authority over showrunners and cannot dictate policy, external activists have to navigate a very different landscape than those who run the broadcast television industry. In Lopez's extensive engagement with Asian media activists, she highlights the fact that the efficacy of any given activist tactic depends on numerous factors, which include "the kind of image being protested, the kind of group initiating the protests, and the cultural and legal landscape surrounding the production and distribution of the image, among others."[79] Lopez notes that the "desire to maintain positive relationships with media producers is a common attribute of activist groups whose main goal is to impact representation in mainstream media outlets."[80] To this end, an activist group might frame their work as educating creatives and offering assistance rather than scolding them. Schilt similarly finds that it is "more productive to employ educational campaigns that provide information for altering future . . . representations than to use hostile tactics, such as boycotts, that tend to only affect the immediate issue at hand."[81] *The Rookie*'s writer/producer Fredrick Kotto shares that he has "had experience with social justice leaders who want to use this medium to make change—and I think that's great, it's smart, it's forward-thinking," but that "there is a finger-wagging element that can sometimes come through, which is counterproductive."

In the case of Color of Change, its status as a racial justice organization in which media is just one avenue for pushing progress likely helped it to be frank and unvarnished when presenting data in its 2020 *Normalizing Injustice* report. This report was fueled by the fact that, as Color of Change consultant Kristen Marston explains, television content "impacts the way we vote, the way that we react to people, and even the way that we either believe Black Lives Matter is a terrorist organization or not."[82] Published mere months before George Floyd's murder, this report demonstrated that crime dramas normalize injustice as a standard practice, misrepresent the criminal justice system in ways that render racism invisible, and exclude BIPOC people behind the camera. In doing so, Color of Change put a spotlight on shows like *Blue Bloods* and *Lethal Weapon* in which concerning representations of police violence and civil liberty violations were the most egregious. Their candor likely did not make them any friends at *Blue Bloods*, but what's unclear is whether there is any context in which a show like *Blue Bloods* might be receptive to these kinds of critiques, committed as they are to blue-line rhetoric (see Figure 1.3). Where they did find success was with series with more diverse casts and BLM advocates and allies. Creatives at these programs proved considerably more open to critique, and their responses

FIG. 1.3. Jamie calls for backup on the *Blue Bloods* episode "Drawing Dead" (2013).

demonstrated a desire to do better, seemingly fueled by the authentic desire to do good while informed by a fear of getting canceled—literally or metaphorically—for failing to do so. Thus, even though its published report was used by news outlets to lambast the cop genre, Color of Change was invited to consult on more than one hundred series.[83]

Various resources, tools, and strategies are available to BIPOC writers that function to educate all writers (but especially white writers) while helping to lessen the burden carried by BIPOC writers who are often dramatically outnumbered. Color of Change offers consulting services to help writers understand, at a macro level, the tropes they rely on and the stereotypes they reinforce when crafting "bad guy" characters. TTIE also offers consulting, as well as fact sheets that put information about racialized tropes and stereotypes into the hands of writers so that, rather than calling writers out as racist for deploying racist tropes, they give writers a way to talk through how to write characters. TTIE's Barb Friend describes these fact sheets as "somewhat of a shield" that can serve as a "sort of defense for someone who might be afraid to speak up or someone who's feeling like they want to stand up for one of their co-workers but maybe they don't have the words for it."[84] In this way, TTIE's fact sheets serve as impartial expertise and easily accessible resources that cut down on BIPOC writers' emotional labor. As Amanda Green explains, mostly white writers' rooms are ripe with racist and biased comments, and a single Black writer in the room can only do so much to educate their white colleagues; with consultants like Color of Change and tools like TTIE fact sheets, BIPOC writers in predominantly white writers' rooms can harken back to the educational information to help bear the weight of those difficult conversations. Beyond this, Green shares, "One of the biggest tools we have is actually the specter of Twitter and going, 'Hey guys, I know we really love this story idea, but how do you think that'll play out on Twitter? Like, will Twitter say we're being racist?' Which is just a covert way of saying, 'Dude, you're being racist. If I call you out, I'm not gonna get a job . . . but what would Twitter say about this storyline? Are we exposing ourselves?'"[85]

Another resource comes from the Geena Davis Institute, which "collaborate[s] with media producers, executives, advertisers, and content creators, providing active guidance to create systems that amplify diversity both in front of and behind the camera."[86] Elizabeth Kilpatrick, GDI's senior vice president, explains the purpose and history of its Spellcheck for Bias program.[87] Numerous studios and brand partners participate, typically because a showrunner or producer will want insight or because a studio executive wants assistance in covering sensitive subjects, and so the program "really took off during Black Lives Matter . . . because people wanted an outside assessment of what they were doing so they didn't get a lot of pushback." In the Spellcheck for Bias program, consultants review scripts and consider factors like race, gender, sexuality, age, and body type, and quantify the inclusion of different groups, but the consultants also "point out the tropes and stereotypes that are being used, or [if] there [is] harmful language," so as to point out opportunities to do better. For example, if a character is a fifty-year-old white man and it is not important to the role that it be a fifty-year-old white man, the consultant might encourage writers to adjust the character. "We're very careful about not wanting to impinge on the artistic integrity of what they're doing," Kilpatrick explains, "but just sort of provide—here's an opportunity . . . there are this many opportunities where you could change those characters." Kilpatrick reports that 150 broadcast scripts utilized the Spellcheck for Bias program in 2023, with some series submitting multiple episodes. It is not that studios require writers to use GDI as a resource, but that after the summer of 2020 "there was a big pushback from studios . . . to make sure that what they were putting out there in the world was showing good representation and not a lot of tropes and stereotypes, particularly in certain areas." This push from studios was part of Hollywood's larger trend of prioritizing DEI, at least for a time: "It went from . . . a division of HR that was peripherally involved in the actual content to a position that reports to the CEO. It's at an enterprise level and they're taking it seriously." Kilpatrick acknowledges that this has started to change in a kind of post-Floyd lull, but that GDI continues to work to help writers understand and think through their options in crafting television narratives.

Conclusion

The 2005 Hollywood Writers Report, as its introduction explains, "replays a story told many times in previous WGA reports: pockets of promise may emerge from time to time, but institutionalized barriers continue to stymie progress on the Hollywood writer diversity front."[88] This holds true for many areas of television development and production and is almost certainly as true now as it was then. Increases in representation in one area are often met with decreases in another. Programs and mandates are developed that recognize diversity as integral to U.S. culture and seek to counteract centuries of institutionalized racism; they are met with lawsuits and claims of anti-white racism. Attempts to make television reflect the United States' 40 percent BIPOC population are derided as symptomatic of Hollywood liberals with a "woke mind virus."[89] Progress, be it a natural evolution or concerted efforts to correct the underrepresentation of BIPOC people, has produced a more diverse creative body; it has also put great pressure on BIPOC creatives to do well, and it takes a toll. Showrunner Aaron Rahsaan Thomas shares, "There's a certain exhaustion when you're a person of color trying to tell stories that are close to you emotionally in a different way than others."

Broadcast television has evolved considerably in the twenty-first century. Brandy Monk-Payton (2021) notes that the commercial medium of television "has seemed to shift from the discourse of promoting racial 'relevance' to that of practicing an active 'reckoning' with race at the level of the industry, text, and audience." In this context, the inclusion of racially diverse characters has been less an afterthought than it once was, and the shift to expand BIPOC people occurred at all levels both on- and off-screen. This is a natural progression in cultural politics, assisted by numerous organizations within and tangential to media industries that are invested in a more colorful symbolic universe on television, including writers, actors, networks, and activist groups. At the same time, mere visibility is not enough, and it is debatable to what extent increases in BIPOC representation signal political gains. Organizations like the Geena Davis Institute and Color of Change provide reports that qualitatively and quantitatively measure on- and off-screen diversity and have proven to be valuable consultants for series interested in producing more representative and nuanced depictions of America's diverse population.

In the next chapter, I turn my focus on the police procedural genre in which BIPOC employment comes with particular challenges, specifically the genre's tendency to overlook police crimes against people and communities of color. I begin by considering the tension between dramatic impulses and discourses of "accuracy," and the role of police officers who work in television in navigating that tension. My findings suggest the limitations of police influence on content despite popular assertions to the contrary. I then trace developments in the depiction of the police from the pre-BLM era to the early BLM era, emphasizing the ways existing cop dramas dipped their toes into conversations about police brutality and systemic racism. Finally, I lay out different approaches to creating cop shows in the midst of the BLM era and demonstrate the potential for showrunners to challenge the consensus ideology of U.S. cop shows.

2

Early BLM Cop Shows (2013–2020)

Adjusting to a New Normal

Television is not an institutional monolith, and it does not automatically reflect dominant ideologies. Rather, it comprises individuals who make decisions informed by myriad factors, including governmental regulations, network corporate cultures, public sentiments, commercial imperatives, expert consultants, and individual tastes and preferences. The genre of police procedurals is ripe for consideration of how ideologies and industrial logics operate around and through these content creators, as those who work on police procedurals do their jobs working under an increasingly intense microscope.

Television's police officers have historically been presented as protectors, albeit imperfect ones, articulated through a sympathetic lens as they struggle to maintain social order.[1] However, it is not as simple as good cops catching bad villains; rather, police procedurals create a space to explore the complexities and contradictions inherent in modern policing.[2] For example, some police officers and detectives in *The Shield* (2002–2008) and *N.Y.P.D. Blue* (1993–2005) were demonstrably prejudiced against Black and Brown suspects, and both racial slurs and excessive violence were regular features of these narratives.[3] This reconceptualization of policing as inherently flawed rather than sacred resulted in a widening of representations of law enforcement officers.[4] The individuals who are responsible for this content, disproportionately white men, are not uniform in their approach to creating television or representing policing, but interviews with them and analyses of the police genre's cultural forum frequently indicate a growing sense of obligation to produce programming that might better serve racial justice. Still, these shifting representations have tended to locate flaws with policing in individual characters instead of treating them as symptoms of a dysfunctional, amoral bureaucratic institution.[5] With the rise of the Black Lives Matter movement came increased scrutiny of both policing and police procedurals.[6]

I begin this chapter by exploring the role of the often-maligned technical consultant and the contested notion of "authenticity" in cop shows, tracing historical shifts in the role of police officers in writers' rooms and on set; in this section I articulate the ways current and former officers are empowered or constrained in their contributions to the genre. I then provide a brief review of pre-BLM cop shows to provide context for the police genre at the beginning of the BLM movement, emphasizing how they typically framed and engaged issues like policing and systemic racism. This survey is not comprehensive, nor is it limited to broadcast series, as select series on cable (*The Shield* on FX, 2002–2008) and premium cable (*The Wire* on HBO, 2002–2008) left a mark in their engagement with police corruption. I follow this with an exploration of early BLM cop shows like *Law & Order: SVU* (NBC, 1999–present), *NCIS: Los Angeles* (CBS, 2009–2023), and *Blue Bloods* (CBS, 2010–2024) that predate BLM's inception and incorporated the movement over time. I close this chapter by analyzing three programs that were created during, and to varying degrees motivated by, the BLM movement. Using interviews with their showrunners, I demonstrate how *S.W.A.T.* (CBS, 2017–present) and *The Rookie* (ABC, 2018–present) take a decidedly antiracist approach and contrast this with how *Chicago P.D.* (NBC, 2014–present), which is one node in a web of Dick Wolf productions, takes a more conventional approach. I tie these varied approaches to the perspectives and creative approaches of their showrunners and shed light on the industrial logics and internal struggles that produce very different tones among BLM-era cop shows.

Cops, Consultants, and the Construction of "Reality"

Consultants are common in numerous television genres, helping to provide realistic jargon for legal procedurals and medical shows, among others. Reasons for using consultants include creators' artistic goal of realism and accuracy, actors' desire to appear competent, and audience preferences.[7] In his study of science consultants, Frank identifies two functions of consultants: furnishing cues that allow creators to give fictional narratives "a greater sense of perceptual reality," and enabling creators "to feel better about the products they create and become part of the studio publicity machine that tries to impress upon us, the viewing public, that their production partakes of the Real."[8] Research on consultants thus theorizes their role and considers the extent to which television can or should be realistic as an art form; in other words, what degree of accuracy should a consultant help a content creator to achieve? When Davis, Savoie, and Longnecker interviewed science experts who consult on science-fiction programming, they found that the emphasis on accuracy is inconsistent, as science is utilized for different purposes in a narrative.[9] Noting that consultants and creators expressed similar beliefs about the use of science in science fiction, Davis et al. propose that "only those consultants whose perspectives generally align with creators will last in Hollywood."[10] This aligns with Fredrick Kotto's take on contemporary police consultants in cop shows, which recognizes the various constraints placed on technical consultants.[11]

Much of the criticism of the police genre focuses on its tendency toward "copaganda," specifically placing blame on the roles of police officers in producing cop shows.[12] This critique seems facile given the realities of television consulting work that active-duty and retired officers do. Police consulting on police procedurals has evolved over the history of broadcast television. *Dragnet* was famously deferential to the LAPD and made liberal use of LAPD officers and resources, but contemporary police procedurals are far more restrained, and LAPD officers serve as consultants or work security. In the writing process, consultants might be invited to review scripts for glaring errors and mistakes or to comment on a narrative's premise or plausibility,[13] and many consultants report having their feedback taken seriously and implemented.[14] *Chicago Fire* and *Chicago P.D.* creator Michael Brandt, for example, might ask a firefighter consultant to provide him with a scenario that gets his characters from point A to point B "because we just don't want to go save cats out of trees and put out fires and then come back to the house and finish the conversation we were having before. . . . That's where the consultants are really helpful . . . help find those scenarios so the personal storylines of the shows keep getting pushed forward."[15] On set, Frank points out, a consultant's presence is "effective only to the extent that the director, and to a lesser extent the producer, want it to be," such that if the director and producer do not value them, the consultant will at best have "some minor impact on the visual aspects" in ways that weakly support the perception of reality.[16] Cop consultants are meant to help with guns, weaponry, and tactics (GAK), which means showing actors things like what they should look like when they go through a door and how to hold a weapon.[17] Thus, while many (though not all) of the television creatives who create cop shows might fetishize police officers, actual police contributions to content are less substantive than mainstream critics are inclined to believe; rather, they are there to lend a production an air of authenticity.

Though technical consultants are ostensibly present to facilitate accuracy, representations of policing are of course only ever "accurate" in the loosest of terms. Brandt, for example, points out that cop shows do not realistically depict the amount of paperwork that police do or their low success rates—"the boring stuff"—but instead show the "fun and entertaining stuff that is the status quo of the genre."[18] Authenticity in cop shows is a construct built around efforts to garner high ratings and rake in advertising dollars. As part of this, police dramas default to depicting officers in a positive light; television writing is an art, but television programs are made by and sold to corporations, many of which tend to frown on negative depictions of the police, regardless of how accurately they capture the uglier realities of policing in the United States. As a result, TV cops are typically the good guys, and activists—both those outside and working within the broadcast industry—must work diligently and strategically to chip away at this glossy facade. My concern is less with the lack of scenes showing police toiling away at paperwork and more with the ways these writ large inaccuracies discursively limit the cop genre's cultural forum, particularly when it comes to issues of racist policing practices.

Fredrick Kotto models an alternative to how former police officers can be useful in the production of cop shows that disrupt the genre's status quo and offer an antiracist alternative. Kotto may be one of the most influential police officers in Hollywood, but he is not a consultant.[19] After nearly twenty years of service with the San Jose Police Department in northern California, Kotto left the force to become a television writer. Kotto had become an officer because, as a Black man, he had had bad experiences with the police, and he wanted to model a different kind of policing: "I always thought, if I'm going to be a cop, I'm going to be a normal person. I'm going to be a good dude and try to be fair with everybody." Kotto recounts an extensive background investigation including psychological exams, interviews with ex-girlfriends and former bosses, a polygraph, and a credit check before being admitted. (It is worth noting that this is not a countrywide standard, and Kotto describes background checks in some regions as "virtually nonexistent"). Though Kotto worked in numerous divisions, his time working undercover gave him experiences that motivated him to try his hand at writing. Kotto read sixty-seven books on how to write a script and wrote some pilots that earned him an agent and job offers. After sustaining an injury that prevented him from further work in the field, Kotto relocated to Los Angeles, where he worked a series of jobs. He tells me, "I think what was really appreciated is that I really try to bring some authenticity because . . . I didn't come up as an assistant. I didn't grow up in the system. I just know good stories and then, thanks to my studies, how to write them."

Though he never worked as a technical consultant, Kotto effectively functions as one. Kotto spent one year as a staff writer on a cable network crime drama that "wanted a detective's experience to help the story along in a realistic way." Still learning the ropes, Kotto recalls, "My whole thing was 'keep your mouth shut and contribute when necessary,'" and so he would chime in with guidance on what a detective might do in any given moment. "And they're like, 'We didn't even think of that—excellent—it goes in the show.'" Technical advisors do not always get this response. They are usually active-duty or retired police officers for whom "this is a second well-paying job . . . and they don't want to lose that job." This means that on-set cops are unlikely to say anything that a producer does not want to hear, for example, by pointing out that "cops would never draw a chalk line outline around a dead body" or other technical accuracies that detract from the dramaturgy of the cop genre; "I can't tell you how many times I've heard, 'We're not making a documentary.'" Producers might describe a scenario and ask if it is possible, and "the consultant will say, 'Not really, but, you know, I'm working on a show and I'm not going to tell you you're wrong. So, yeah, why not? I mean, it's Hollywood, right? It's make-believe.'" When a writer/producer has the experience of working in law enforcement, it is a different dynamic. Like a technical consultant, a cop-turned-writer is useful because "most cops don't know how the stories are told, and most TV producers do not know how crimes are investigated. All they really know is what they've seen on cop shows, and that's why you get the same thing over and over again. And I figured out a way to make myself valuable in Hollywood is to know both sides." Very few people have taken this path, with Kotto and *Criminal Minds* showrunner Ed Bernero serving as rare exceptions. However, Kotto knows "a number of Black officers . . . who want to become writers" because they recognize numerous myths about policing, and "we can dispel a lot of them, we can get rid of a lot of these tropes, these tired, old, dumb, boring ideas that get played over and over."

Kotto is not interested in churning out the same de rigueur representations of policing that can be found in most cop shows. Frustrated with producers, studios, and networks that want content dumbed down for a mass audience, Kotto has found a home as a writer/producer at Alexi Hawley's *The Rookie*. Kotto recalls an interview in which Hawley expressed a desire to be "authentic" and explore what policing looks and feels like, because "that wasn't really going on" in other cop shows. Rather than reminders that "we're not making a documentary," Kotto shares, "Alexi will ask me in earnest, 'What would police do in this situation?' And I will tell him in earnest, 'Well, they would do this, or they would do that, and they certainly wouldn't do *that*.'" Kotto goes on to explain, "I feel fortunate and blessed in the way that I'm able to bring what I think is a commonsense decency police aspect to television, and Alexi's had the smarts, the kindness as a person to actually put that on television." While he acknowledges that some police officers must surely beat information out of suspects as is so commonly seen in countless cop shows, "in reality that's 100 percent unacceptable. . . . Is that what we're gonna promote as the right thing to do? I think we'd be foolish and short-sighted to do that."

Kotto believes in the power of media to shape and improve law enforcement, having seen it firsthand. "In every police academy, myself included . . . we teach potential police officers how to deal with situations by showing movies and TV shows. We absolutely lift scenes out of shows and show them in the academy . . . as either correct or incorrect," and he hopes *The Rookie* is adopted as a model for what to do. This push to model a different kind of policing—one that is no less entertaining than *Chicago P.D.* or *Blue Bloods* but that finds newer, more compelling ways to drum up drama—aligns with the goal of activists who want to see an expanded range of voices and perspectives included in cop shows. Such diversity of perspectives can be fostered by using alternative sources for consultants. For example, as I will discuss in chapter 3, Hawley consulted with representatives from Color of Change in crafting narratives for *The Rookie* that provided more nuanced engagement with the repercussions of policing for the communities being policed.[20] Expanding the consulting pool for a cop show creates greater possibilities for expanding the broadcast medium's cultural forum by introducing perspectives that might not come naturally to writers and technical consultants.

The generic status quo, with all its inaccuracies, prevents the entertainment broadcast medium from cultivating a space where audiences might come to terms with the ideologies and proposed policy changes that are needed in order to systemically change policing in the United States. Activists promote more "accurate" or "realistic" representations of policing that confront the myriad ways implicit bias and other racist perspectives manifestly influence policing practices, and this proposal is at times misinterpreted—sometimes belligerently so—to mean activists want cop shows to emphasize realities like paperwork and do away with the dramatic elements. However, the real goal is not to create boring cop shows filled with paperwork but cop shows that honestly reflect on systemic issues that disproportionately target BIPOC people: police dramas in which cops are held accountable when they act in racist ways, use excessive force, or break the law to solve the case, all while being heralded as the heroes. This kind of antiracist policing would likely read as "inaccurate" and aspirational, or perhaps as "woke" and pandering, depending on the ideological leanings of the viewer. It might also be read as commercially dangerous for challenging the status quo of a wildly successful genre. And yet, as some programs developed in the pre-Floyd BLM years will show, inaccuracies can be more interesting and socially compelling. Moreover, there is an audience for nontraditional, antiracist police procedurals.

The Status Quo of Pre-BLM Police Procedurals

The police genre is as old as television itself, having transitioned from radio with the medium's invention. Broad patterns can be identified in how police and policing have been depicted over time, from the undisputed hero to the maverick to the complicated man to the aspirational figure. The genre has developed from the time of the prototypical police procedural *Dragnet*, which "depicted the police officer as a public hero who always got his man," to the 1980s and *Hill Street Blues*, in which "the police officer has been shown to fail occasionally and even to question his or her own self-worth."[21] With this evolution came the loss of what John Sumser terms "moral certainty," which had long been a hallmark of the police procedural throughout the 1960s, '70s, and '80s.[22] In the 1990s the genre expanded its growing emphasis on complex serial narratives that focused on the officers and detectives in character-driven dramas.[23] Nineties' cop shows like *Homicide* (1993–1998) and *NYPD Blue* (1993–2005) "were produced with a keen awareness of the genre's past, through which they opened up and explored specific core elements of the genre: realism, melodrama, and issues of justice."[24] As Nichols-Pethick points out, this blending of generic tradition and novelty allowed cop shows to "participate in the ongoing forum about crime, community, and citizenship that is so central to the police genre." It is perhaps not surprising that so many cop shows take a similar approach in their depiction of policing, as there is something of a revolving door within the cop genre, with writers, producers, and actors working on numerous projects throughout their careers. For example, after working on *Colombo* (NBC, 1971–1978), Steve Bochco created *Hill Street Blues* (NBC, 1981–1987), which writer/producer Billy Finkelstein dubs "a kind of turning-point police drama,"[25] before going on to create *NYPD Blue* (ABC, 1993–2005) with *Hill Street Blues* writer David Milch; Shawn Ryan would later hire writers and producers from *NYPD Blue* and *Homicide: Life on the Streets* for *The Shield*.[26]

FIG. 2.1. Sipowicz interrogates a witness on the *NYPD Blue* episode "Guns 'n Rosaries" (1994).

Cop shows in the 1980s and 1990s increasingly leaned into melodrama and seriality, with series like *NPDB Blue* primed to use "contemporary social discourses to explore the concept of virtue" and present "the figure of the detective as the model citizen: responsible for oneself and *obligated to others*."[27] Writing in 1997, Pribram described *NYPD Blue* as taking viewers "into a world where we rarely see film and television cops go: the emotional dilemmas and interpersonal conflicts of human relationships."[28] Similarly, Finkelstein suggests that *NYPD Blue* "pushed at the parameters of what constituted a cop show and how dramatically complicated you could make characters," specifically the Dennis Franz character of Andy Sipowicz: "That was a portrayal of a cop, the likes of which I don't think we had ever seen on television." Sipowicz belongs to a breed of cops that are "'loose cannon' iconoclasts . . . willing to compromise the tenets of law, and even risk their careers, for the more ennobling goal of ridding society of a criminal evil that the justice system seems ill-equipped to handle."[29] Such cops are intuitive, skilled, and focused on getting justice for victims. Notably, however, Sipowicz was also an angry alcoholic who regularly enacted linguistic and physical violence against people of color, including the frequent use of racial slurs (see Figure 2.1). The gritty realness of this character might be attributed at least in part to the fact that early seasons relied narratively on a consultant named Bill Clark, a detective whom creator David Milch hired to act as technical consultant. In this role, Clark read and commented on scripts, supervised the set dressing, and made himself available to advise actors in technical aspects of their performance. Clark's friendships throughout the NYPD also, Milch recounts, "solved or simplified countless production problems."[30] This was a more in-depth form of consulting than the contemporary model described to me by *The Rookie*'s writer/producer and former detective Fredrick Kotto.[31]

Milch stated he "wanted *NYPD Blue* to be about race" and that "one of its most important aspects was the opportunity to address race, among other issues, in the kind of complexity [he] hadn't seen in other television drama;"[32] Sipowicz thus functioned as an illustration of this complexity, his racial biases serving "as a way to grapple with the contradictions that frame discourses about race in urban America: where the responsibility for racism lies, and what might be done about it."[33] Rather than pretending racist cops do not exist, *NYPD Blue* puts one front and center as part of the series' commitment to realism, as "*not* to portray racists in a series about New York cops would have made the show incredible."[34] One reason for *NYPD Blue*'s apparent legacy seems to be Sipowicz's growth over the course of twelve seasons, as he begrudgingly adapts to change and comes to accept and respect his BIPOC colleagues and supervisors while also breaking the habit of hurling racial insults at suspects.[35] Writer Niceole Levy celebrates flawed cops like Sipowicz over the heroes of more contemporary programming, noting that "every time Andy Sipowicz said something racist, he got called out . . . and it didn't mean he grew every single time, but it happened enough that you saw him grow; you saw him as a person who realized that that mentality needed to change."[36]

Premiering less than a year earlier, *Homicide: Life on the Street* (NBC, 1993–1999) adapted journalist David Simon's 1991 book *Homicide: A Year on the Killing Streets* for television. Simon's book chronicles a year spent with Baltimore homicide detectives, and the series captures the book's "factual complexity, narrative density, and sociological precision."[37] The *Homicide* series pulled extensively from the *Homicide* book in terms of characters, criminal cases, and plotlines such that producer Tom Fontana notes the production "had pretty much sucked every comma and question mark out of [Simon's] book" by the end of the series.[38] Simon's role as a crime reporter lends both a certain amount of authenticity and a grain of salt to the depiction of policing, capturing and confronting the realities of policing as observed firsthand by an impartial journalist in ways that Clark's reports to *NYPD Blue* creatives could not; as Simon notes in writing his manuscript, "I was fully aware that my detectives were, at moments, racist and sexist and homophobic . . . I very purposefully kept those moments in the manuscript . . . as guideposts for readers seeking an honest view of inner-city cops."[39] *NYPD Blue* consistently earned higher ratings and mainstream popularity, which *Homicide* producers attributed to their show's "more realistic, variegated, and accurate view of detective work . . . a depiction that generally eschews car chases, gunplay, nudity, and profanity"[40] and their investment in creating "a thinking person's police show."[41] *Homicide* therefore challenged traditional generic norms and embraced social realism over staid expectations of what would make for commercially successful television, avoiding cop-show formulas and breaking with conventions more than it obeys them,[42] and reports suggest ongoing negotiations between this approach and NBC's desire to improve ratings through increased depictions of romance or action.[43] *Homicide*'s drama instead came from detectives' considerable commitment to tackling moral questions around racial animus and cultural dislocations throughout the crime-solving process, resulting in "a complex discourse about the social, economic, and political policies that sometimes foster crime in the first place."[44] This approach "remorselessly punctures the hope—sustained, if not created, by the hundreds of television cop shows broadcast by American networks since the 1940s—that homicide detectives wish to do right by murder victims" by showing detectives to be intellectually engaged while emotionally shut off, treating crime-solving as a bureaucratic endeavor to change names on the murder board from red (unsolved) to black (solved).[45]

Breaking even further with the tradition of moral certainty in cop shows, *The Shield* (FX, 2002–2008) was created by Shawn Ryan and was inspired by the Rampart scandal, which exposed corruption among an LAPD anti-gang unit in the 1990s. Ryan crafted FX's flagship program around Vic Mackey (Michael Chiklis), the self-serving leader of the ultraviolent Strike Team in the fictitious Farmington area of Los Angeles.[46] The series pilot sets the tone for a very different kind of cop show, with Mackey famously informing a suspected pedophile, "Good cop and bad cop left for the day. I'm a different kind of cop," before violently beating the suspect with his fists and a large phone book (see Figure 2.2). David Aceveda, Mackey's captain, reluctantly makes use of Mackey as a tool of blunt force, conceding that "Mackey isn't a cop—he's Al Capone with a badge." When Mackey's violence results in a confession that saves a little girl's life, everyone is relieved and Mackey's tactics are tacitly condoned, but viewers see a different side of the Strike Force at the end of the episode when, after breaking into a drug dealer's home to rob and kill him, Mackey uses the dealer's gun to execute a fellow officer who he knew was investigating him for corruption. With its depiction of the worst kind of offenders Los Angeles has to offer and the Strike Team as a

FIG. 2.2. Mackey interrogates a suspect in the pilot episode of *The Shield* (2002).

necessary evil for keeping those offenders contained, *The Shield* constantly "set a new low for police behavior on television" and "forced viewers to rethink and redefine their notions of justice and morality."[47]

Scholars have been divided on whether *The Shield* celebrates bad cops, and Ryan admits the writers struggled with that as well.[48] Suspecting that viewers "of different ideological bents like the show for different reasons," Ryan also felt "there was a visceral enjoyment a lot of people . . . had at seeing the strike team get away with some of the stuff that they did." Moreover, the writers liked their actors and "tried to write them as human beings, not just soulless villains." Ultimately, Ryan suggests, people who think *The Shield* celebrated cops' bad behaviors were not paying attention. The "horrible details" that came to light with the Rampart scandal conflicted with television's decades-long lionization of police officers, so it felt only right that *The Shield* depict "the not-so-good cops, to sort of explain what's going on and to help explain [why] communities of color look at the police departments in their cities with suspicion."

Ryan sheds light on how the showrunner of a cop show, a creative scribe with no first-hand experience in policing, can come to learn about and understand the perspectives of police officers in ways that inform the world they create on television. Ryan's experience writing television cops was informed by his time doing ride-alongs and observing police officers. Ryan reports being shocked by an us-versus-them mentality, "a bit of dehumanizing that begins to happen over a period of time in police officers' eyes—'I can't believe these animals live this way'—and it becomes a gateway to mistreat these people." While shocked by this revelation, Ryan also admits, "I can't say that I blame them, and I can't say that I would be any different if I worked one of those jobs." Ryan recognized the history of racism historically built into institutions like the LAPD and was interested in the contradictions whereby white officers like Vic Mackey can "elevate the brotherhood of police officers" and defend Black cops against racist criminals, only to turn around and racially profile throughout his own investigation. Recalling time spent in a predominantly Black neighborhood with a high homicide rate with ten white homicide detectives, Ryan learned that "they learn very quickly to factor race into things" and that when "the people that you're spending time with are often murderers and people covering for murderers, it's hard to balance that with the larger picture of race relations." Therefore, in writing police shows, Ryan felt it "disingenuous not to acknowledge that race plays a factor to a larger degree than it does in other aspects of our society."

The ways American cop shows like *Homicide*, *N.Y.P.D. Blue*, and *The Shield* reflected on policing demonstrates an interest in exploring how police behave, both in actuality and in theory. Their approaches were largely shaped by actual police officers and detectives whom they either knew personally or had read about extensively, be they technical consultants as in *NYPD Blue*, sources from prolonged studies as in *Homicide*, or the combination of acquaintances and dirty cops detailed in news coverage as in *The Shield*. They showed diverse precincts where BIPOC people and women (and the occasional member of the LGBTQ community) could work alongside straight white men to protect the innocent. There were some bad apples who were occasionally held accountable for their actions, though if they came from a rotten orchard, there was not much anyone could really do about that. While they operated in a world where racism in policing was a serious problem, it was sufficiently mundane to avoid too much attention in entertainment television. More than twenty years after Rodney King was brutally beaten by four LAPD officers, the Black Lives Matter movement would start to move the needle.

Early BLM Engagement: Adapting to a Budding Movement

Numerous police series permeated broadcast airwaves at the time of the first outpouring of national support for the Black Lives Matter movement and thus found themselves in a position to participate in amplified discussions about policing and systemic racism. A review of three such shows—*NCIS: Los Angeles* (CBS, 2009–2023), *Blue Bloods* (CBS, 2010–2024), and *Law &*

Order: SVU (NBC, 1999–present)—illustrates different approaches that established cop shows took to dealing with a changing sociopolitical landscape in which the police's treatment of Black people was increasingly part of national discourses. These three programs had established a tone long before George Zimmerman's acquittal prompted the first #BlackLivesMatter tweet in 2013, and there was no cultural mandate to immediately engage the budding movement. The movement eventually influenced each show to some degree but was not consistently evoked by their characters or narratives.

Writers on these shows frequently expressed concern about how to address the movement "authentically" through the lens of established characters and tone, which are shaped largely by a show's premise. *NCIS: Los Angeles* follows a diverse team of naval law enforcement officers led by Chris O'Donnell and LL Cool J, and though police officers might appear from time to time during an investigation, they were not featured in any meaningful way. Speaking to its tone, a writer and producer for *NCIS: Los Angeles* suggested that this spin-off was "a little bit more of an action comedy" and "a little bit lighthearted" as compared to the original *NCIS* series. As a result, the writers took a more escapist approach in their storytelling that emphasized banter and action and was less predisposed to tackle heavier issues like challenging institutionalized racism in policing. This was not due to any kind of official rule or mandate; rather, "that was just kind of the way that we viewed the show ourselves." It was not until Color of Change published its 2020 *Normalizing Injustice* report that *NCIS: Los Angeles* made a more concerted effort to engage, as I will discuss in chapter 3. That said, it is worth noting that this series fared relatively well by Color of Change metrics. Specifically, Color of Change measured the ratio of wrongful actions committed by "good guys"—that is, criminal justice professionals (CJPs)—versus "bad guys." As the organization's *Normalizing Injustice* report notes, in depicting bad behavior as committed by good people, cop shows are guilty of "framing bad actions as relatable, forgivable, acceptable and ultimately good."[49] Color of Change dubbed this the "Good Guy Endorser Effect" as "most series conveyed the idea that whatever a CJP does is inherently 'right' and 'good' by virtue of it being done by a CJP, especially a beloved main character." By this measure, the police are de facto heroes and their actions categorically heroic, regardless of the legality of those actions or their negative consequences for others. With an eight-to-one ratio, *NCIS: Los Angeles* was by far less egregious than shows like *Blue Bloods* and *Law & Order: SVU.*

In contrast to *NCIS: Los Angeles*, *Blue Bloods* was interested in discussing the nuances of policing at length, but in ways that would earn it scorn from

Color of Change. *Blue Bloods* has "earned heaps of praise from police officers" due to the unflinching support it provides the profession and has been described as a fantasy world of idyllic officers.[50] While *The Rookie* and *S.W.A.T.* specifically took an aspirational approach to showing what policing could look like, they deviate from the *Blue Bloods* approach of overlooking, ignoring, and deriding criticisms of the institution. When a sea of NYPD officers turned their backs on mayor Bill de Blasio in December of 2014 after he committed the treacherous crime of "acknowledging systemic racism and asking for police accountability,"[51] their demonstration captured *Blue Bloods*' approach of backing the blue above all else. *Blue Bloods* is perhaps the most pro-police cop show in recent history, focusing on the multigenerational Reagan family and starring Tom Selleck as patriarch Frank Regan, commissioner of the NYPD; his father Henry is a retired commissioner, his son Danny is a detective, his son Jamie is an officer who marries a fellow officer named Edie, and his daughter Erin is a lawyer in the district attorney's office. Danny is particularly guilty of the kinds of concerning behavior Color of Change seeks to address, and he echoes *The Shield*'s Vic Mackey in the pilot when he violently attacks a suspected child predator while his Black partner looks on, implicitly condoning police brutality. This approach to representing policing earns *Blue Bloods* the dubious distinction of being the most egregiously problematic cop show of the BLM era according to the Good Guy Endorser Effect: For every wrongful action committed by a "bad guy," *Blue Bloods* showed thirty-six wrongful actions committed by a "good guy."

A review of select *Blue Bloods* episodes provides a troubling concept for this alarming statistic. On Friday nights the show's cases "offer constant reassurance that there are no true racial issues within the criminal justice system that can't be solved by a speech about colorblindness or the steely resolve of Tom Selleck's mustache."[52] More pernicious than this devotion to the NYPD is the tendency with which *Blue Bloods* introduces characters—often BIPOC individuals—who speak up against the police but are revealed to be malicious and deceptive. For example, the 2011 second-season episode "Black and Blue" sends Jamie and his partner to a Black church after receiving an anonymous 911 call about an armed gunman inside, only for the officers to be pushed down a flight of stairs and injured; after the Black church leader makes a big splash in the news with accusations that Frank and the NYPD were racially targeting Black neighborhoods, Danny's investigation reveals that the reverend arranged for the 911 call in order to provoke an incident and get press attention. When an officer is accused of shooting an unarmed Black teen in the back two years later in the fourth-season episode "Drawing

Dead," Frank's and Erin's diligent efforts to get to the bottom of things reveals that a witness to the shooting immediately grabbed and hid the victim's gun, proving the officer's innocence in the "clean shooting" and providing a reason to be skeptical of claims of excessive force. The pinnacle of this narrative approach has to be the fifth-season episode "Excessive Force" in 2014 in which Danny chases an unarmed Black man into an apartment building's second-story hallway and tells the man to put his hands up or get thrown out the window; cut to the man flying through the window, crashing to the ground and howling in pain before yelling that Danny pushed him and repeatedly screaming the words "police brutality!" The same Black reverend from "Black and Blue" returns to soak up media attention and stir up disdain for the NYPD and says he has a witness—a boy who is ready to say he saw Danny push the Black man out the window. In true *Blue Bloods* fashion, the investigation reveals that the Black man threw himself out the window and that the reverend bribed the child's family to lie about what the child saw. Though the reverend's actions constitute a felony, Frank tells him, "I'm gonna give you one last chance to honor the cloth you wear and the title you put before your name," further solidifying his position as the morally righteous arbiter of justice.

Laura Hudson describes *Blue Bloods* as a "white-privilege lullaby" in which "accusations leveled at police by citizens are almost always revealed to be fraudulent, and concerns about racial bias are almost always manufactured, deceitful, or overblown."[53] This is concerning when it functions as copaganda for an audience—older, mostly white, and skewing conservative—that buys into the narrative that the police are always right and that Black people's complaints about police brutality are illegitimate. This mythical ideal of police officers is not simply aspirational to its viewers but "a reaffirmation of how the show's viewers already think they are," Hudson said. This is not to say that *Blue Bloods* refuses to engage with issues in contemporary policing, including the use of bodycams and presence of citizens with smartphones, the evolution of stop-and-frisk practices, the police union's threat of "blue flu," and the expectation that officers never apologize for shooting people, even when it was an honest and regrettable mistake. However, the forum of ideas about policing that plays out at the Reagan family's multigenerational Sunday dinner table inevitably reinforces the myth that there are very few bad apples and that a few decent cops—especially Frank—can excise the rot with a strong backbone, moral grounding, and the uncanny ability to think seven steps ahead.

Whereas *NCIS: Los Angeles* was inclined more toward witty banter than institutional critique and *Blue Bloods* was more prone to defending the

FIG. 2.3. Jolene looks down at the boy she shot on the *Law & Order: SVU* episode "American Tragedy" (2013).

institution than challenging it, *Law & Order: SVU* is famous for its "ripped-from-the-headlines" approach to storytelling. The first *Law & Order* spin-off, *SVU* follows detective Olivia Benson (Mariska Hargitay) and her diverse team as they solve sexual assault cases. Benson's longtime partner Elliot Stabler (Chris Meloni) was often violent with suspects, helping to set the tone for a series that would eventually garner a twenty-to-one ratio for Color of Change's Good Guy Endorser Effect. While this was not exactly novel in the cop genre, writer/producer Amanda Green notes that it felt empowering in a culture that habitually ignores or downplays violence against women; Green describes Stabler as "a poor example of men being validated for breaking the rules because there was a moral impulse—they did it in the context of a broken system for women.[54]

The headline-ripping approach would seem to lend itself to engaging national conversations about policing, and it did so quite early on in the BLM era, just months after Trayvon Martin's killer was acquitted. *SVU*'s fifteenth season included "American Tragedy" (October 2, 2013), which blended two recent news stories, inspiring Newsone (2013) to characterize the episode as one in which "Paula Deen Shoots Trayvon Martin." Here, a celebrity chef named Jolene (played by Cybill Shepherd) shoots Mehcad Carter, a Black teen in a hoodie (see Figure 2.3). The neighborhood has been the site of a string of violent rapes of white women by a Black man, and Jolene claims Mehcad followed and attempted to attack her. The evidence shows Mehcad was at least five feet away from her when Jolene shot him and that he was unarmed—literally a choirboy—but Jolene claims she feared for her life, and two of the rape victims identify Mehcad in a photo lineup. The police practice broad racial profiling in their stop-and-frisk procedures, failing to differentiate among Black men just as the survivors did, as the actual rapist is soon caught in the act while Mehcad lies dying in his hospital bed. Director Fred Berner explains that the episode "played on one's prejudices" and that while Jolene was "easy to hate out of the gate," their goal was "not to be pedantic about any one state of mind but to try and complicate the issues so that the conversation gets kickstarted."[55] Berner understands a political climate of entrenched ideological positions in which "it's very hard to get anybody to listen to any opposite point of view or anything that might go against their own sphere of thinking." Though Berner asserts, "I have no desire to make that big change—that's not my job; I can't do that," he acknowledges that by broadcasting an episode in which creators "allow people to be vulnerable, allow them to be confused, allow them to see a slightly different side of something," they can essentially encourage viewers to be more open-minded to competing viewpoints. "My chosen vocation is to just plant little seeds in people and hopefully they grow." Echoing this sentiment, director/producer Norberto Barba describes the emotional fulfilment viewers look for in *Law & Order: SVU* and articulates the brand as one that successfully raises cultural issues, presents various ideological positions, rolls with the times, and mirrors society.[56] Still, looking back at decades of work on police procedurals, Berner admits to feeling bad "that the conversations have not been had . . . the understanding of what implicit bias is and what institutionalized racism is, and . . . what happened is that it become good business for the networks" to simply avoid tackling these subjects. Berner attributes this in part to a relatively liberal talent pool of actors who "want to be working in the interest of what they perceive to be the greater good," with studios and liberal-minded producers writing stories that promote those working relationships.

These three series demonstrate the variety of approaches that programs about law enforcement might participate in and contribute to the cultural forum around Black Lives Matter and systemic violence, as well as the extent to which they might opt out of such conversations as being outside of their scope. In each case, the established characters would need an organic entry point to engage in these topics, and writers might not develop those entry points if they do not feel so inclined. To Color of Change's point, more diverse writers' rooms would likely be more invested in telling those stories, or at the very least would not be surprised or intimidated when those stories were proposed. While many white writers and producers grappled with if and how to broach race-related storylines about policing and abuses of power, the Black writers I spoke with expressed a degree of relief that more honest stories about racial profiling and the like could be shared on a national stage. Many of these writers worked on shows that premiered after #BlackLivesMatter rose to prominence in 2014, a time in which cultural microscopes were increasingly turned to representations of policing in America.

Entering the Fray: Creating Cop Shows in the BLM Era

While the events of 2020 would put a temporary halt to new shows about cops, the murders of Eric Garner and Michael Brown by police officers in the summer of 2014 did no such thing. *Chicago P.D.* had already expanded Dick Wolf's *Chicago* franchise in January, building a police show around the corrupt Detective Hank Voight, who had begun terrorizing firefighters on *Chicago Fire* in October of 2012. *NCIS: New Orleans* (CBS, 2014–2021) premiered in September 2014, followed the next year by *Rosewood* (Fox, 2015–2017) and then *Shades of Blue* (NBC, 2016–2018) and *Lethal Weapon* (FOX, 2016–2019) in 2016, *S.W.A.T.* and the miniseries *Shots Fired* (Fox, 2017) in 2017, *The Rookie* and *FBI* in 2018, and *FBI: Most Wanted* in spring of 2020. Cop shows during this era were unafraid of showing bad cops and did so in numerous ways. For example, *Shades of Blue* revolves around lieutenant Matt Wozniak (Ray Liotta) and the racially diverse detective squad he leads astray; like Vic Mackey and his strike team, Wozniak's crew keeps the peace among criminals while taking a cut for themselves until one team member cuts a deal to save herself at the expense of the rest. By contrast, the "bad cops" in *Lethal Weapon* blend the integrity and exceptional ability of *NYPD Blue*'s officers with the violent, maverick behaviors of 1970s gunslingers, making them the second-worst offenders of Color of Change's measure of wrongful actions by "good guys"—criminal justice professionals—compared to "bad guys" at a ratio of thirty-four to one. Whereas *Blue Bloods* peripherally included BIPOC characters who could condone white officers' regular violence and civil rights violations, the greater diversity of this era allowed BIPOC characters to both condone and commit these bad acts.

The men who created cop shows after the BLM movement was established did so in a different sociopolitical landscape than their predecessors, as the movement offered a frequently deployed shorthand for police brutality and institutionalized racism. These creators typically served as showrunners, a title that encompasses head writer and executive producer and is reached after working one's way up the ranks.[57] As Landau explains in *The*

TV Showrunner's Roadmap, a showrunner's success is contingent upon their ability—among other things—to stay on time and within their budget, forecast story needs, and predict production problems, balancing both creative and economic responsibilities. While showrunners work with writing teams, those writers are tasked with collaborating to realize the vision of the showrunner, who is ultimately seen as responsible for the series and the source of its meaning.[58] Though the term had not yet been coined, Cantor focused on people who would now be identified as showrunners and emphasized social and industrial structural impacts on producers' motivations and values,[59] and Newcomb and Alley highlighted showrunners' agency within these structures as "self-conscious creative producers."[60] This approach to conceptualizing showrunners recognizes their role as cultural intermediaries, not in the Bourdieusian sense of critics,[61] but as people who use their platform to offer critiques of society, and implicitly the role of television, in and through the content they create. Herbert, Lotz, and Punathambekar outline how scholars might consider these writer/producers as individuals, asking what role they play in television production, what their work entails, what resources they have, and what challenges they face.[62] Scholars might also investigate production culture by asking, What do showrunners think about their work, and how do they understand their role? What are the motivations and cultural values that shape their daily decisions, and how are those motivations and values expressed, both to themselves and others? All these questions seek to better understand the external messages showrunners receive and the ways those messages are internalized and in turn shape production practices. Furthermore, these questions recognize the significant role played by showrunners as cultural intermediaries who must balance creative impulses and commercial mandates in an increasingly complex sociopolitical context. Insight from showrunners can clarify how motivations, including creativity, money, and cultural value, can be informed by ethical or moral considerations.[63]

In this section I focus on three contemporary police procedurals that premiered in the years following the establishment of the Black Lives Matter movement: *Chicago P.D.* (NBC, 2014–present), *S.W.A.T.* (CBS, 2017–2024), and *The Rookie* (ABC, 2018–present). Spanning the three largest broadcasters, these series constitute a valuable site of analysis for examining showrunners' conceptions of their roles and responsibilities in creating police procedurals against the backdrop of increasing media coverage of police violence toward people and communities of color. These three programs illustrate a range of responses to incorporating themes of systemic racism and policing in the BLM era. The representations in *Chicago P.D.*, *S.W.A.T.*, and

The Rookie signal an awareness of the expectation, and sometimes perceived responsibility, that they address institutionalized norms in policing that disproportionately affect Black and Brown citizens. Notably, the original idea behind each series was instrumental in framing how each might address these themes, and showrunners were also affected by notes from their networks. Interviews with the showrunners Alexi Hawley (ABC's *The Rookie*), Michael Brandt (NBC's *Chicago P.D.*), and Aaron Rahsaan Thomas and Shawn Ryan (CBS's *S.W.A.T.*) serve as the basis for this analysis. These showrunners spoke candidly about the values, responsibilities, and challenges they faced in producing police procedurals after the BLM movement became part of American popular culture. Our interviews demonstrate a complex negotiation of creativity, moral responsibility, and corporate interests.

Michael Brandt had already created and was showrunner on the first season of *Chicago Fire* when he was inspired to create *Chicago P.D.*. In the third episode of *Chicago Fire*, two detectives—one of them the crooked Captain Voight—were brought on as guest stars, and "their characters really just popped . . . everybody really gravitated to those characters." These characters made numerous appearances throughout the season, culminating in a police-heavy episode that functioned as a free pilot. NBC greenlit the new series, and *Chicago P.D.* was built around the premise of a dirty cop in a position of power who broke the law as he saw fit. Brandt explains, "He really was a dirty cop . . . we weren't thinking about ten years later . . . [that] we were gonna have to now service this character forever." That said, Brandt did not "want to make a show about a cop who's just bad and dirty all the time . . . that's not going to last very long," so they rounded out Voight's character to explore his background and motivations. Brandt was excited by the challenge of having to make someone so problematic into someone the audience could "at least respect . . . and find interesting." Still, this unintended origin story for *Chicago P.D.* lent itself to a different framework for representing policing, one more akin to *The Shield* with its corrupt law enforcement officers than is typical of police procedurals.

In contrast to the dirty cop at the core of *Chicago P.D.*, *S.W.A.T.* was created to consider race and policing. *S.W.A.T.* creator Aaron Rahsaan Thomas is a Black man who grew up in an urban neighborhood with a love/hate relationship with the police.[64] Having been raised on television and having picked up on the lack of representation of officers who looked like him—especially as created by Black writers and producers—Thomas wondered what it would be like to be a Black officer who fully understands the experiences of both police officers and Black Americans. Thomas felt he "hadn't seen any show really in earnest tackle . . . the sociopolitical aspect of what it means

FIG. 2.4. A shocked Hondo is promoted to team leader by Commander Hicks at a press conference as camera bulbs flash on the pilot episode of *S.W.A.T.* (2017).

to be caught between two worlds." Knowing that proven intellectual properties with familiar titles were more likely to find success on television, Thomas hunted through titles until he found *S.W.A.T.*, which originally aired two seasons (1975–1976) before being adapted into a 2003 feature film. Two key elements made *S.W.A.T.* ripe for the kinds of stories Thomas wanted to tell. One was that the film had cast Samual L. Jackson in the role of team leader Hondo, a role originally held by a white man, and so Thomas knew "that fight's already been fought for me" and that he could continue to increase diversity in the cast. The other element was the rich and complicated history of LAPD's SWAT, a militarized police force created in Los Angeles, because "LA does race riots better than anything else. . . . What better place to set a Black cop in the center of all of that and have him deal with that even as he's trying to be a good cop?" Unlike the many Black officers on television who are "just a cop who happens to be Black, which has been the main approach for the most part," Thomas set out to present "a Black man who works as a cop, meaning that when he looks at situations, he's looking at it through the lens of a Black man." In addition to featuring a Black lead, *S.W.A.T.* also set itself apart from the typical cop show in its pilot, in which Hondo's squad leader accidentally shoots a Black teenage boy and is fired the following day (see Figure 2.4). Thomas describes *S.W.A.T.* as "my opportunity to do my own version of a mainstream network procedural where, yes, you get some comfort food, they get the bad guys, they do really cool action things . . . but at the same time there's nutritional value." As this was Thomas's first foray into acting as showrunner, Sony proposed that *The Shield* creator Shawn Ryan come on as co-showrunner to lend his expertise.

The Rookie is like *S.W.A.T.* in that it was intended to show good police dealing with real issues. Alexi Hawley created *The Rookie* "in the shadow of Philando Castile's killing."[65] Hawley had been affected by "what the police officer brought to the car, the way he'd been trained, the sort of . . . us versus them mentality that he came in with." In creating a series about patrol officers and recognizing that "police killing Black men in America has been going on for a very long time and . . . it wasn't a new thing," Hawley's goal was to create an aspirational series that reflected the diversity of Los Angeles and "would sort of address policing as it should be." This meant showing a particular approach to policing, one based less on gunplay and more on talking to people in crises, and "without hanging a lantern on it . . . just try and internalize that sense of . . . a good thing happened because [the officer] talked to a guy in crisis as opposed to escalating it to something else." While this aspirational approach has been consistent throughout the series, Hawley admits that after George Floyd's murder "it became clear very quickly that being aspirational alone was not enough—that ultimately we were representing a view of policing that was alien to a pretty big segment of society," and from this he developed a stronger sense of responsibility as a storyteller within the police procedural genre.

Varying degrees of a perceived sense of moral responsibility can be found across the showrunners I interviewed, ranging from a strong sense of duty to do good on one end to a rejection of any such obligation on the other. At the crux of this conversation is a debate around the role of television in society. Thomas recognizes that a cop show inherently contains "support for the existence of cops . . . but do we currently have the best version of a system of police?"[66] *S.W.A.T.* tries to contribute to "the national conversation on cop shows . . . to add more layers to the conversation" and get away from the polarized thinking that either fetishizes police as infallible or seeks to dismantle it entirely as an irredeemable, unsalvageable system. This creates a textual backdrop that recognizes the need for "some form of law enforcement" while simultaneously acknowledging that "there's gotta be a better way to do it."

Similarly, Hawley wanted to tackle policing practices from the premise that U.S. policing is full of flaws.[67] Believing that most police understand that the system is "f——up, it doesn't work, that 911's a catch-all . . . for everything; you're just dumping everything in the police's lap but not training them for it." Hawley wanted to create a place to highlight and reevaluate the norms and practices in policing that have proven so problematic. Hawley was also frustrated by the status quo within the police procedural genre, whereby law enforcement is rarely held accountable for using weapons or otherwise engaging in violence. Hawley's challenge was this: "As a patrol show, who engage with the community a hundred different ways a season, how do we at least be self-aware enough that every case, we're thinking about what the repercussions are, how we talk about policing . . . but not in a way that's on the nose, not in a way that's hitting you over the head with it, because we don't do anybody any favors if we get canceled because people think we're strident or people think we're, you know, giving you your medicine or whatever. So how do we still keep the fun of the show . . . the connection to the show the audience has, but start talking about stuff?" Hawley tackled this problem by working to maintain the sensibility of the series, including moments of humor and irreverence, but also to depict consequences. "Most police shows, they fire bullets all the time, they kill people all the time, and . . . then you go to commercial and you come back and it's all wrapped up," he points out. In *The Rookie*, viewers watch as officers are relieved of their weapons and reminded that they do not have the right to remain silent and may in fact be fired if they refuse to speak with investigators.

Thomas and Hawley are overtly and morally invested in fueling conversations that might be sensitive or controversial but necessary for improving relationships between law enforcement and civilians. By contrast, Ryan, who had created *The Shield* and was brought on to *S.W.A.T.* to lend his expertise through developing the new series and serving as co-showrunner, was a bit more circumspect. Ryan specifically stated that even though the series has "message" episodes, "I try not to have an agenda," though his comments ultimately demonstrate that he, too, feels the pull of the moral economy, if only in service of *S.W.A.T.*'s original premise.[68] Ryan recognizes that much of the show comes from Thomas's attempt to reconcile the Black versus blue antagonisms, but he resists this when he argues, "It's not up to us as showrunners, as show creators, to solve society's problems. . . . What I'm trying to do is just increase awareness with our viewers while simultaneously entertaining them." Ryan goes so far as to suggest it would be wrong of him to try to make audiences believe something he believes, yet at the same time he recognizes "a certain obligation" as one of the few police shows centered on a Black character to address these themes, especially in the wake of George Floyd's murder. The centrality of race to the show's premise was therefore instrumental in fueling engagement with police brutality. Ryan suggests that other police shows "that are a little bit more generic, they're just about the crime and the crime solving" might more easily avoid these ideologically complex topics, but that central to *S.W.A.T.*'s DNA is "the internal struggle of a Black police officer . . . and the aspirational idea that if he can figure out a way to make these two communities come together, maybe we as a society can do that as well." Despite Ryan's earlier rejection of a moral duty in his work and his many comments disavowing his responsibility to effect change, this final comment suggests that the esteemed showrunner does in fact recognize the power of the showrunner to contribute to the greater good, albeit through critical discourse and complex narratives rather than dogmatic ideological lectures.

Brandt shared Ryan's overt rejection of the moral duty and the sentiment that he did not want audiences to feel any one way by the end of an episode, but he went even further in that direction, stating, "I don't think I ever felt like there's a moral obligation to what I, as a writer, need to be saying."[69] His emphasis was instead on being authentic to the characters and the world he'd constructed; here, Brandt identified authenticity as "a construct, one that is built around trying to get high ratings and make money off advertisers" rather than the true "authenticity" of showing paperwork and other low-stakes aspects of policing. While Brandt was interested in the scenarios that might naturally arise in the narrative world of *Chicago P.D.* and which may or may not relate to the themes of racist policing, he did not communicate an impulse to reflect on the institution of policing or its place in contemporary society in the same ways Hawley and Thomas did. If such themes should emerge organically, Brandt would "authentically" explore the different perspectives each officer might have, and those perspectives might in fact be informed by the character's race, but having those explorations at all was incidental.

While these showrunners have served as the head writers and producers and have been instrumental in shaping the narrative world of their programs, they have also operated within a network studio system that has its own opinions and preferences. According to these showrunners, network executives and other key figures were generally—but not always—supportive of their attempts to tackle sensitive subjects like police brutality. In the case of *S.W.A.T.*, Thomas reports, "I was a bit penalized by my own background, and not in the way you'd expect," because he expected antagonism for anything outside of the norm.[70] With a draft of the pilot script in hand, Thomas expected studio executives to push back against the kind of honesty he was aiming for and to advocate for providing their imagined audience of white Midwesterners with televisual comfort food, and so he "erred on the side of being too safe, initially." Instead, Thomas found CBS executives to be quite supportive and "willing to go further than I ever expected" to create something that fit their audience without shying away from real conversations. CBS endorsed his pilot, which begins with the SWAT team's white commander mistakenly shooting a young Black civilian and shows the commander immediately resigning, with the job then transferring to the Black SWAT officer Hondo. *S.W.A.T.* went on to address historical events like Rodney King and George Floyd in a process Thomas describes as "learning . . . bit by bit what people are ready for." At the same time, Thomas recognizes that networks have business models and audiences they must serve, and the showrunner's "job is to grab as many eyeballs as possible." With that comes a necessary compromise, but Thomas found that he had consistently "been able to go further than I expected." Ryan also reports support from CBS, but he ties it more directly to diversity and the bottom line, noting that the "more inclusion in a show, the greater ratings potential. . . . When you open your show's universe to a lot of perspectives and people who look different from each other, it invites a whole wider range of audiences to come in."[71] Executives at ABC were similarly supportive of both diversity and thematic engagement. Hawley notes that "ABC has been a champion of diversity from the very beginning on the show in terms of cast and the crew" and has developed programs to help underrepresented writers and directors find work and make career advancements.[72]

While all three series were subject to feedback from the networks, *Chicago P.D.* had the additional element of being part of Dick Wolf's extensive programming. Brandt recalls having a peculiar experience writing an atypical episode of *Chicago P.D.* that comprised almost entirely a conversation about race, racism, and policing between white patrol officer Kim Burgess and a Black man as the two are trapped in a room (see Figure 2.5).[73] Normally, Brandt explains, writers will create an outline of an episode and pitch it to NBC and executive producer Dick Wolf so that the studio knows what's in store; the writers then receive notes that they use while writing the episode. In this case, "we just wrote the script because it was . . . very different and off-pattern of the show." Wolf was displeased because "his way of doing things is very much on pattern. . . . Our shows push certain buttons at certain times in certain ways," and part of the showrunner's job on Dick Wolf Productions is to exercise creative freedom but still "stay within those constructs." Despite Wolf's disapproval, NBC approved the pitch, and the episode's ratings "were huge, like big ratings for that time of the season for that episode; and the reactions, it was really, really positive." NBC could have vetoed the episode, but Brandt feels the network trusted him and his team because they had "a very, very respectful working relationship" and "the shows did well." Similarly, Brandt suspects "Dick wanted to veto it but

FIG. 2.5. Kim discusses race relations at gunpoint with her captor in the *Chicago P.D.* episode "What Do You Do" (2015).

didn't because he respected us and wanted us to take a shot at it." Following the episode's success, Wolf conceded that he had been wrong to doubt Brandt for breaking pattern and prioritizing blunt discourse over action sequences.

Conclusion

Early BLM cop shows varied in the degree to which they strayed from generic conventions of the time. Some aligned with the history of maverick gunslingers and noble cause corruption, in which law enforcement officers break the law when it suits them in order to save the day. Others specifically aimed to show policing as it ought to be: careful, deliberate, responsible, and compassionate. When television's police officers pulled their guns and used deadly force, some series continued in their failure to depict "the truth of police officers' reactions when they fire a fatal round," showing them as unaffected after taking a life and overlooking post-shooting procedures for officers.[74] Others made a point of highlighting these moments, as when *The Rookie*'s Officer Nolan is relieved of his weapon, interviewed by Internal Affairs, and reminded that he does not have the right to remain silent after shooting and killing an armed assailant. Thus, series were positioned differently to account for the global response to George Floyd's murder. If the cop show genre has historically been a rotten orchard that condones or celebrates racist policing, then many cop shows are bad apples, but the occasional showrunner arrives with tools for cutting away at that rot.

The spring of 2020 was a tumultuous time for U.S. cop shows. The release of the Color of Change report *Normalizing Injustice* put many police procedurals on blast for their handling of police violence and civil liberty violations, giving many in these writers' rooms pause. A global pandemic threw a wrench into television production, forcing many series to end earlier than intended and leaving storylines unfinished. George Floyd's murder then triggered international protests against police brutality and systemic racism, bringing heightened awareness and urgency to issues that were typically ignored or made mundane in their presentation. Amid public cries against copaganda, the long-running Fox series *COPS* (1989–2020) was canceled. Writers and producers for police procedurals were under a microscope. How did they understand their responsibilities at this point, and to what extent would it be possible to avoid engaging the issues highlighted by the BLM movement? The following chapter explores the cultural forum of police procedurals' responses to the events of 2020.

Interviews with numerous writers, directors, producers, and showrunners across broadcast television's police procedurals allow for a deeper examination of how knowledge and power are formed in and through the genre, specifically how ways of knowing are organized into industrial logics about how the genre can and should operate. This approach foregrounds the material consequences of the commonsense discourses that emerge through police procedural production practices. As these interviews demonstrate, resistance and power are mutually constitutive, providing insight into the degree of agency these individuals experience as cultural intermediaries within the industrial constraints imposed by the broadcast television industry. Program creators struggle to varying degrees with the moral and political implications of the stories they tell, actively participating in meaning-making through continuous, complex negotiations among competing interests.

All told, showrunners are navigating ideas about who their audiences are, what messages and conversations viewers will tolerate and how best to present them, cultural criticisms of the police procedural genre, pressures from studio executives to earn the network high ratings and good press, and their own instincts to tell certain kinds of stories in contributing to the televisual landscape. Ryan describes audiences as "very sophisticated and they can tell . . . when someone's trying to manipulate them into believing something," and so a police procedural can successfully take on issues of systemic racism so long as it approaches it correctly; Hawley surmises, "I think because we weren't just flatly on the nose, sort of preachy about stuff, that we didn't get the kind of pushback" they might have otherwise gotten.[75] This approach aligned with the goals of networks and studios that were being increasingly skewered for contributing to the normalization of police brutality through their many police procedurals and were desperate to, at the very least, appear to be interested in redeeming themselves in the moral economy. Within this framework of constraints, BLM-era showrunners have produced a range of series with differing degrees of critical cultural engagement, informed in large part by the individual showrunner's sense of moral duty. In this way, some showrunners adopt the view of showrunner as an auteur, creating culture by "crafting expressions of their own concerns within the constraints of a commercial medium."[76] These constraints of course evolve over time and across contexts and can include factors intrinsic to moments of cultural reckoning like the ones experienced in 2020.

Findings from these interviews suggest that even in the commercial broadcast medium, a culture of morality can take root and be developed through showrunners, particularly when those showrunners internally experience an ideological imperative to contribute to society's well-being by having tough conversations. Even so, generic conventions that fuel pro-police discourses, including excusing "rogue cop" behavior and condoning problematic laws that protect police at the expense of citizens, can be hard to escape. To that end, it is worth noting that one of the major criticisms of "copaganda" in police procedurals is that the cops are predominantly the "good guys," and their misdeeds are forgiven as being in service of the greater good. This critique is often oversimplified to the first point—that the cops are the heroes. For shows like *The Rookie* and *S.W.A.T.* that take an aspirational approach to representing policing, there is a very real risk that they will fall into this same trap. An important distinction must therefore be made between aspirational content and "copaganda." The latter was an accusation frequently aimed at police shows after George Floyd's murder, the genre thus being charged with celebrating and even fetishizing police. A key element to this criticism was that police were represented as morally righteous even as they broke laws and violated civil liberties, and that they seldom if ever faced consequences for their actions, a charge substantiated by activist organization Color of Change's in-depth examination of crime dramas.[77] While aspirational content also treats officers as the good guys, it does so while carefully avoiding the kinds of violence and law-breaking perpetuated by cops in other series and consistently depicts consequences for those behaviors, including justified shootings in life-or-death situations. This representational strategy demonstrates that in the police procedural genre, depicting police as heroes and critiquing the police institution are not mutually exclusive. The key, it seems, is to align viewers with officers and detectives who expose corruption, challenge institutional flaws, and actively work to hold bad police officers and policies accountable. Recognizing the challenge, Hawley admits, "I came in knowing that I wanted to be aspirational, that I wanted to do things the right way," but even he was susceptible to copaganda's influence on police procedural storytelling.[78] During the summer of 2020 as he prepared for *The Rookie*'s third season, Hawley tasked two writers with reviewing the first two seasons and providing insight into how well they had previously dealt with policing, considering recent events. Hawley was reminded that his characters had celebrated the execution of a no-knock warrant "because that's cool shit that cops do, and so that was on us . . . and then of course Breonna Taylor gets killed and you're like—yeah. No-knock warrants are bad. There's no reason for no-knock warrants." The regret Hawley expressed at this example points to the struggles that come with infusing a showrunner's work with moral economy, a renewed commitment to thinking through the implications of different policing practices, and a reevaluation of the representational norms that constitute police procedurals.

If within television-culture morality it is important that police procedurals contribute to well-being, and if the generic conventions of police procedurals—particularly violence without accountability—do not promote well-being, then police procedurals' generic conventions must evolve to highlight a broader, more diverse range of perspectives. The interviews in this chapter demonstrate that some showrunners, based largely on their individual personalities and proclivities, will categorically engage, reflect, and feel a greater sense of duty in their role than others; some will embrace the opportunity to tell new stories in new ways, while others will primarily reinforce the status quo. This newer breed of showrunners can be developed through the ranks in writers' rooms that are diverse and that promote morality right alongside creativity and commerciality in creating content. Networks and studios can help by promoting and supporting diversity, not just in staffing writers' rooms but in rising through the ranks so that more diverse voices can reach the rank of showrunner, and by greenlighting series from those underrepresented groups. In the following chapter, I turn to the 2020–2021 season to explore how these showrunners and writers handled cop show narratives following the "tectonic shift" in the tenor of conversations about racism and police brutality.

3
Post-Floyd TVPD
How Policing Is Broken and Why It Will Never Be Fixed

When it comes to our criminal justice system, there is a fierce, life-and-death battle playing out between the forces of the status quo and the forces of reform and change. Why is it so contentious, and why does it remain so unresolved? One reason is that there are fundamental differences in belief and motivation underlying those different forces.
—*Normalizing Injustice* (2020), 11

On November 11, 2020, *S.W.A.T.* kicked off its seventh season with depictions of protests inspired by the deaths of both George Floyd in 2020 and Rodney King in 1992. Black SWAT officer Hondo Harrelson argues with his father about how much has changed in the interim and how much hope there is for the future, but they come together to march in the streets past a mural of George Floyd, Breonna Taylor, and three other victims of police violence. That same night on another network, *Chicago P.D.*'s eighth season picked up where it had left off when COVID-19 derailed production months before: with a multiepisode story arc about a Black officer taking on a crew of "bad apples." The ensemble cast discussed race and policing throughout the episode, using George Floyd's name as well as fictional analogs from their narrative world. The next night, NBC's *Law & Order: Special Victims Unit* (*SVU*) opened its twenty-second season with "Guardians and Gladiators," an episode in which a Black man is arrested while a growing crowd captures the scene on their phones. The premiere was heavy with discussions of policing practices and explicit references to George Floyd, Breonna Taylor, and

Black Lives Matter protests. These series and others offered reactions to the events of the preceding months.

As the previous chapter demonstrates, police shows were already incorporating themes and narratives from the Black Lives Matter movement into their programming before George Floyd's murder sparked international outrage. *Chicago P.D.* had a multiepisode arc on the subject interrupted by COVID-19, and *NCIS: New Orleans* was in the process of breaking a similar storyline when Floyd was killed. However, the crescendo of criticism toward police shows and the corresponding accusations of "copaganda" forced showrunners, in many cases, to sit up and take stock of their approach to televisual storytelling. For some, this was compounded by the January 2020 report from Color of Change that levied strong allegations against the crime genre. Networks also responded; *The Rookie* showrunner Alexi Hawley found his studio "very engaged, and they pushed a lot on, 'How are you planning to deal with this and talk about this?'"[1] Hawley had already begun the process of grappling with how to do a police show in light of these events, and the studio supported his efforts to tackle problems in policing related to recruitment, training procedures, overzealous unions, and more. Broadcast television's prime-time police procedurals thus gave renewed focus to issues of systemic racism and problems in U.S. policing practices, as well as reinvigorated calls from the public to defund the police.

I begin with an overview of the Color of Change report, which identified troubling patterns in representation and called on television showrunners and writers to do better, followed by an exploration of the conversations among cop shows' creators, producers, writers, directors, actors, executives, networks, and agencies in preparing for the post-Floyd landscape. I then shift my focus to ten U.S. police procedurals that aired during the 2020–2021 season, just months after what might be considered the peak of the BLM movement: *Blue Bloods* (CBS), *Chicago P.D.* (NBC), *FBI* (CBS), *FBI: Most Wanted* (CBS), *Law & Order: Organized Crime* (NBC), *Law & Order: SVU* (NBC), *NCIS: Los Angeles* (CBS), *NCIS: New Orleans* (CBS), *The Rookie* (ABC), and *S.W.A.T.* (CBS). My analysis here highlights the ways in which that season's police dramas addressed (and ignored) the central issues of Black Lives Matter.

"Normalizing Injustice"

Color of Change is a racial justice organization that works to "move decision-makers in corporations and government to create a more human and less hostile world for Black people in America."[2] In addition to fighting for criminal, economic, and other forms of justice, Color of Change promotes what it calls "media justice" by ensuring accurate and diverse representations of Black people in media, achieving meaningful diversity and inclusion behind the scenes, and ending inaccurate representations of the criminal justice system on TV. Its report *Race in the Writers' Room: How Hollywood Whitewashes the Stories That Shape America* is detailed in chapter 1. As a follow-up of sorts, in January 2020 Color of Change released a report titled *Normalizing Injustice: The Dangerous Misrepresentations that Define Television's Scripted Crime Genre.*

In the foreword to this report, Color of Change's president Rashad Robinson makes the case that "today's police, prosecutors and prisons are under increased public pressure to change how they operate, and in many cases are being forced to make long-stalled system changes,"[3] but that progress is slowed by a lack of public consensus. While politicians and news producers reinforce roadblocks to change with race-baiting and fear-mongering tactics, "there is no stronger public relations force working against reform than scripted television," particularly those "defending the system, especially the police." Many police series "continue to miseducate the public about crime, race and the system itself. They do so in ways that undermine reform, demonize people of color and serve to legitimize debunked policies, discredited arguments, corrupt decision makers and (what should be) indefensible actions. In short, they are helping to normalize injustice." Echoing this after the events of 2020, Color of Change's deputy chief marketing and storytelling officer Amity Paye notes that those events made racial justice "a majoritarian issue" but that while "more people in each writers' room are thinking about it, storytelling became more intentional but not necessarily better."[4]

Crime shows are ripe with depictions of noble cause corruption: law enforcement officers engaging in wrongful behaviors, including civil rights violations and violence in the pursuit of justice, such that the ends justify the means. The report identifies specific representational patterns that work to condone or even celebrate these actions. One pattern is that these wrongful actions are committed far more often by the narrative heroes (i.e., "good" or beloved cops) than by criminal justice professionals who have been configured as the "bad guys." Good cops behaving badly are therefore framed as relatable and forgivable for their actions. A second pattern is that when this bad behavior is acknowledged, it is most frequently among BIPOC people and women, while white men are typically free to behave badly without criticism. Only 3.7 percent of wrongful actions in this study were shown to be investigated, and in just half of those instances the actors were charged—half of those successfully, and suspended with pay as a result.

Moreover, several programs used BIPOC characters to validate wrongful behavior, either by having them commit bad acts themselves or by showing them to condone it among white colleagues. Notably, the vast majority of instances of noble cause corruption are presented as occurring independently of race; the Color of Change report states that "wrongful actions specifically associated with racial bias—and prevalent in real life—were conspicuously absent . . . as were general wrongful actions being carried out in a racially biased way."[5] Daily practices were presented as race-neutral, the change was dismissed as unnecessary, and only six discussions arose that mentioned innovations or reform in criminal justice—all of them advocated by BIPOC characters.

Color of Change released this report not to chastise writers and producers but to highlight troubling patterns that they argue effectively distort public perceptions of race and criminal justice, and to encourage writers and producers to behave more responsibly. Robinson writes, "We hope this report will speak to all those writers who want to be part of telling stories in a way that influences viewers to have a more authentic understanding of the characters, forces and factors that shape the justice system, and in a way that helps viewers reckon responsibly with all the complicated issues bound up in it."[6] Robinson's hope was well received by at least some of the writers and showrunners responsible for re-presenting U.S. policing to the public, who made use of Color of Change resources and opportunities. Color of Change offers to serve as consultants for television shows, and, while their presence does not preclude racism or microaggressions from filtering into writers' rooms, they help to alleviate pressure on writers who would like to see shifts in representations. As one writer for a *Law & Order* series asked, How often can the sole Black writer stand up to and educate the white majority on race? By bringing in Color of Change to consult, the onus for BIPOC writers is lessened because of the framework they suggest; rather than confronting white writers with a personalized sense of indignation, BIPOC writers and white allies can now point to the resources and data with which they were presented to reframe ignorant comments as counterproductive and harmful to the production.

The relationship between Color of Change and a writers' room typically starts with training on the *Normalizing Injustice* report, in which they review highlights and consider factors such as, Who are the consultants for the show? They will pull stats on the show in question and demonstrate, for example, whether police are the sole consultants or if other stakeholders' perspectives are invited. These sessions invite writers' rooms to reconsider problematic examples of their own work, emphasizing egregious examples, and putting those examples into conversation with industry statistics. In addition to leading writers' rooms through seminars meant to improve representation both on- and off-screen, Color of Change has developed relationships with numerous crime shows. Color of Change sets expectations beforehand, receives scripts, does line-by-line comments, and recommends changes when they find examples of racism. Those shows can submit scripts for review so that they can get expert advice on areas in which they might, often unwittingly, perpetuate harmful stereotypes and racist representations. These activists are also available to meet with writers' rooms about potential angles to include in storylines, helping programs to respond to the *Normalizing Injustice* report in realistic ways and present issues as they ought to be presented.

Because most studios and networks have made major commitments to racial justice, many opt to invite Color of Change to weigh in as part of that commitment, but Paye acknowledged that some specific writers can become defensive. Color of Change's work relies in large part on critiquing writers' scripts and programs, but they make an effort to build a relationship based on a growth mindset, emphasizing the ways writers can make changes going forward. Thus, Color of Change offers critique rather than criticism, focusing on racial justice and racial perspectives on scripts and promoting conversations that lead to more intentional storytelling. They typically see more engaged conversations once they have identified opportunities to change and to have more dynamic and realistic storytelling. For example, Paye notes, almost every program features a forty-something Black officer who has not experienced racism before, whereas statistics show that Black children know about racism by the time they are six years old; their focus is therefore on telling better, more honest stories, and they have found that writers are occasionally defensive but are far more likely to own their mistakes.

While many writers demonstrate a familiarity with the *Normalizing Injustice* report and a desire to be part of a shift within the genre, others are decidedly uninterested. Paye describes *Blue Bloods*, for example, as exemplifying all the challenges and problems that Color of Change has been highlighting from the start. The report shows that, during the time of their study, the *Blue Bloods* writers' room comprised six white men and two white women; they were the worst offenders in the ratio of "good guys vs. bad guys" committing bad acts, and their storytelling comes from a singular viewpoint, heavily informed by their relationship with police consultants. Their perspective is thus completely shaded by what police tell them and how police want to be portrayed. This is not to say that an all-white writers' room cannot write the right story, but it is considerably more difficult to do so when writers and executives only consult with representatives from one side of a complex cultural issue. This is compounded by financial elements. Paye argues that "just like in politics, you gotta look at where the money is coming from. These shows are getting a lot of money; they're getting a lot of support from police. It's not an accident that there's gaslighting. It's actually a concerted effort by police departments and the police unions to have their work portrayed in this way." Inviting consultants like Color of Change, then, is an important step in combating that particular impulse within the police genre. Color of Change advocates expanding a show's consultant pool beyond blue-backed groups and has created a mechanism—a database—for writers to find potential consultants. The Writers' Room Database of Experts promises to help writers "find the experts you need to inform authentic, anti-racist portrayals of Black people and communities, the reality of race in all our daily lives, and the most pressing social issues for today—especially criminal justice." One series that embraced this opportunity was ABC's *The Rookie*, which brought in not just Color of Change but other community activists and expanded the range of perspectives included in their post-Floyd season. They subsequently created a special narrative committed to telling the other side of the story of American policing, and their multiepisode arc about a law professor highlighted groundbreaking efforts around the country to remove racist cops from their positions.

Many of the police procedurals that aired during the 2020–2021 season made use of Color of Change in one respect or another, if only as a wake-up call. Regarding narratives, *NCIS: New Orleans* writer Talicia Raggs states that Color of Change "had the idea, rightfully so, which we all seemed to miss, that the way the TV showed how police work, the quote-unquote complication of cops but ultimately the good guys, were excusing civil rights violations across the board."[7] The concern, Raggs notes, is that "when a police incident occurs, people's minds are for the officer because the officer is always portrayed on television as the good guy" (see Figure 3.1). Though her program was not among the worst offenders, she states that "it was jaw-dropping and eye-opening and really sort of devastating to a lot of us in the business, particularly those that write for cop shows, especially those of us who were people of color." Speaking to that relationship between writers' racial diversity (or lack thereof) and representation, which is also addressed in the report, a writer on *NCIS: Los Angeles* remembers that it highlighted the lack of diversity in so many police shows' writers' rooms, and that most writers subsequently hired for *NCIS: Los Angeles* were women and people of color.

FIG. 3.1. An officer stares in shock at the man he shot on the *NCIS: New Orleans* episode "Biased" (2020).

The Color of Change report and the global BLM protests fueled many writers and showrunners to make changes. Raggs describes these creatives as making an effort "to understand what it actually meant and how we could still tell good, effective, entertaining stories and yet not be as damaging to the communities that they were damaging." Having read the report, Alexi Hawley utilized Color of Change as a consulting group for his series *The Rookie*, which premiered in the fall of 2018, just a few months after the television season that had been analyzed for the 2020 study. After some initial conversations, Hawley made a point of sending scripts to Color of Change for feedback, most of which he incorporated before going into production. Hawley dismissed the occasional suggestion in order to act in the service of characters, but he states that he generally engaged with Color of Change in an open and honest way. Speaking in 2022, Paye held up *The Rookie* as an exemplar of antiracist and inclusive storytelling.

Published five months before George Floyd died, the report notes that the crime genre "is far behind so many of the conversations taking place across the country today when it comes to race, gender and the criminal justice system, rather than out in front of them."[8] Moreover, the report argues that the "stray storyline about the corrupt or racist actions of an individual cop usually comes around to validate the system as a whole. The flawed character who is wrong in one scene and then the hero in every other scene and episode all year, likely does not give viewers pause as much as writers may hope."[9] How, then, did police procedurals respond to the *Normalizing Injustice* report, George Floyd's death, and the acute focus on the cop show genre in the 2020–2021 season?

Racial Reckoning in 2020

Regardless of whether they included Color of Change directly, broadcast networks, studios, production companies, and even talent agencies brought people together to explore next steps. Director John Behring felt that after the video footage of Floyd's murder resulted in massive demonstrations, the studios and networks "said to themselves—and were told by their top-tier alliances of . . . the ACLU and other people that are communicating with them on that level—'You have to do better with regard to these issues.'"[10] There was thus a mandate to improve both numbers and representation of people of color, and "those kind of mandates from the network and the studio forced the showrunners to think in those terms." Rather than defaulting to white characters in any given role, writers and producers were encouraged to increase diversity when possible. "The network and the studio basically have been pushing for inclusive casting as a response to Black Lives Matter and . . . sort of forced people to wake up and face the reality of what's been happening over these many years."

Seminars were quickly convened to bring people together to prepare for what lay ahead. Fred Berner, who directed and produced across numerous Dick Wolf series, recalls a webinar convened by Peter Jankowski, head of productions at Wolf Films, with civil rights activist Connie Rice, Bill Bratton (former chief of the LAPD and commissioner of police in New York City and Boston), and *Law & Order: SVU* star Ice-T.[11] Wolf Films engaged Rice as a consultant so that "Wolf Films could continue to be relevant and a force for good in the conversation," Berner explains, though he suggests they failed in this goal as often as they achieved it. Berner describes the webinar as an attempt to bring together all the writers, directors, and producers and educate them on BLM as well as "where this catharsis was, and what the obligations were and what the desires were amongst those creators to do right by putting forth storylines and newly minted characters in a more contemporary and 'woke' vein." He recalls "a recognition that . . . we're a bunch of old white people who have been telling stories pretty much the same way for decades." Jann Turner, a television director represented by the Creative Artists Agency (CAA), also describes how CAA quickly responded with huge seminars that explored race, representation, and inclusivity; Turner felt there was a bit of breast-beating but also a genuine realization that they needed to contribute to changes that decentered white men's voices.[12] The Wolf webinar was meant "to shake this shit up" and help writers understand the needs inherent in "writing a Black character with some specificity and nuance and reality."

Such seminars promoted increasing diversity, and individuals who had always worked to increase diversity among writers and casts found it less difficult to do so after the summer of 2020, as Behring indicated. Behring noticed, for example, that "there's more diversity expectations with regards to casting of shows I direct, which I'm happy and eager to do." Similarly, Turner registered a concerted effort to help her be more inclusive in her role as an episodic director, a position with some say in terms of casting episodic characters. While her past attempts to include more women and people of color had been met with eye rolls and "didn't earn me any friends," Turner noticed an increased willingness from all directions as writers, producers, and executives became invested in facilitating progress. Berner had also prided himself on helping underrepresented folks get work in a network television environment that was designed by and for white men and saw a dramatic shift in which "we would submit our roster of directors to Wolf Films and to the network and they would go, 'No, not enough diversity. You need more people of color.'" While the networks and studios seemed to think an add-diversity-and-stir approach would suffice, Berner insisted that setting these directors up for success would require inviting them into the fold early enough and providing quality mentorship and guidance so that they would do the job well.

At the same time, as with early BLM cop shows, there was not a unified or singular dedication to incorporating BLM after the summer of 2020. Some series had these themes baked into their DNA and would very naturally address them in the 2020–2021 season. Others, particularly those that focus not on city police officers but rather naval police or federal agents, had more narrative leeway to avoid diving into this narrative terrain. For example, *NCIS: Los Angeles* takes place in Los Angeles, and the LAPD has a long history of corruption; while the protagonists of *NCIS* are not themselves the kind of police officers who were the focus of global protests, their characters would naturally intersect with those officers in the series, and because the LAPD and LA sheriff's officers were not the protagonists, there was greater ability to highlight and critique institutional problems. The writers and producers had discussions about how best to address racist policing and authentically acknowledge recent events while recognizing the show's role as more escapist fare and not sharply departing from the series' established tone.

Though their series had varied in the extent to which they previously engaged the Black Lives Matter movement, industry professionals were uniform in their duty to participate in these broader cultural conversations in the 2020–2021 season. Even *Blue Bloods* showrunner Kevin Wade was "aware they are being scrutinized in an America battered by . . . deaths and debates over the role of law enforcement" as well as the potential blowback he and *Blue Bloods* might earn based on the series' direction.[13] *The Rookie* creator Alexi Hawley states, "We had a responsibility as a show to address it, and I had a responsibility as a showrunner with a diverse cast. . . . We had some very hard conversations because it was hard for them to put on that uniform on TV."[14] In the wake of 2020's summer protests, Hawley's dedication to challenging norms in policing spurred a shift in the lead character, officer John Nolan, from wanting to be a detective to wanting to be a training officer so that the series could better engage training as the most influential way to prepare future generations of police to do better. Similarly, *S.W.A.T.* co-showrunner Shawn Ryan describes feeling "a certain obligation because . . . so few police shows are centered on a Black character," and because lead actor Shamar Moore "was struggling with what it meant to be an actor who went and put on a police uniform for work."[15] Aaron Rahsaan Thomas, *S.W.A.T.* co-showrunner and creator, was interested in asking, "Do we currently have the best version of a system of police?"[16] This meant not only creating a space for Moore to unpack the trauma of being a Black officer, but also for the good white officers on his team to confront their own blind spots (see Figure 3.2). The character of Deacon, for example, has been taught to believe the system generally works, with the occasional exception; in this season, Thomas wanted Deacon to learn that "sometimes you need to step outside of yourself and hear perspectives from people who don't have your life experience in order to really have a smart and fully informed conversation." Thomas continues, "That's in some way what the show was trying to do for the national conversation on cop shows. . . . Let's present a perspective that maybe other shows have not provided . . . to add more layers to the conversation." Similarly, *Law & Order: SVU* producer Norberto Barba thought it important that the lead character Olivia Benson admit and take responsibility for her own implicit bias: "We didn't want to show superhero cops. We wanted to show them as human, some good and some bad, and some not realizing they were doing something they shouldn't."[17] In the *NCIS: New Orleans* writers' room, Talicia Raggs recognized, "We have this pulpit right now, so let's just go at everything. Let's go at all the problems in New

FIG. 3.2. Hondo and his family take a knee in front of a mural of Breonna Taylor, George Floyd, and others on the *S.W.A.T.* episode "3 Seventeen Year Olds" (2020).

Orleans. . . . There's this underbelly of injustice in all different kinds of ways, particularly in the justice department, and not just in policing."[18] That they were already breaking a storyline about police corruption when Floyd was murdered "juiced us more into knowing we were doing the right thing."

One of the themes within this forum became finding a middle ground between blue lives rhetoric and calls for the outright abolition of policing. Thomas characterizes this polarity as unrealistic, noting, "Most people I know are somewhere in between where it's a sense of, alright, you need some form of law enforcement, but there's gotta be a better way to do it, and what's that way, and let's have that conversation."[19] Similarly, for *The Rookie* showrunner Alexi Hawley, the series' established aspirational approach was revealed to be insufficient. Hawley admits that after George Floyd's murder, "it became clear very quickly that being aspirational alone was not enough, that ultimately we were representing a view of policing that was alien to a pretty big segment of our society, and so we had a responsibility."[20] *S.W.A.T.*, *The Rookie*, *Chicago P.D.*, and others created spaces for their cop characters to find common ground and have candid, respectful conversations about the state of U.S. policing. *Blue Bloods*' showrunner makes a similar pitch when he reports, "Maybe I'm kidding myself, but I do believe that when we've had issues [between two opposing groups], we would build a platform of equal dimensions for the other side of the argument."[21] However, it is worth considering to what extent showrunners are in fact kidding themselves—whether two sides of arguments are both respectfully allowed a nuanced platform for discussion, as well as the limits to how two opposing positions can reasonably be presented in a show, particularly when the issue at hand is police brutality that results in the death of unarmed civilians.

A key element worth considering is that, in most cases, these programs had to find a way to participate in BLM-themed discussions that were authentic to their preexisting narrative worlds. Some series were thus better primed than others to dive into the deep end of these conversations, which largely threaten to delegitimize the very institutions around which their programs are built. For shows such as *NCIS*, where the main characters—the heroes—are law enforcement officers but not part of the police department, they were able to introduce and narratively deal with bad officers. For series where the police are indeed the heroes, guest stars might similarly be introduced for the purposes of disposal. *Law & Order: Organized Crime* was in a unique position, as the series premiered its abbreviated first season in April 2021; however, it followed the return of Chris Meloni as Elliot Stabler, the beloved NYPD detective from *Law & Order: SVU* who committed untold acts of noble cause corruption in the name of getting rapists and pedophiles off the streets. Recognizing that Stabler's behavior would be a harder pill to swallow on post-Floyd television, executive producer Fred Berner describes their approach in modifying the established character. Specifically, it was important for the established fanbase to watch Stabler struggle "because if he struggles and he's my boy, he's my guy, then his struggles become my struggles, and only when you can really emotionally connect to what that character is going through, [the character] becomes the ambassador to beginning to change the synapses and how you perceive the issue." Rather than pretend Stabler's bad actions were good, they forced the character to realize—"you're a bad guy and you gotta learn new ways, and policing is different . . . he's coming back to a world that has changed . . . and you put him into a policing environment that has significantly changed since he left ten years ago." In this way, *Organized Crime* was able to highlight questions of policing, positioned as simultaneously part of and apart from generic police procedural conventions of the 2010s. By contrast, *Blue Bloods* struggled to engage a movement it had previously derided by featuring claims of police brutality as a useful weapon for criminals to employ against honest police officers, and its showrunner Kevin Wade stated that "the respect and affection of the 12 million people that watch [*Blue Bloods*] frankly take precedence over the twelve pundits who may watch it for the first time because it's a show about white cops";[22] though Wade also acknowledged a need to address the events of 2020 in some way, this comment indicates a determination to maintain the series' status quo in embracing blue lives rhetoric and delegitimizing criticisms of the NYPD or the institution of policing.

Issues of racist policing and systemic reform were given varying degrees of attention across series, with some series providing multiepisode narratives (e.g., *The Rookie*, *S.W.A.T.*) while others touched on them very little (e.g., *FBI*, *FBI: Most Wanted*). Within this season of content, my analysis considers (1) how these shows articulate problems in contemporary policing, (2) the suggestions they propose for improving U.S. policing, and (3) the impediments they identify that render police reform difficult if not impossible. As with the previous chapter, my analysis blends textual criticism with testimonials from showrunners, writers, producers, and directors. My analysis demonstrates that this forum is ultimately quite limited, emphasizing individualized problems and solutions as opposed to systemic ones. Furthermore, the consistent lack of resolution works as a cop-out whereby American police procedurals appease calls for reform—of both the police institution and the impulse toward copaganda—without sacrificing generic strategies that have proven so successful.

These series contextualized themselves within the climate of increased scrutiny and calls for police reform, many of them making specific reference to George Floyd, Breonna Taylor, and other Black individuals who were killed by police. *Blue Bloods* reports a significant drop in recruitment and the need for good PR, and law enforcement officers in *NCIS: Los Angeles* are quick to correct individuals who conflate them and their tactics with police and police brutality. The summer of 2020 is articulated as a moment of significance, and many series reflect on the "old playbook" that led the United States to this point, and which must be thrown out (*Chicago P.D.*, *Law & Order: SVU*, *The Rookie*, *S.W.A.T.*). At the same time, there are beleaguered suppositions that the United States has been here before, and that since little was improved in the past, we should not be optimistic now (*Law & Order: SVU*, *S.W.A.T.*); notably, these conversations tend to occur between Black men.

Policing in the United States has a documented history of political support for right and even far right candidates, but the growing number of Black officers and minority-led police associations have fueled progressive reform.[23] In a similar vein, the increased inclusion of BIPOC officers in recent decades has worked to dilute—though not eliminate—police prejudice toward BIPOC communities,[24] as has the shift in police training to place a greater emphasis on multiculturalism.[25] At the same time, there is evidence that some white officers maintain a deeper level of prejudice and resent reform efforts.[26] Because the main characters of police series are in law enforcement, it should come as no surprise that some lament the ways public sentiment toward the police has changed in the past few years and express resentment at the scrutiny placed on them (*Chicago P.D.*, *The Rookie*, *S.W.A.T*), even as others acknowledge the power police have and the need for change (*Chicago P.D.*, *NCIS: Los Angeles*). It is also worth noting that main characters, though flawed, are generally interested in combatting racist policing, and new characters are introduced to represent racist cops in ways that can be dealt with by season's end. In this section, I map out the ways American procedural series articulate the problems in modern policing, potential solutions for improving policing for the police and public alike, and the myriad impediments to progress.

HOW WE GOT HERE: PROBLEMS IN POLICING

One explanation for the large number of "bad apples" in policing is the nature of the training they receive. *S.W.A.T.* showrunner Aaron Rahsaan Thomas considers these officers and asks, "How did that bad apple, so to speak, become bad? Where did that individual learn that behavior from? Was that person just born a bad seed . . . or was that something they learned over time?" Notably, the three series that broach this topic are the ones with multiepisode arcs in which racist or white supremacist men on the force are discovered and pursued by "good" cops. In *The Rookie*, a series that follows earnest and well-meaning guardian Officer Nolan as he joins the LAPD, Nolan learns from James (played by Arjay Smith), a Black inner-city community leader, that rookie cops are routinely brought to his neighborhood "because the arrests are easy." Like his character James, Smith takes issue with the failures of police training that produce officers whose misconceptions and skewed perceptions lead them to target and discriminate against Black people.[27] Pulling from first-hand experiences of having guns drawn on him by cops "fitting the description," Smith was invested in James's functionality in *The Rookie*—namely putting the white knight in his place. James explains that rookies are taught "this is what a junkie looks like and this is what a dealer looks like. And from that moment on, that's how cops see us." Nolan assures James that he was not trained that way, and James points out that Nolan's training officer (TO) was a Black woman, suggesting that Black and white TOs train rookies to police differently. When *S.W.A.T.* officers suspect a new teammate is a white supremacist, their investigation reveals the subject disproportionately arrested Black people, and they reflect on how bad training might teach an officer to equate Blackness with criminality and thus find more reasons to arrest Black citizens. The *N.C.I.S.: New Orleans* team uncovers a gang of white supremacist officers who were all trained by an instructor named Campbell who practiced warrior training; this program encourages an "us versus them" mentality that promotes a gladiator approach to policing and is described as prevalent throughout the country. The *N.C.I.S.* team learns that Campbell's trainees receive a considerably above-average number of complaints. Training is thus presented as an important factor in an officer's approach to policing. This is not to say that officers cannot be trained well by white TOs. In *The Rookie*, white veteran TO Bradford reminds a new rookie, "The people we come up against on the street aren't enemy combatants, they're our fellow citizens," and that treating the public as the enemy is doing the job wrong.

Though training is not always discussed, these series consistently recognize the prevalence of police who treat citizens—particularly Black citizens—as the enemy. This problem is articulated as a dehumanizing perspective that shapes how officers approach their job, use their discretion, and see themselves. Stanton, the racist TO highlighted in *The Rookie*, is shown racially profiling and acting aggressively toward people of color; when Stanton is called to the scene of a dead gangbanger, he tells his young Black rookie Officer West that there were "no victims involved," meaning the victim had no value or worth. In *S.W.A.T.*, racist officers gather to lament a cultural obsession with political correctness that wants to hold police responsible for a few "split-second bad decisions." Officers in *Law & Order: Organized Crime* pursue a group of Black teens and, upon running into a Black teen unrelated to the group, violently attack him without provocation. This approach to policing is perhaps most problematic when it results in an officer killing a Black person because the cop feared for their life, as is discussed repeatedly in *S.W.A.T.* and depicted in *Chicago P.D.* and *FBI: Most Wanted*. In the case of *Chicago P.D.*, which handled this kind of shooting in a one-episode narrative, Officer Wheelan is introduced when the ensemble cast sees a video of Wheelan killing an unarmed Black man. Wheelan complains after the shooting that people see the police as an occupying force and that he is very familiar with "those faces, the 'I hate cops' faces," crying out, "I did thirty years in a warzone!" Wheelan insists he was doing his job and that the victim reached for his gun; when faced with video evidence to the contrary, Wheelan believes it was altered because he is so convinced of his integrity, though he eventually realizes that his fear blinded him to reality. In such cases, *S.W.A.T.* showrunner Thomas suggests, we see that officers with good intentions are "over time . . . taught to fear for your life or in your in neighborhoods where you fear the people that are there . . . and you start to then assume that everyone's a threat," resulting in a system that encourages an us-versus-them mentality.[28] This is in contrast to what *The*

Rookie showrunner Alexi Hawley recognizes as more community-based policing, wherein officers live and work in the same neighborhoods and consider the people they police and protect their neighbors.

American police procedurals offer various perspectives on how officers should treat each other in response to poor behavior, invoking discussion of the "blue wall," a reference to police culture's code of silence that prevents officers from bringing each other's illicit behaviors to light and holding them accountable.[29] Bowling, Reiner, and Sheptycki note that cop culture is built on a tendency toward solidarity whereby officers "back each other up in the face of external investigation."[30] In all cases, those in management within the police ranks are tasked with projecting to the public a defense of policing as rational, acceptable, and legally sound. As an irate Sergeant Kenny explains in *Chicago P.D.*, "Blue wall is there to keep us together; it keeps us safe. It's a bible, our Ten Commandments. . . . If someone chooses to violate that code, he's gotta pay the price. Way it's always been. Way it always will be." When officers misbehave, cop culture calls on those in positions of authority within the force to defend officers by acting in ways complicit with misconduct, turning a blind eye; when this becomes impossible in the face of public outcry, management among police organizations can balance intentional ignorance of the problems with the sacrifice of select individuals as "bent" and in so doing ratify the institution's effectiveness in self-policing. In addition to perpetuating a process that "ratifies the effectiveness of the disciplinary process as a whole,"[31] this approach treats racist cops as "bad apples" rather than recognizing the police institution as a "rotten orchard" in which racist policing practices are a system-level failure.[32] Thus, racist police and policing practices that are common in the United States,[33] albeit expressed less openly and virulently than in the past,[34] can generally go unchecked, with a predominantly white police force resisting efforts toward police reform.[35]

This aspect of U.S. cop culture is frequently represented in cop shows. Officers repeatedly support each other, for example, by characterizing racist rants as blowing off steam (*S.W.A.T.*), chalking up the violent beating of a protestor to an error in judgment (*Chicago P.D.*), and giving an officer the benefit of the doubt that he believed a cell phone was a gun when he shoots an unarmed Black man (*FBI: Most Wanted*). Bad cops are also protected when their superior officers close complaints against them (*Chicago P.D.*, *NCIS: New Orleans*) and when medical examiners are pressured to label excessive-force deaths as accidents rather than homicides (*NCIS: New Orleans*). And yet, this season of American procedurals features various instances of "good cops" speaking up against "bad apples." Representing a range of responses

FIG. 3.3. Captain Grey and Officer Bradford place Officer Stanton on administrative leave on the "Lockdown" episode of *The Rookie* (2021).

spoke to the truth that, as *Law & Order: SVU* producer Norberto Barba explains, "There are some bad cops, and there are cops who support those bad cops by keeping quiet, and then there are good cops who want change." When *The Rookie*'s Officer Bradford admits he has been giving cops like Stanton a pass, his trainee Lucy says, "It wasn't a pass. You gave him permission. Silence is complicity." Bradford responds by supporting Officer West's complaints about the racist Stanton to the captain, and the three work together to bring Stanton down (see Figure 3.3). In *S.W.A.T.*, Deacon similarly realizes he has been ignoring fellow officers' questionable (i.e., racist) comments for years and secretly records the racist cops in order to get them off the streets. *Chicago P.D.*'s Detective Atwater gets charges dismissed against two Black men who killed the white Officer Doyle because, as Atwater witnessed, Doyle had no probable cause in instigating a gun fight, and the men fired in self-defense. Still, these series depict the consequences for officers and other public figures who challenge the status quo of protecting the police, including the threat of losing their job (*Law & Order: Organized Crime*, *Law & Order: SVU*) and being targeted for retribution (*Chicago, P.D.*, *NCIS: New Orleans*).

HOW TO IMPROVE: SOLUTIONS FOR POLICING

If modern policing faces a crisis built on poor training, a warrior stance, and a blue wall that protects bad cops from facing consequences for their actions, then we must consider what can be done to improve conditions. Various solutions or tools are considered across these series, alternately pointing to steps already being taken and advocating for new changes. Some of these are about who makes it onto the force, and others focus on how officers do the work of policing once in uniform. Some locate the power to change among officers, and others place it at higher institutional levels. No clear-cut solutions are presented, as these series demonstrate the ways each solution is flawed or has unintended consequences.

Part of the conversation around how to improve policing is about who should be the ones affecting change. The push to defund the police and thus redistribute city funding to social workers and others would have to come from local politicians, likely spurred by public outcry. Some shows (*Blue Bloods*, *Law & Order: SVU*, *The Rookie*) make the case for a more limited police mandate, as relying on police as a catch-all for society's ills when they are trained for very little has led us to the current crisis. For example, *The Rookie* describes cases involving people with mental health crises in which the arrival of an officer with a gun is not as helpful as a trained mental health professional. By contrast, Deacon (*S.W.A.T.*) takes offense at "this whole defund-the-police nonsense," which he interprets as a lack of gratitude for officers who risk their lives every day, but he is challenged by his troop leader Hondo, who points out that not all problems need a gun as part of their solution. Change, *Law & Order: SVU* suggests, can also result from lawsuits. When a Black man named Jayvon is wrongfully arrested, he synchronizes his lawsuit against the NYPD with other pending cases so that they can collectively demand systemic change, fueled in part by a report on how the NYPD handled #BlackLivesMatter protests in 2020 (see Figure 3.4). Though the series does not establish whether these lawsuits are successful, they are built on insider information, suggesting that change is dependent upon the insight of officers including those in internal affairs (IA); one IA officer explains to Detective Benson that systemic changes like de-escalation training and civilian oversight must come from within if police are going to accept it, and Benson in turn counsels Jayvon on specific changes he can demand, assuring him that he has may allies in the force who are frustrated by their inability to get rid of bad cops, a sentiment echoed by Harper (*The Rookie*).

Some attention is given to issues of who gets to be a police officer. One solution is a more diverse force, with many Black officers (*FBI: Most Wanted*, *Law & Order: SVU*, *S.W.A.T.*) detailing how they joined the force in order to be part of making it better. *S.W.A.T.* explores this in more depth when Hondo, a Black officer, struggles with the mayor's request that he be the poster boy for recruitment efforts in the African American community. As Hondo explains to Erika, a young Black woman on his team, "It's the same old show and it doesn't stop. And the gap between Black and blue is even wider now." Erika wonders what will happen when there are no Black

FIG. 3.4. Olivia and Christian watch news coverage of Jayvon Brown's lawsuit on the *Law & Order: SVU* episode "Guardians and Gladiators" (2020).

officers, leading Hondo to propose a series of recruitment meetings where Black officers can speak openly about the unique challenges they face and the mistakes made by the LAPD. Another approach appears in *Chicago P.D.*, which suggests the value of early intervention strategies that might detect implicit bias among officers; however, some white officers take offense to the questions they are asked, and the episode concludes by revealing that Officer Wheelan had passed the screening with high marks a week before killing a young Black man. A more radical solution proposed by *The Rookie*'s police reform advocate Dr. Ryan is the Camden Experiment, in which officers are fired and must reapply for their jobs, subject to new background checks, including screening of their social media accounts. Officer Harper finds this to be an extreme solution that would gut the force, but Dr. Ryan reiterates that they "would be coming back to a *better* force" and that "without major action, things will never get better."

In terms of how policing is done, these shows offer various correctives, but with mixed messages. One is a reliance on body cams (*The Rookie*), which might be used to keep officers from stepping over the line. Dr. Ryan points out a flaw with body cams, specifically that they are "always broken whenever the cops cross the line," but Officer Nolan insists that cops want body cams because "it makes it easier to disprove complaints." Thus, body cams are presented as being useful, but mostly for protecting cops; bad cops can turn off body cams to avoid evidence of their bad behavior, as Stanton does, and good cops can rely on body cams to protect their own reputations against false accusations of police brutality. Another corrective is an end to the mindset of noble cause corruption, which Officer Nolan explains is when "an officer justifies bending or breaking the rules if they believe that infraction is being done in the name of justice." Nolan's captain characterizes this mindset as a cancer that will no longer be tolerated, and *Chicago P.D.*'s Deputy Superintendent Miller also takes a firm stance against this approach to policing. However, *Chicago P.D.*'s narratives repeatedly show officers breaking rules in this way. Moreover, when they do not, or when they are held accountable for doing so, the consequences are shown to be tragic; a serial rapist who is set free because the arresting officer was deemed too aggressive goes on to attack multiple women, and Miller's own son is killed by drug dealers after she refuses to let officers proceed without a warrant. Finally, the governor in *Blue Bloods* proposes that cops who slip up even once should lose their pension. While the police commissioner agrees that pension laws need to be modified, he wants a case-by-case review rather than the automatic loss the governor proposes. Many of the solutions to police corruption that are proposed in these series are thus raised only to be exposed as flawed.

Why We Are Stuck: Impediments to Progress

As the previous section demonstrates, potential solutions to the problems of policing are not clearly articulated or uniformly supported. A problem cannot be addressed if those involved are unwilling to admit the problem exists, and numerous characters across these series admit to being part of the problem. An FBI special agent in charge gives a press conference addressing the long history of homicides committed by a handful of police officers against people of color and takes steps to make amends for the sins of the past (*FBI: Most Wanted*). Detectives recognize and speak up about their implicit biases and their commitment to confronting those biases in order to better serve the public (*Law & Order: SVU*). Police superintendents recognize that critiques of policing are not a personal affront and work with community leaders to address systemic inequalities (*NCIS: New Orleans*). At the same time, they face officers who complain that pushes to change policing "make it harder for good cops to do the job" (*The Rookie*) and lament, "We're all trying our best" (*Chicago P.D.*), as if they can't do better, as well as high-ranking officials who think the public is equally to blame for the events of 2020 (*Blue Bloods*). Thus, many of the options presented in these series face backlash as the public, officers, police commissioners, deputy superintendents, police unions, and mayors struggle to come to an agreement regarding the problems this country faces and the steps that should be taken.

American police procedurals articulate impediments to progress in ways that emphasize systemic concerns. Internal affairs officers in *Law & Order:*

SVU, *NCIS: New Orleans*, and *The Rookie* detail how difficult it is to hold cops accountable for abusing their authority, and *The Rookie* and *Blue Bloods* point out how cops who police other cops are treated as rats and prevented from doing their job. *The Rookie* also details the Police Officer Bill of Rights, and *NCIS: New Orleans*, *The Rookie*, and *S.W.A.T.* address the role of police union lawyers who are highly effective at protecting bad cops. Instead of punishing officers for abusing power, these series explain, gladiator cops are moved around, and cities settle financially with complainants rather than admit fault. Police officials with the most power are presented as "more interested in the optics than actual change" (*Law & Order: SVU*).

These larger systemic roadblocks to progress are reinforced by the blue-wall mentality, paired with officers' belief that they are powerless to improve things. Deacon (*S.W.A.T.*) recognizes that racist cops are a problem and does not want them protected but has internalized the belief that "cops don't turn on other cops." Though Deacon, a white man, eventually helps to bring down the racist cops in his field, the same is not true for Stanton's old partner (*The Rookie*), a young Black man who not only refuses to turn Stanton in for his racist behavior but warns him that others are gunning for him. After all, he reasons, "Blue protects blue. . . . The system is not gonna change, so what's the point of me throwing myself off a cliff? I gotta get what's mine." In *Law & Order: SVU*, white police chiefs harangue a Black chief for going on record and apologizing for systemic racism at the NYPD and calling for bias training and an end to qualified immunity, accusing him of throwing "every cop in this department under the bus."

In the face of such stalwart systemic impediments, the threat of negative publicity becomes a tool, even as a scare tactic. When Detective Atwater is persecuted for crossing the blue line, he threatens to go public about the coordinated attacks against him, and the orchestrator of the campaign against him stands down (*Chicago P.D.*). Hondo goes public about racist cops in *S.W.A.T.* only after the Board of Rights declares a lack of tangible evidence, correctly guessing that outside pressure would overturn the decision, but Hondo is then disciplined for going outside the chain of command. Similarly, Officer West (*The Rookie*) wants to go public when he learns that the police commissioner and the Board of Rights allowed Stanton to keep his job, asking his captain why he should protect a police department that cares more about a lawsuit than his life. West's captain predicts that publicity would hurt West without leading to any real change, and they settle for sharing video evidence of Stanton's unacceptable behavior with his new squad, effectively identifying him as a racist cop. Thus, the greatest tool for effecting change appears to be public pressure on policing institutions, but even this is presented as a flawed solution that will often fail or even backfire against guardian cops who try to utilize public outcry.

Conclusion: Progress, Not Perfection

The cultural forum surrounding policing in American procedurals, particularly in the 2020–2021 season when attention to these issues was more frequent, demonstrates the complexity of policing and police reform in the twenty-first century. Television's police cannot be uniformly characterized as good or bad, guardians or gladiators. Rather, law enforcement officers debate among themselves about what constitutes a "bad apple" and how best to address problematic officers—if at all. In particular, these series emphasize the hurdles officers face when they try to challenge and change the status quo, facing both systemic barriers and backlash from fellow officers when they cross the blue line. Within this framework, Black officers, of whom there are one or two per series, face a unique challenge, fighting an impossible battle as they try to navigate the blue line in Black bodies.

A prominent finding across the themes I analyze is that problems and solutions are articulated at the level of individuals rather than as systemic. The presence of "good" cops who do not shoot unarmed Black citizens, and who do not train new officers to police in racist ways, outweighs "bad apples" who are largely presented as anomalies. The blue wall that protects so many bad officers is shown to be surmountable by tenacious and morally righteous protagonists. Because the police institution produces so many upstanding officers and detectives, many of whom will stand up to others who take a gladiator approach to policing Black communities or otherwise let their racist feelings affect their work, cop shows suggest that it is not the case that the system needs major reform; instead, more good cops can and should work to excise the rare bad apple. In the world of these American police procedurals, there is no rotten orchard, and a few bad apples do not spoil the bunch.

It is also worth considering differences in the ways racist cops are framed. As noted earlier, these series feature ensembles in which the main characters are imperfect but not maliciously racist, and many of the "good" cops either espouse antiracist discourses or at least consider the ways in which they have contributed to a problematic status quo. "Bad apples" are introduced to these contexts, and the good cops are able to provide a united front against them. The explicitly racist cops in contemporary cop dramas differ noticeably from racist cops like Sipowicz from *NYPD Blue*, not just because they are peripheral characters but because their racism is less overt and therefore harder to confirm and thus hold accountable. Whereas Sipowicz would use the N-word,[36] racist cops in shows like *The Rookie* and *S.W.A.T.* use coded language to communicate their meaning, signaling their racism to like-minded colleagues while often leaving others oblivious. Additionally, Sipowicz evolves as a character and learns to deal with his racist instincts productively. By contrast, many of the racist officers in these series act like martyrs, unrepentant and uninterested in changing; they are not looking to learn and grow and diminish their racism but rather seeking ways to maintain their sense of white supremacy by shoring up support for their racist attitudes. As peripheral characters, they are quickly dispensed with, though often without justice having been fully served. Again, the issue of systemic racism in policing is narratively brushed aside when these specific characters' racist beliefs are exposed.

Another pernicious pattern across the themes analyzed above is that larger-scale solutions are discredited almost as soon as they are raised. Such solutions are narratively and discursively articulated as flawed, often because they will result indirectly in harm that outweighs the good they will do. American police procedurals thus amplify discourses from U.S. culture that explain why conditions cannot or will not improve, often in the form of structural impediments throughout the institution of policing. Factors that structurally hinder real-world policing are, in a sense, replicated by the television industry, which faces its own impediments to challenging the status quo in the American police procedural genre, such as a reliance on the genre's narrative structures and inequity among the industry's decision-makers. This begs the question of whether the scripted entertainment programming industry is truly capable of engaging radical reform, or if the industry is instead destined to cater to demands placed on it as a business. Even after resounding calls for police reform and a spotlight on cop shows, the 2020–2021 season did not cease in its depiction of copaganda. Instead, these series featured shining examples of good cops catching bad apples without solving the systemic issues that have produced so many bad apples over the years. By highlighting the ways good officers triumph over bad, police series get credit for acknowledging their complicity in the status quo without having to dismantle, or even push hard against, the structures from which they benefit.

The lack of resolutions within and across these series aligns with the cultural forum model, which values the existence of dialogue around cultural issues over the presentation of narrative closure.[37] By contrast, Gitlin suggests that hegemonic ideology is systematically preferred by, and reinforced through, programming features like genre and slant, which introduce and domesticate alternative or oppositional values.[38] This book reconciles the two disparate theoretical strands, articulating both the dialogue of American police procedurals' cultural forum and the reliance on narrative closure; the lack of resolution—of any clear answer of how to curb racist policing in the United States—functions unto itself as a form of ideological closure that defers to the status quo.

Lotz questions the effectiveness of counter-dominant perspectives on television, asking, "If a series . . . presents a view contradicting or negotiating dominant ideological perspectives, and no one but those critical of the dominant ideology sees it, is its challenge to hegemony diminished?"[39] In the current study, messages that oppose the dominant U.S. ideology of valorizing police are being circulated in the American police procedural genre, whose audience is broadly regarded as supporting that dominant ideology. Therefore, we might conclude that the very genre that long protected the public image of police and therefore contributed to the current state of U.S. policing is also the genre best positioned to effectively communicate messages of progressive police reform to America's more conservative viewers. The potential for these scripted series to sway viewers' perspectives on such issues is amplified when the conversation continues from one episode or series to the next rather than in isolated moments of representation. At the same time, viewers are presented with only part of the picture, teased with introductions to larger calls for reform, only to have those calls silenced by television's structural reliance on the tried-and-true success of the American police procedural genre.

We might perceive the increase in on-screen discourses of police reform as indicative of cultural progress, but this also may simply signal how the media taps into activism in order to avoid getting dragged for being culturally insensitive or tone-deaf. We should also keep in mind that this forum is cultivated for broadcast audiences by a none-too-diverse group of writers and producers; as Edwards points out, the population of low-level writers may be increasingly diverse, but the superiors they report to are overwhelming white, and the companies that own television shows are not historically interested in exposing systemic racism within police institutions.[40] The 2020 Color of Change report similarly highlights the lack of diversity among television writers, showrunners, creators, and executives, and argues that this overwhelmingly white (and male) community is a major factor in the limited perspectives offered by U.S. crime dramas. And yet, whatever a program's motivation, be it writers' support for social justice or executives' demand for commercially viable programming, the inclusion of explicit criticisms of U.S. policing is an important step toward making those concerns a greater part of public discourses.

Annual Hollywood Diversity reports from UCLA's Entertainment and Media Research Initiative suggest that the networks make changes when the pressure is on, as BIPOC individuals made up just 13.1 percent of show creators on scripted broadcast series in fall of 2020—these series having been greenlit prior to Floyd's death—up to 23.2 percent for fall of 2021 in the aftermath of global protests.[41] We can celebrate this indication of progress while lamenting that the record 23.2 percent BIPOC show creators is still far below the 43.1 percent BIPOC U.S. population, and even when diverse writers' rooms produce diverse programs that challenge the status quo, they do not all gain a sufficient following to stay on the air. For example, *East New York* featured a diverse ensemble cast with Black and Latino leads, challenged generic conventions, and was canceled after one season on CBS. There is therefore no formula for success, but incremental progress continues to be made.

4

Beyond the Police Procedural

Black Lives Matter in Comedies and Dramas, Too

The cultural forum of Black Lives Matter exists far beyond the police procedural genre. While cop shows are primed to engage with issues of police brutality and systemic racism, comedies and other forms of drama can avoid these topics with greater ease, and some certainly choose to do so, but others deliberately incorporate ongoing discussions about race in America. These programs, which Brandi Monk-Payton dubs "BLM TV," consist of content that has "remarked on this history of violence in explicit and implicit ways" by "interrogating structural racism and anti-blackness on- and off-screen."[1] For those series that constitute BLM TV by participating in the forum, contributions vary in both quantity and quality of attention given, with some series addressing BLM themes regularly and repeatedly, while other series broach the subject in a "very special episode." The "very special episode" has been "both a staple of television and the bane of its existence" because it acknowledges that "television can provide insight on and sympathy for a timely and/or emotionally resonant issue," but it can also "be unbearably cheesy and clumsy, which can do more harm than good."[2] As Framke explains, the VSE often fails because "it's just so much easier to get on a high horse than it is to explore a complicated issue in 40 minutes or less," resulting all too frequently in self-righteous moralizing. Even when engagement is sustained beyond a single episode, Monk-Payton notes that there can be "a disconnect between the promise of such content's engagement with social justice and what it actually delivers," for example, when it "reproduces a kind of white imagination of black terror and suffering under the guise of critical commentary."[3] More promising are programs that "have the tendency to combine expressions of trauma and joy, striving to depict the complexity and fullness of black experiences."

This chapter explores BLM's cultural forum and BLM TV beyond the cop genre by exploring broadcast comedies and nonpolice dramas. In the first part of the chapter, I provide an overview of different kinds of sitcoms—Black-cast and multiracial sitcoms—and the ways they addressed BLM, articulating the relationship between casts, writers, and activist engagement. Multiracial sitcoms like *New Girl*, *Superstore*, and *The Neighborhood* can organically introduce BLM into their narratives, using the casts' diversity to authentically voice numerous competing perspectives on changing race relations in the United States. Black-cast sitcoms like *The Carmichael Show* and *black-ish* are also naturally suited to engage BLM, but the conversations among networks, showrunners, writers, and actors inevitably take on a different tenor. I conclude my discussion of comedies with a more detailed study of *Brooklyn Nine-Nine*, a multiracial cop comedy created by two white men that was groundbreaking in many ways and yet demonstrably guilty of "copaganda." I then turn to the numerous dramatic subgenres outside of cop shows, including legal dramas, political dramas, and medical dramas, that make up a sizeable amount of prime-time programming. My attention to dramas' expansion of the BLM cultural forum features an in-depth case study of *Station 19*, a firefighter drama that made full-throated, if rocky, inroads in its engagement with racist policing practices and its modeling of a path toward defunding the police. Drawing on interviews with writers, producers, and actors for *Station 19*, I illustrate how a progressive leadership style can produce collaborative creativity that challenges the status quo of television's most popular genre.

No Laughing Matter: Black Lives Matter in Broadcast Comedies

While the goal of sitcoms is ostensibly to make audiences laugh, comedies have long addressed serious issues and participated in conversations around moral and ethical issues that concern citizens. The titular character in *Maude* was the first leading lady in prime time to have an abortion in the 1972 two-part episode "Maude's Dilemma," and *All in the Family* featured TV's first attempted rape in the 1977 two-parter "Edith's 50th Birthday," in addition to regularly tackling racism. In 1990, six months before Rodney King was violently beaten by the LAPD, *The Fresh Prince of Bel-Air* featured an episode titled "Mistaken Identity" in which two young Black men are pulled over for driving too nice a car; *Family Matters* featured a similar storyline in the 1994 episode "Good Cop, Bad Cop." When Black officer Terry Jeffords (played by the famously muscular Terry Crews) is stopped by a white officer while roaming his neighborhood looking for his daughter's missing toy in

Brooklyn Nine-Nine's fourth-season 2017 episode "Moo Moo," it was the first time the police sitcom genuinely acknowledged ongoing issues of racism in policing.

Notably, Black-cast sitcoms like *The Fresh Prince of Bel-Air* and *Family Matters* are better positioned to raise issues of systemic racism and police brutality, as the presence of Black bodies on screen functions as an entry point to such topics, similar to how police procedurals are better primed to engage these issues as compared to other forms of dramas like medical dramas or political dramas by virtue of featuring numerous police officers. Black-cast sitcoms regularly acknowledge and reflect on race in ways that white-cast sitcoms like *Friends* and *How I Met Your Mother* do not, so while more emotionally intense episodes may appear "very special" in their presentation, they are not a stark contrast from the general depiction of the lives of Black characters. Multiracial sitcoms like *The Office*, *Superstore*, and *Brooklyn Nine-Nine* fall somewhere in the middle in their acknowledgment of and engagement with racism, taking for granted a diverse American landscape and frequently acknowledging characters' ethnoracial identities but rarely making those identities and the struggles they face the theme of the episode.

New Girl (Fox, 2011–2018), one of the few multiracial sitcoms on broadcast television to feature two Black men—Winston (Lamorne Morris) and Coach (Damon Wayans Jr.)—has Winston explore numerous career paths before becoming a police officer. Though race is regularly acknowledged by the series, it is typically used to make fun of white people and poke fun at stereotypes. However, in one "very special" B-plot initiated by Morris, *New Girl* addresses what it is like to be a Black cop in the twenty-first century. Airing on April 7, 2015, "Par 5" shows Winston awkwardly approaching an attractive Black woman named KC at a restaurant and asking her out, only for her to invite Winston to a rally to protest the police. A predictably nervous Winston gets KC to agree to meet him for lunch instead, over which she explains that there was a kid at the rally "who was arrested last week because he 'fit a description.' I mean, he's fourteen—he doesn't even fit into his jeans." Winston chuckles awkwardly, and KC asks him what he does for a living, at which point two officers passing by greet Winston by name. When KC asks if he is a cop, Winston insists that he is a stripper and implies that their uniforms are, in fact, tear-away costumes. Later, Winston confides in his white friend Nick, "With everything that's going on I just—I feel like she wouldn't respect me." Nick asks if Winston wants his opinion, and Winston unequivocally responds, "No, Nick, I don't. This is something you can't understand" (see Figure 4.1). Winston understands where KC is coming from because he

FIG. 4.1. Winston talks to Nick about being a Black police officer on the "Par 5" episode of *New Girl* (2015).

ran away from the police as a child out of habit. Coach pops up at this point to second Winston, but it becomes a joke: "As the only other Black man in this loft, I feel like I should weigh in. This issue really hits home with me, and I feel like I have a lot of thoughts and ideas that I need to get off my chest. . . . But I'm hungry." Coach then heads to the kitchen while singing to himself, "Race talk snacks, race talk snacks, gotta get me some race talk snacks, gonna be super uncomfortable." Deeper discussion is thus precluded, saving both Nick and white viewers the discomfort of having to deal too much with the dark realities of racism in this comedic context. Winston eventually goes to KC's office and comes clean, and KC says she is not mad about his being a cop but about his lying. This scene is marked by additional awkward jokes from Winston and concludes with KC suggesting that it is only fair that Winston strip for her and her colleagues—again, without larger themes of systemic racism in the police institution being addressed or unpacked.

The subplot of "Par 5" is the extent to which *New Girl* deals with race and policing and resulted from Morris feeling "he was 'betraying' the Black community by playing a police officer," leaving him "with 'a weird mental state' as more cases of police brutality came to light."[4] Morris had received numerous tweets about Winston becoming a police officer and was upset by the Darren Wilson verdict following Michael Brown's murder in Ferguson, Missouri. Morris reports thinking, "I should address this, without being too preachy or too militant."[5] Morris brought the idea to producers, acknowledging the need to balance "the desire to address the topic with the responsibility to be funny." He was unsure what to expect from the three white producers and was surprised to learn they had also wanted to address it, and the producers invited Morris to tackle writing the episode. Not everything Morris wrote made the cut, including the assertion that "Black people are being slaughtered," presumably because it is hard to incorporate truths that dark into a comedy series led by a white woman who proudly "rock[s] a lot of polka dots" and has regular contact with glitter. Morris shares, "We wanted to take a neutral stance. I have friends that are police officers, and they're great individuals; when one officer does something wrong, law enforcement as a group takes the fall."[6]

Superstore (NBC, 2015–2021) is another multiracial sitcom that regularly brings up race in order to ridicule racism, though most episodes only feature one Black character, Garrett (Colton Dunn). While *New Girl* ended before 2020, *Superstore*'s final season was created in the aftermath of the global protests. The first few episodes primarily addressed COVID-19, and *Superstore*'s first engagement with BLM is when a shipment of "safety supplies" turns out not to be the much-needed personal protective equipment they were expecting but instead antilooting procedures and a sign reading that their parent company Zephra "believes in the Black community," to which Garrett retorts, "What are we, ghosts?" *Superstore*'s approach is ultimately to criticize racist corporate procedures like locking up Black hair-care products, as well as the self-congratulatory tone companies take when they end their racist practices, and poking fun at well-meaning "woke" white colleagues who can't seem to shut up about antiracism book clubs. After Garrett points out other racist rules that dictate his behavior and appearance to his oblivious white supervisor Dina, she convinces him to take on the free labor of compiling "a list of all the racist stuff that corporate needs to talk about." At a meeting where Black employees are encouraged to contribute—and where white employees are presumably there to represent white audiences—Dina says, "I think a lot of us want to help, but we just have blind spots when it comes to this stuff. I mean, when I was growing up, we were told the goal was to not see race." Garrett is sure this "goal" was developed by white people, and that the goal should instead be awareness of how race affects Black people's daily lives, prompting a slew of jokes at the expense of white people who struggle to do so. As Garrett grows frustrated, he tries to pawn the job of compiling the list onto his Black colleague Nia but takes it back after she laments that "once again, Black women are the ones everybody expects to drive social change." Garrett later points out to Dina that she put the burden on him, and she agrees to take over and explains that she'll send it "up the chain" and that they should get an answer in three to five weeks. When, in the episode's final scene, Dina storms in with a crushed cutout of the store's racist mascot M. C. Cool Cloud and demands an explanation, Garrett says, "It's racist and I was tired of looking at it, and I wasn't gonna wait three to five weeks for someone else to come fix it." Dina takes a beat before she simply responds, "Got it." The takeaway here is that institutional change is slow and that small acts of antiracism are an alternative so long as white people with authority allow it.

Whereas *New Girl* and *Superstore* feature diverse casts beyond Black and white characters, *The Neighborhood* (CBS, 2018–present) moves the white Johnsons—Dave, Gemma, and their young son Grover—into a Black neighborhood next to Calvin and Tina Butler, whose adult sons Marty and Malcolm are frequently present. The series revolves around the growing relationship between the two families, with issues of race featuring prominently, especially early on; this is often in the small ways the Johnsons learn about Black history and cultural practices, including white flight, women's wigs, appropriation, and teaching Black history in schools. The term "Black Lives Matter" comes up in the second episode when Gemma wants to try on Tina's wigs, and Marty tells Gemma that she has to say "Black lives matter" first. A startled Gemma says, "Of *course* Black lives matter." Tina laughs and says Marty was just messing with Gemma, "but good answer, girl."

Though the premise that Black lives matter permeates *The Neighborhood*, the third season premiered with a very special episode on November 16, 2020. Malcolm arrives at the Butler home and announces that he was playing basketball at the park with his friend Trey when police officers showed up, started harassing them, and beat and arrested Trey; Malcolm tried to say something, but one officer reached for his gun and Malcolm stopped talking. When Dave and Calvin go to the police station to investigate, Dave wonders what Trey "did to get arrested," believing it to be Trey's fault for being "not exactly a Boy Scout." Calvin counters, "Just because Trey had some run-ins with the law don't mean he did something today, and even if he had, it doesn't give them the right to whoop his ass." The police insist on holding Trey over the weekend, prompting Malcom to organize a protest to march on the precinct. Meanwhile, Gemma tries to explain to her very confused son Grover about the double standard by which he can safely rely on the police for help while Black people live in fear of police violence. Calvin and Tina return from the protest and report that "everything was peaceful, and then the cop showed up in riot gear" and "started pushing us off with their shields and then firing tear gas, and all hell broke loose." They realize Malcolm is missing, and Calvin and Dave go off in search of him while Dave continues to be perplexed by the situation. Calvin asks, "What do you expect?

You arm the police like they're going to war, that's exactly what they're going to do. I mean, those guys were itching for a fight." Dave insists that "it's not like all cops are bad," and Calvin encourages Dave, "Tell that to the people being choked out and killed in the streets. . . . Of course there's some good cops, but they're part of a system that was created when we weren't even considered people." Calvin ties the history of slavery to systems that keep Black Americans "undereducated or incarcerated and out of the voting booth." Dave concedes, "Maybe you're right; maybe the system is broken," to which Calvin counters, "No, the system is working exactly the way it's designed." When Calvin and Dave find Malcolm, he is agitated and wants to escalate because he doesn't know how else to channel his feelings of helplessness and anger; Calvin tells him to fight not with his fists but with his mind, by organizing the community and effecting change because "you can't help nobody if you're dead or in jail." In the closing scene, Trey has been released due to the protests, and the cops who attacked him are being investigated and potentially face charges. Calvin leads Trey, the Johnsons, and his own family in prayer as they ask for "the strength to lead the world towards justice, peace, and love for all God's children." Race remains a central theme of the series, but the immediate threat of police brutality recedes from the central narrative in subsequent episodes.

The Carmichael Show (NBC, 2015–2017) and *black-ish* (ABC, 2014–2022) are more solidly Black-cast than *The Neighborhood* with their focus on Black families, but similar to *The Neighborhood* in that they contain ongoing engagement with racial issues as well as the occasional episode that more seriously considers systemic racism and policing. *The Carmichael Show*, which focuses on Jerrod Carmichael, his mixed-race girlfriend Maxine, his brother Bobby and former sister-in-law Nekeisha, and his parents Cynthia and Joe, tackled the BLM movement in its second episode, "Protest," which aired August 22, 2015; unlike *The Neighborhood* and *black-ish*, this episode didn't feel "very special" in the context of the series, which habitually tackles heavy issues like gun rights, date rape, domestic abuse, and Islamophobia through a comedic lens. Instead, *The Carmichael Show* is a Black sitcom and a black comedy, ripe with gallows humor (see Figure 4.2). As with all its episodes, the subject at hand was discussed at length by the cast that constitutes their own mini cultural forum on each topic, providing an impressive range of nuanced perspectives after the six characters learn that an unarmed Black man has been shot by the police. The heavy cultural commentary is interspersed with jokes, "as if to defy the idea that this awful incident should bring the episode to a screeching halt."[7] For example, Jerrod says there is no point to protesting because it is a waste of time that accomplishes nothing, and when Maxine

FIG. 4.2. Jerrod annoys his parents in the pilot episode of *The Carmichael Show* (2015).

argues that protesting led to gay marriage, Jerrod counters that Neil Patrick Harris had more to do with passing legislation than anything protesters did. Jerrod later recounts a story about being cuffed, thrown to the ground, and scraping up his face because he "fit a description" by wearing a hoodie while out on a coffee run, but is reluctant to admit how scary it was until realizing that he could have been the one killed. Again, comedy is infused into this drama as Jerrod's pain fuels a joke at the expense of his light-skinned girlfriend.

Six months later, the second-season *black-ish* episode "Hope" similarly brought a Black family together to grapple with police brutality, raising many of the same questions and concerns as *The Carmichael Show.* In an episode that creator Kenya Barris reluctantly admits definitely "fit under that category" of very special episode, Dre Johnson, his wife Bow, his parents Pops and Ruby, and his four children—Zoey, Junior, Jack, and Diane—follow national news coverage on the potential indictment of a police officer in the fictional McQuillan case while discussing police brutality and the failures of the justice system. Pops describes the police as "damn thugs," but when Bow counters "not all police," Dre confirms that it is "only 92 percent—the other 8 percent are advisors on *Law & Order.*" Zoey needs a reminder of which example of police brutality the McQuillan case is, and the family rattles through a list of conflated cases, including "the one where they shot the kid in the middle of the street," "the one where they shot the guy in front of the college at the traffic stop," "the unarmed guy who got shot in the back," "the traffic stop," and "the unarmed guy who was selling cigarettes that got choked" before confirming that McQuillan is "the unarmed guy who was selling DVDs that got tased thirty-seven times." In crafting the fictional McQuillan case, Barris wanted "an aggregate of all the cases that have happened in the past five years," and his approach to the whole episode did not receive any notes from the network beyond what images would be permitted during their prime-time slot. The episode's forum centers on how to explain policing and racism to the youngest children, as well as whether they should have faith in the justice system, with the failure to indict the police in the McQuillan case suggesting that faith would be misplaced. Dre declares, "The system is rigged against us," and Zoey feels helpless and lost; of course, the Johnsons don't solve racism, but the twins encourage Zoey to keep fighting for a better future, and Dre and Bow take their teenagers to join the protest.

In addressing "Hope," Barris said, "My hopes are that it starts a great conversation and, at the same time, makes people laugh and think. My fear is: I don't want to piss anyone off. I don't want to politicize the show."[8] Given that *black-ish* is ostensibly quite political with its regular engagement with sociopolitical issues, Barris counters that his series is "politically adjacent" because it doesn't land on a singular point of view; rather, it crafts a variety of thoroughly developed perspectives. To that end, he did not include the words "Black Lives Matter," which he feels is "a politicized movement" that "has nothing to do with what the show is." Though Carmichael had tackled police brutality almost immediately and clearly included BLM in the narrative, Barris felt the need to wait until the second season, when an established audience would see it as a natural topic for the Johnson family to discuss. The emphasis was not on the BLM movement but on the difficulty of raising Black children in a world where images of violence against Black people are too ubiquitous to avoid. In bringing comedy to the VSE, Barris says, "We wanted to make sure that we had some levity to make the seriousness of the topic something that you could swallow, but at the same time we didn't want to have so much levity that it trivialized the issue." Barris reports that Lawrence Fishburn ("Pops") and Jennifer Lewis ("Ruby") were tearful and thanked him after the table read, which he wasn't expecting as a comedy writer.[9] The show *black-ish* thus illustrated the cultural forum's power to host meaningful and nuanced engagement with complex sociopolitical issues. As the following section will show, the cultural forum around race and policing was possible—though perhaps not inevitable—even when the comedy came from the cops themselves.

CASE STUDY: *BROOKLYN NINE-NINE*

Created by Mike Schur and Dan Goor, *Brooklyn Nine-Nine* (*B99*) has the peculiar distinction of being a workplace comedy set in a police precinct. As a "cop show" it would be expected to engage with issues in policing, as is commonly found in police procedurals like *S.W.A.T.* and *The Rookie*—especially as it boasts a diverse cast—yet its status as a sitcom works to avoid too much in-depth consideration of serious topics. Schur explains the original nugget of an idea for *Brooklyn Nine-Nine* wasn't even about police; rather, it was about "a goofball who didn't have a dad and who suddenly was confronted with a guy who he . . . knew instantly could be his new father figure."[10] Schur also points out that "the setting of the show is kind of less important ultimately than the characters and their relationships," and once he has figured out how to make those relationships funny, he figures out what setting or vocation works for that relationship. Though this dynamic between goofball Jake Peralta (Andy Samberg) and father figure Raymond Holt (Andre Braugher) could have been captured in any number of workplace settings, Goor explains that police work "felt like an exciting area to tackle, just in terms of telling stories," with the additional benefit of being more accessible to the public—and therefore requiring less exposition—than the setting of a parks department, as Schur and Goor discovered with their previous hit *Parks & Rec*.[11] Schur and Goor wanted their characters to be good at their jobs rather than incompetent detectives who let criminals get away, and they focused more on the ensemble's intergroup dynamics and the cleverness or stupidity of the criminals rather than the victims of the crimes. For their consultants, Goor relied on a friend in the NYPD who could share insight into what kind of experiences a gay Black man like Captain Holt would have had during his career. *B99* also utilized a technical consultant in the form of a former Glendale police officer and private security consultant who had dealt with the NYPD and could provide tactical expertise regarding the proper way to get through a locked door or hold a gun.[12] That said, the cops in *B99* rarely pull their guns, aligning closer to the reality that most NYPD officers have never pulled a gun, much less discharged it, and diverging from "the language of a television show" that regularly features gun-wielding officers.[13]

Even aside from being a comedy, *B99* differed from the cop shows described in the previous chapters. In a 2016 interview, Goor acknowledged that *B99*'s cops are very much a part of and fond of the community they serve, which is not often the case portrayed by U.S. cop shows. Goor shared, "I think the risk is that it seems like we've got our head in the sand in terms of what's going on with the world and with the community," and he expressed a desire to better "address the tension between communities, currently, and the police." Like *The Rookie* and *S.W.A.T.*, *B99* took an aspirational approach in "modeling what a good police-community interaction would be like," while also conceding that "the world has changed so much in the four years since we started this show" and that "if we were designing this show from scratch now, we might have built in more of the current tension." For example, much of the humor surrounding the character of Jake Peralta is that he was drawn to policing after falling in love with *Die Hard* and wanting to live out fantasies of being John McClane; his antics are rendered harmless by his sincere dedication to helping people, but his gleeful suggestion that they get a tank did not age well after Trump reportedly suggested that tanks be used against BLM protestors.[14]

It wasn't until the fourth season that *B99* considered contemporary issues with racism in policing in the episode "Moo Moo," in which Terry Jeffords (Terry Crews) is harassed by a white patrol officer Maldack while innocently scouring the streets of his neighborhood for his daughter's missing toy. Goor had struggled to find a way to tell such a story because "our guys are cops, and we portray the cops as good guys."[15] Maldack essentially practices "stop and frisk," which Goor suggests *B99*'s protagonists would never do, in an episode written and pushed for by writer Phil Jackson. Though multiple versions of this story were considered, actor Andre Braugher predicted that Holt would warn Jeffords against filing an official complaint for fear that it would prevent Jeffords from securing a position for which he was being considered; the episode ultimately took this approach, allowing the show to make use of being the rare ensemble cop show with two Black officers and unpacking the feeling of being alien in two cultures. Jeffords is disappointed to learn he did not, in fact, get the job, but Goor "felt like this ending was really the best, truest, meatiest ending. This ending of the two of them saying, 'It's tough—there is no answer.'" Though affecting, this episode took on the flavor of a "very special episode" as *B99* largely set aside its concern with systemic issues in policing until its post-Floyd final season in 2021.

Before the events of 2020, serious consideration of race in policing was limited to "Moo Moo" and to flashbacks showing the racism Captain Holt experienced rising through the ranks in the twentieth century. Then, like the more serious cop shows on television, *B99* faced charges of copaganda in 2020, even though the NYPD's top brass is almost uniformly represented negatively and "shown to be incompetent, soulless careerists, malicious, or even outright criminals" who are "constantly portrayed as racist, sexist, and homophobic."[16] The first seven seasons depict the NYPD "as flawed, but redeemable" and "an institution that's seriously trouble[d], but worth fighting for," as well as feature an ensemble that only occasionally violates suspects' rights, rarely acknowledges these violations, and quickly forgives them.[17] Being a comedy rather than a drama did not save *B99* from criticism, and showrunner Dan Goor responded with a year-long hiatus.

The cast and crew of *Brooklyn Nine-Nine* were demonstrably alert to the implications of George Floyd's murder for what had long been a lighthearted comedy about a diverse police precinct full of witty quips and hijinks. In June of 2020, one week after Floyd's death, the cast and crew donated $100,000 to the National Bail Fund Network. Actress Stephanie Beatriz, who plays detective Rosa Diaz, encouraged other actors: "If you currently play a cop? If you make tens or hundreds of thousands of dollars a year in residuals from playing a cop? I'll let you do the math," inviting them to join her in donating to antiracist, projustice causes.[18] Later that month, actor Terry Crews gave an interview in which he shared insights into conversations happening among *B99* writers and actors. Crews began by explaining his history of experiences with the LAPD, where he was deemed a threat and had guns pulled on him. Noting that the problems highlighted by the 2020 protests were nothing new, Crews stated, "We always knew this was happening, but now white people are understanding" and have now experienced Black America's trauma, in a sense, with the video capturing Floyd's final moments.[19] The mainstream circulation of these images permeated the *B99* community, with the cast having candid conversations about both racism and its inevitable influence on their police-based sitcom. "We've had a lot of somber talks about it and deep conversations, and we hope through this we're going to make something that will be truly groundbreaking this year," Crews shared. "We have an opportunity, and we plan to use it in the best way possible," with showrunner Dan Goor electing to scrap the four episodes that had already been scripted for the final season. Crews had no idea at the time what direction the eighth season would take after all those involved recognized that business as usual would be impossible because the national shift in consciousness required a reexamination of their role in contributing to public perceptions of police.

Though he cocreated *Brooklyn Nine-Nine*, Mike Schur was not involved in its day-to-day operations past the second season, and so he introduced me to Dan Goor on the Paramount picket line in July of 2023 so that I might inquire about their final season. I explained the reason for my interest in the subject, only to be met with a pained expression. Though I don't recall his exact words, Goor communicated no small amount of anxiety regarding the final season. When I reassured him that I had enjoyed the series and that my goal was not to tear him or the series down, Goor suggested that was "almost as bad" because praise felt inappropriate. Goor appeared uncomfortable revisiting what was a tumultuous time for the cop genre, all the more so due to the complexities of balancing beloved police detectives and the comedic mandate with anticopaganda sentiments. I suspect there is no approach he could have taken to handling *B99*'s final season that would have saved him from feeling the weight of his responsibility. It, in fact, took a bit of time to figure out what approach to take, as *B99*'s seventh season aired its finale in April of 2020 and did not premiere its eighth season until August of 2021 with an episode aptly titled "The Good Ones."

Upon its return, *B99* immediately established a new normal of thinking critically about systemic issues in policing and gently mocking white allies. Flashbacks reveal that the sardonic detective Rosa Diaz (Stephanie Beatriz) "quit after George Floyd was killed because she thought that she could do more good by becoming a PI that helps victims of police brutality," as Holt explains to Jake, but Jake takes her resignation as a personal criticism of policing and of himself. Wanting to rebuild his relationship with Rosa, Jake volunteers to help Rosa with a client—a Black woman who was assaulted by two officers at a nearby precinct—and thinks he can help because he knows the captain there and believes "the system can still work sometimes when good people are involved." Jake meets the client and awkwardly explains that he is "one of the good ones," parroting white ally language about how he is *actually* one of the good police officers and not the bad ones who just say they are good ones, while Rosa and the client look at him with unveiled skepticism. After hearing the client's story about two officers demanding to know what was in her bag, grabbing her, yelling at her to stop resisting, "which I wasn't, I was just scared," and throwing her against a squad car, Rosa and Jake conclude that the officers must have been looking for an arrest at end-of-shift so that they would have an excuse to make overtime. They go to Captain Lamazar at the Seven-Four, who confirms the arrest is problematic and that the officers have received numerous complaints, and Rosa is unsurprised to learn their body cam footage "was mysteriously corrupted," with Lamazar confirming "they probably tampered with it" (see Figure 4.3). Lamazar alerts them to the presence of a witness—a rookie cop—but when Jake and Rosa arrive at the rookie's apartment to interview her, they are stopped by the head of the patrolmen's union, who states, "I'm here to stop your heartless crusade against our heroes in blue" before blaming the victim for escalating things and claiming marches lead to rioting and looting. Eventually, they access the body cam footage proving the client's innocence, but when they show it to Captain Lamazar, she immediately destroys it, shocking Jake ("Oh no, you're

FIG. 4.3. Rosa and Jake tell Captain Lamazar about dirty cops in her precinct on the "The Good Ones" episode of *Brooklyn Nine-Nine* (2021).

a villain!") but not Rosa. Lamazar explains that she really *is* one of "the good ones," causing Jake to shrivel under Rosa's knowing glare, before detailing the myriad institutional steps and roadblocks that would prevent her corrupt officers from ever being held accountable; the best-case scenario is that the officers drop charges against Rosa's client.

The head of the patrolmen's union is a blowhard named Frank O'Sullivan (John C. McGinely), who returns throughout the season as a villainous personification of blue-line rhetoric. A grown man who lives with his mother and has an alarming obsession with Bruce Springsteen, O'Sullivan believes police officers can do no wrong, and thus, if a police officer did something, it cannot be a wrong action. After butting heads for the first half of the season, O'Sullivan takes Jake's side in the sixth episode when Jake arrests a man without probable cause and is sued. O'Sullivan defends Jake and argues that cops have to make split-second, life-and-death choices every day, and that they cannot do that if they are afraid of being fired for every little mistake. While this does not sound inherently unreasonable, it comes from a character established to be irrationally single-minded, and Holt counters that this was not a life-and-death situation; moreover, when cops are not held accountable for their bad actions, the community loses faith in the police, which in turn makes it harder for officers to do the work of protecting the community. Much to O'Sullivan's dismay, Jake admits that he made bad choices and that he deserves to be punished, and he is suspended.

O'Sullivan's pro-police machinations have the unintended consequence of disrupting the institution he is hell-bent on protecting and defending. In the third episode O'Sullivan manufactures a media stunt to imply that officers are under threat and orchestrates a "blue flu" where hundreds of police officers call in sick using falsified medical reports. This plan backfires when, with fewer cops on the street, Captain Holt compiles evidentiary data that complaints against the police have dropped dramatically and that crime rates did not rise; as he explains to O'Sullivan, "the Nine-Nine just became a case study for how a police force can work better with fewer police." As a result, detective Amy Santiago develops and pitches a police reform initiative, which is approved by the New York police commissioner in the eighth episode. Holt reminds her, "It is exciting, but there's no guarantee it will work. There's a lot of resistance to change; nevertheless, it's our duty to try because if we don't then we are truly lost." Holt is appointed deputy commissioner of police reform, and the series ends with Holt and Amy leaving the Nine-Nine to work on police reform full-time. Viewers are left to imagine that police institutions are capable of reform and that officers like Holt and Amy can slowly effect change.

Dramas Beyond the Precinct

Outside of the police procedural, dramas include nonpolice crime dramas like *Magnum P.I.* and *The Blacklist*, political dramas like *Scandal* and *Madam Secretary*, legal dramas like *The Good Wife* and *All Rise*, medical dramas like *Grey's Anatomy* and *New Amsterdam*, family dramas like *This Is Us* and *Parenthood*, and teen dramas like *All American* and *Riverdale*. In keeping with the increased recognition that "diversity sells," most of these series feature racially diverse ensemble casts, albeit frequently with a white lead. The amount of diversity in their writers' rooms is another issue altogether. As the previous chapters have shown, the makeup of a writers' room and production team has ramifications for what stories are told, and how. Isolated writers' rooms tokenize writers and frequently produce racialized tropes, and liberated rooms produce varied and nuanced representations of BIPOC people, with included rooms falling somewhere in between. By surveying a range of dramas across subgenres, I illustrate how showrunners' identities and attitudes cultivate certain kinds of writers' rooms; these rooms in turn produce distinct approaches to representing the BLM movement, systemic racism, and police brutality.

The reboot of *Magnum P.I.* (CBS, 2018–2022; NBC, 2022–2024) is positioned as a more diverse iteration of the intellectual property, replacing Tom

Selleck with Latino actor Jay Hernandez and featuring four BIPOC actors among the six primary characters. However, the reboot came under fire early on, not just for its writers' room but for the showrunner's ignorance. When asked whether he had staffed a Latinx writer in his writers' room, showrunner Peter Lenkov said he did not because "it's incredibly hard to find writers."[20] The next day, Lenkov tweeted that he'd been mistaken and there was one Latina in his seven-person writers' room, noting that she had completed CBS's Writers Mentoring Program. His forgetfulness has been attributed to the suggestion that since she is a diversity hire who works for "free" through the program, this lapse is indicative of a belief that inclusion "is a nuisance, minority writers are a burden to hire and promote, and experienced minority writers are nigh-impossible to find."[21] This was further borne out by his firing in July 2020 after CBS Television Studios found that Lenkov had "spoken inappropriately to women and people of color."[22] It should come as no surprise, then, that *Magnum P.I.* does not particularly engage the BLM movement. While not strictly a cop show, *Magnum P.I.* does include a police officer among its ensemble, opening the door to at least one frank discussion about policing. In the third-season 2021 episode "The Long Way Home," detective Gordon Katsumoto discusses policing with his teen son, who is frustrated with a broken policing system. Detective Katsumoto agrees "it's failed a lot of people, and they have every right to be angry. We need to do better. Period." He goes on to equate activism with patriotism and concludes that "change, real change, needs to come from the inside," so while he is proud to be a cop, he will work every day to be better at his job. Despite Lenkov's ousting, *Magnum P.I.* did little to address systemic racism in policing, as this episode represents the show's most overt contribution to BLM's cultural forum.

Of course, police and policing are not the only ways entertainment programming has engaged with concerns highlighted by the BLM movement. *New Amsterdam*, a medical drama with a white lead and diverse cast, was more considerate in its engagement with race, if slow to participate. This is perhaps due, at least in part, to the makeup of the writers' room in early seasons, in which white writers made up 50 percent of writers but all of the upper-level positions of showrunner, executive producer, and co–executive producer. Showrunner David Schulner discusses how it took until the middle of the third season for the series and its characters to wake up to the realities of systemic racism as it relates to their terrain of medicine.[23] After coming to recognize these blind spots, Schulner admits "we haven't tackled it head-on until now." The lead character, a white man named Dr. Max Goodwin, seeks to address the racial inequalities that permeate American medicine and, in doing so, turns to Black colleagues who explain "that you don't always have to have the answer or be the one to implement the change yourself, that it's about making space." This approach reflexively acknowledges the position of white writers and other creatives in Hollywood, inviting white people to think about their role in creating, participating in, and benefiting from racist problems, as well as how to appropriately respond.

Like *New Amsterdam*, *Grey's Anatomy* is a racially diverse medical drama that was slow to address race in meaningful ways. The first of Shonda Rhimes's many hit broadcast dramas, *Grey's* "made use of racialized bodies as signifiers of historical progress in the struggle of televisual racial representation" while also "undermining the diversity of those bodies through a laundering, or whitewashing, of social and cultural specificity" through the practice of blindcasting, or not writing race into a character's breakdown so that actors of all races can audition for each role.[24] While appearing to be a progressive, well-intentioned, and financially prudent push "to reinforce a multicultural society that could attract a number of audience demographics," Kristen Warner explains how failing to address race once BIPOC actors are cast effectively creates neutral—read white—roles with diverse casts in which BIPOC actors play white characters.[25] Kiley Donovan, who served as writer and co–executive producer for *Grey's Anatomy* and later its spinoff *Station 19*, describes *Grey's* as "what the world could be if people didn't get hung up on race," which is why its Black doctors were so rarely depicted enduring racial struggles.[26] This is not unlike *The Rookie*, which took an aspirational approach to showing working professionals. Creator Shonda Rhimes famously described herself and her friends as "post-civil rights, post-feminist babies" who "take it for granted [they] live in a diverse world,"[27] and this quote has been used to explain the absence of race-based stories in early seasons of *Grey*'s; however, some people who have worked in Shondaland, including director Jann Turner, suggest that it was not a lack of desire on Rhimes's part so much as pressure to maintain a race-neutral status quo.[28] Turner posits that Rhimes was in a vulnerable position as one of few Black women with power at a broadcast network, and that she had to be subversive and sneak in content until she was powerful enough to be more overt. With rare exception, as in the fourth-season episode "Crash into Me" in which Dr. Mirada Bailey (a Black woman) and her intern Dr. Cristina Yang (a Jewish Korean American woman) have to treat an EMT with a large swastika tattooed on his stomach, issues with contemporary racism are generally omitted from narratives in the first decade of *Grey's Anatomy.*

The growth of the BLM movement prompted changes in the ways *Grey's Anatomy* told stories, including racial disparities in medical treatment and the BLM movement itself. In the 2015 twelfth-season episode "Something Against You," the white Dr. Amelia Shepard is surprised to learn from her Black colleague Dr. Maggie Pierce that racism is ongoing. Amelia gets some insight into how (not) to deal with race when speaking with Black people, for example, not asking Black people to make white people feel better about messing up. Maggie counsels Amelia, "One piece of advice I can give you is if you feel uncomfortable having done it, check your white privilege and don't do it again." Two seasons later, in 2018, the episode "Personal Jesus" is described by writer/producer Zoanne Clack as "an opportunity to explore the conversation she has with her son when they pass police on the road" in more overt ways than had previously been done on *Grey's Anatomy*.[29] Clack, who has been with *Grey's* since it premiered, explains, "We've been portraying other-than-white groups in a very good light and trying to change the basic attitude of unconscious bias," acknowledging that they have always dealt with these issues "unconsciously by generally portraying the antidote to these misconceptions by portraying people as people with regular problems." This episode, however, took a more straightforward approach through a story in which the doctors treat a Black child who forgot his key and was shot by a police officer while breaking into his own home. This episode was meaningful for the Black actors and writers who got to tell more explicit stories about surviving American policing, but also for then-showrunner Krista Vernoff, who was confronted with her own white privilege. Vernoff reports, "I don't think there's one single thing that has had more impact on me personally and professionally than when [Dr. Miranda Bailey's Black son] Tuck puts his hands on his head and has to practice what he'll say when stopped by police," saying that it has changed her understanding of privilege and the differences between her and Clack, "that I don't have to have that conversation with my child" while her Black colleagues and characters do. Clack had been determined to talk about unconscious bias and the ways it can be changed so long as it is acknowledged and addressed, and she gives Vernoff credit for "empowering the writers to lean into topical subjects." Recognizing that police are the focal point of the problem of unconscious bias because they carry guns, Vernoff also points out that there are police departments "where chiefs have acknowledged implicit bias exists and put new protocols and training in place—and radically decreased the number of shootings" of Black men.

Like Clack on *Grey's*, *All American* (CW 2018–present) creator Nkechi Okoro Carroll was invested in telling authentic stories about Black experiences during the BLM era. *All American* is a primarily Black-cast teen drama that explores issues of race and class. Carroll wrote the series' third episode in which the Black lead and his mixed-race friend get pulled over, prompting discussions of colorism and privilege. Then, in February of 2020, Carroll pitched an episode about a young Black woman who is shot and killed by police after being found asleep in her car; this episode would air more than a year later.[30] Carroll hoped that, by this point, "the thing I'd be battling the most is that it would feel outdated"; the slew of events in 2020 "breaks my heart because it means we haven't made the forward movement that I was hoping." In this episode, one woman is shot for sleeping it off, while another (Olivia Baker) is let go because her white mom is a district attorney, prompting a speech to defund the police. Carroll has always hoped seeing these characters means "somewhere out in the world there's someone who maybe looked at Black youth differently. . . . You hope what you're doing is making a difference, and my goal for this episode was that hopefully it would lead to people understanding the pain and that we're at the point where enough is enough. But I don't know. It seems like nothing seems to make a difference sometimes. I try not to be disheartened by that, and I try to put the authentic truth of that in the show, because we pride ourselves on these characters authentically portraying what it's like to be youth, and specifically Black youth, in America nowadays. And we hope that it makes a difference."

While *All American* shows what liberated writers' rooms can produce, *All Rise* (CBS, 2019–2021; OWN, 2022–2023) imparts different but equally important lessons, not just about the number of BIPOC people in writers' rooms and on screen but the extent to which they are empowered to tell authentic stories. *All Rise* is a legal drama focused on a Black judge named Lola Carmichael who is determined to make sure "blind justice" is in fact blind by ensuring the rights and equal treatment of BIPOC Los Angelinos. Though the book on which it is based is about a white man, creator Greg Spottiswood made the lead a Black woman, and *All Rise* became part of CBS's response to criticisms of a whitewashed prime-time lineup.[31] Institutionalized racism and racial justice were foregrounded by this show from the very first episode, despite contentions behind the scenes. Early in the series' first season, five of the seven original writers, including co-showrunner Sunil Nayar, left the program after clashing with creator Greg Spottiswood over the show's depiction of BIPOC people.[32] Shernold Edwards, one of the Black writers who left the show, reported that the writers "had to do so much behind the scenes to keep these scripts from being racist and offensive," and Nayar shared that Spottiswood "seemed more interested in having him appear at public events than in giving him duties that matched his job title" of executive producer, concluding, "Greg hired me to be his Brown guy."[33]

Writers who left also stated that Spottiswood would ignore, reject, or resist their attempts to make BIPOC characters and storylines authentically reflect the experiences of BIPOC people; Edwards reports that white writers wondered why the Black protagonist's race mattered, and she told producers before leaving, "The fact that I'm still being asked that question tells me that there are people on the show who are incapable of writing for people of color and should not be writing for people of color."[34] Warner Bros. TV investigated at the time and didn't find cause to fire Spottiswood but did hire a Black woman to work with the creator as a corporate coach.[35] Edwards proposes that Spottiswood kept his position because his approach to storytelling "makes race palatable for a CBS audience and the CBS brass" because he, like the brass, "doesn't know anything about it. . . . So there is this strange tone of nothing being said, but the visual representation is there. It's safe, and it's empty." The mass exodus of writers, primarily BIPOC writers, occurred in 2019, but it wasn't until after George Floyd's murder that these details broke in trade publications. The virtual post-COVID-19, post-Floyd writers' room reported similar problems, and Spottiswood was fired at the end of the second season in 2021 following "allegations of unprofessional conduct in the series' writers' room, including the use of offensive and racially insensitive language."[36]

Though their characters spent less time reflecting on and challenging systemic racism than *All Rise*, political dramas like *Scandal* and legal dramas like *The Good Wife* also addressed the BLM movement. These two examples' narratives actively engage issues of justice and the roles and behaviors of governmental officials, and their writers' rooms did so with considerably less turmoil than *All Rise*. On the surface, *The Good Wife* and *Scandal* don't appear to be overly similar. *The Good Wife* was created by a white married couple, Michelle and Robert King, and follows Hillary Clinton–like lawyer Alicia Florrick, who returns to work after her husband, the state's attorney, is caught in a sex scandal. The mostly white cast operates out of a Chicago law firm, and race is only an occasional passing issue outside of the very special episode "The Debate," which aired January 11, 2015. By contrast, *Scandal* was created by Black showrunner Shonda Rhimes and follows a Black political fixer, Olivia Pope, and her racially diverse team of "gladiators" in Washington, D.C., as they help the powerful to avoid the kind of ruin that Governor Florrick faces. Still, as in fellow Shondaland series *Grey's Anatomy*, discussions of race in *Scandal* are woefully absent prior to their very special episode "The Lawn Chair," which aired March 5, 2015 (see Figure 4.4). These two special episodes were ripped from the headlines as they dramatized the slayings of two unarmed Black men and the immediate aftermath of those events.

FIG. 4.4. Olivia and Clarence discuss his dead son's innocence on the "The Lawn Chair" episode of *Scandal* (2015).

In the opening scene of *The Good Wife*'s "The Debate," handheld footage captures two white officers confronting a Black man in a mall and meeting his accusations of racial profiling with the lethal use of their tasers. When the grand jury elects not to hold these officers accountable, their verdict sets off protests across Chicago, disrupting the debate between the two white candidates for state's attorney. The candidates—protagonist Alicia Florrick and her competitor—retreat to the hotel kitchen, and their conversation about the events at hand draws a racially diverse audience of hotel staff. While *The Good Wife* references Eric Garner as its nexus, *Scandal* references Michael Brown. "The Lawn Chair" focuses on the shooting of a Black teen, Brandon Parker, by the white Officer Newton, who claims Parker "fit the description" and was pulling a knife when Newton shot him. Parker's father arrives at the scene armed with a shotgun and sets up a lawn chair over his son's body, refusing to leave until his son's innocence is proven and Newton is held accountable. Despite having a Black lead, *Scandal* had largely operated in a post-race landscape prior to this episode, and the protagonist is forced to confront this while investigating the crime and trying to keep the peace between increasingly hostile officers and a growing crowd of protestors. After discovering the knife under Parker's body was planted, Olivia Pope and the attorney general confront Newton at the police station, and he reacts with a racist tirade about the lack of respect Black people have for the police, to the apparent disgust of his diverse team of fellow officers.

Appearing on the heels of and evoking pressure points in the BLM movement, these episodes in preestablished series invite consideration of the use of real-world trauma for entertainment purposes in numerous ways. For one, viewer responses largely championed entertainment programming's dramatization of these events as painful but necessary, but they were also accused of exploiting the movement or pandering to Black viewers, and network executives were excoriated for financially benefiting from the deaths of Black men.[37] Notably, both series faced criticism for so rarely addressing race in explicit terms, but ironically, it was *The Good Wife* and not *Scandal* that featured the words "Black Lives Matter." We can also consider the role and reputation of showrunners: *Scandal* creator Shonda Rhimes was lauded for using her platform to air such controversial content, even as the episode called out its lead, Olivia Pope, for being so removed from the Black community. Meanwhile, on CBS, critics suggested that *The Good Wife*'s white creators and overwhelmingly white cast were ill-equipped to do the topic justice. Finally, both episodes depicted governmental bodies in which white men with great power were interested in seeing change—at least within the scope of the episode. In this way, these episodes modeled good allyship and pointed toward a pathway to progress. Rather than offering escapist fare, *Scandal* and *The Good Wife* took an hour to recognize the significance of the BLM movement for a growing number of Americans. In the following section, I turn to another Shondaland drama that went even further in expanding the cultural forum of BLM by advocating for and illustrating systemic change.

CASE STUDY: *STATION 19*

Station 19 (2018–2024) is a Shondaland production set in a fictional Seattle fire department. It was introduced as a spin-off of *Grey's Anatomy*, bringing *Grey's* alum doctor-turned-firefighter Ben Warren (Jason George) and guest star Andrea "Andy" Herrera (Jaina Lee Ortiz) to a new time slot on ABC after a backdoor pilot that aired in March of 2018. *Station 19* was helmed by a series of *Grey's* writer/producers beginning with Stacy McKee for the first two seasons, Krista Vernoff starting in season three, and Zoanne Clack (joined by Shondaland newcomer Peter Paige) in the seventh and final season. Like *Grey's*, the cast comprises an apparently incidentally diverse group, though producer Kiley Donovan points out that a fourth-season conversation offers a rearticulation of this unrealistically diverse group by suggesting that the Mexican American captain Pruitt Herrera intentionally recruited a diverse team, including Latinx men (himself) and women (his daughter Andy), Black men (Ben Warren and Dean Miller) and women (Victoria Hughes), white men (Jack Gibson) and women (Maya Bishop), and Asian

American (Travis Montgomery) firefighters.[38] Early seasons of *Station 19* were reminiscent of *Grey's Anatomy* in that they featured a diverse cast but spent little time engaging racial identity politics, instead emphasizing the melodrama of romantic relationships and the excitement of fire effects. In one rare exception, George recalls an episode where his character, Dr. Warren, is pulled over: "I didn't push for [that] but was elated when it came up . . . because, you know, for America, Ben is one of the 'good ones'. . . . You need to see Ben Warren get arrested, or harassed by police, because he's the definition of 'did not bring it on to himself other than the fact that he was Black and driving a vehicle.'"[39]

As with so many shows, *Station 19* shifted approaches in the fall of 2020 with their fourth season, but their approach proved something of an uphill battle. Any number of Americans have lamented television's engagement with BLM, including members of Donovan's own family, and have wondered why television can't just be an escape from the "real" world; Donovan recognizes that entertainment television is supposed to be entertaining, but that for her and Vernoff and Rhimes, "that's not why we make television."[40] These women are not alone in actively wanting their programs to contribute to the greater good and having to figure out how to do that. Creating liberal propaganda might be straightforward, but it accomplishes less than content that appeals to a broad political spectrum and promotes introspection and growth. As actor Jason George points out, "Preaching only works in church. . . . You've got to have a good story first to get people's attention, and then you slide in some stuff through the back door. . . . The story's got to be on point first, otherwise you lose everybody."

Donovan explains that the world changed, as did social media, and it became clear that the production could not ignore trending issues. At the same time, actors became more collaborative and made their voices heard. When Vernoff took over *Station 19*, she had stipulated to the studio that she enjoy the same freedom she had had previously on the more established *Grey's*, suggesting that such freedom would allow her to make *Station 19* as good as *Grey's* and thus enjoy similar ratings and commercial success. Vernoff was uninterested in the constraints of studio network notes, and success on *Grey's* meant she had enjoyed the privilege of being able to tell the studios that she did not want external input, operating more like a cable series that put control more soundly in creators' hands. There are some who claim the distinction between broadcast, cable, and streaming matters very little anymore, but Donovan articulates her experience with broadcast as marked by "a freedom that only comes with the proven . . . the numbers, it's all about the numbers," and that the only reason Vernoff "was able to kind of demand that capital was because the shows had earned it" by bringing in high ratings. Their numbers offered them a bit of protection as high ratings mean higher income from advertisers; Donovan says they try not to think about the financial aspects in the writers' room, but that as an executive producer, she does eventually have to "tap into that side of things."

In addition to advertisers, broadcast content creators must navigate their studios and networks. While content constraints have relaxed over time and studios and networks have proven to be valuable collaborators, there is still a fear that studios and networks might prohibit creators from doing, saying, or dealing with certain things, and Standards & Practices (S&P) offices, of course, keep an eye on legally and commercially concerning content. Beyond the legality of what words can and cannot be spoken on broadcast television, there is the matter of what can be said and shown, for example, when airing storylines about misbehaving police officers. When they tackled this topic, *Station 19* producers had to be careful in how they represented the Seattle Police Department as a real organization. Vernoff and Donovan brought in police consultants as well as leaders of the LA chapter of Black Lives Matter and representatives from Color of Change. This was typical for both *Grey's* and *Station 19*, as both programs actively research and educate on topics, pulling from the expertise of writers who represent relevant parties as well as relying on experts who can help them to understand what kinds of messages activists and experts would like to see introduced to the cultural forum and what approaches to the topic would be best avoided.

Once *Station 19* entered into storylines in which they named George Floyd and engaged in protests, there were questions about whether it was disrespectful (or not) to name the victims of police violence in the commercial context of entertainment television. Writers wanted to be respectful to viewers and to families of the victims and "do it right"; there is certainly no one right or wrong way to represent national tragedies, but there are certainly better and worse, more and less harmful, ways to do so. Though there have certainly been instances of showrunners clashing with network executives about whether and how to address controversy, *Station 19* and Vernoff had the support of their network and studio alike, as everyone seemed to realize that the status quo was no longer an option. Everyone had a responsibility to push for honest, even uncomfortable, conversations through representation. The duty of writers was to tackle these conversations in ways that were not gratuitous and did not add to the collective trauma of Black Americans. One woman, Kasha Foster, worked in Vernoff's production company as director of diversity and inclusion, a new position that Vernoff hoped to normalize on television; Foster's job was to act as liaison between the cast, producers, and writers in order to facilitate conversations not just with outside organizations like Color of Change but among themselves. For example, if a cast member read a line of dialogue that did not feel culturally authentic but was afraid to communicate their discomfort to their white showrunner, Foster could help to mediate this discussion. Foster has dubbed herself "hardconversations.com" and has proven useful because writers' rooms have historically been predominantly white, with the effect of precluding many difficult conversations from ever taking place.

In determining how to respond to the BLM movement, Donovan recounts many pitches about firefighters responding to police shootings and consciously decided that they did not want to present their audience with yet another Black body dying in the street: There was enough of that in the news. Instead, *Station 19* was in a unique position to provide an organic perspective on what it is like to be firefighters—Black, white, Latinx, and Asian—who work with the police every day and are friends and essentially colleagues with the police when they don't necessarily agree with policing as an institution. Their main consultant was a former LA firefighter chief who introduced the writers to numerous Black firefighters, paving the way for conversations about what it is like to see what's happening in the United States and to have to protect the very people being protested against. As *Station 19* writers learned, it is a complex situation for firefighters, who benefit from police protection and assistance through the course of their jobs but who disapprove of so much of how policing operates. Donovan also points to a distinction that is often overlooked: Stating unequivocally that Black lives matter is not inherently, yet is often treated as, an indictment of police.

Station 19's fourth season started with an emphasis on COVID-19, airing four episodes emphasizing the global pandemic before introducing BLM to the narrative in ways similar to the 2020 timeline. In its fifth episode, "Out of Control," *Station 19* enters the conversation with an illustration of just how grossly implicit bias can play a role in policing. The squad of off-duty firefighters helps two Black women look for their missing daughters, whose phones have been traced to the house of a belligerent white man named Bob; Bob has in turn called the police to complain that the women are causing a disturbance by banging on his door. Two officers arrive on the scene, and one seems reasonable while the other's treatment of the women can only be the result of racism. These officers refuse to intervene, but the girls—who are indeed locked in his basement as part of a human trafficking ring—manage to start a fire, and the firefighters rescue them. Bob accuses the girls of lying and of breaking and entering, and when one mother lunges at Bob, the racist officer accuses her of assaulting an officer and violently slams her onto the back of a squad car. Chaos erupts as multiple firefighters try to intervene, and the scene ends with the racist officer pulling his gun on one Black firefighter while another is tackled to the ground and restrained by a pile of officers. Following this episode, *Station 19* went on hiatus for nearly three months, during which it became clear to the writers and producers that people were talking about the show and encouraging others to watch it because it was doing something different in tackling BLM-related issues.

Rather than treat these issues as a one-off, addressed in a single episode and quickly put in the rearview, *Station 19* doubled down for the rest of the season—and beyond. As Donovan explains, some people were emotionally fatigued by the program's ongoing engagement and questioned, "Why are we still talking about this?" But "it's not a one-off . . . for people of color; it's not a thing that they can just be like, 'Oh . . . I'm glad I learned that and I feel enlightened, and now I'm going to move on.'" This dedication to ongoing engagement was felt not just by the producers but by actors as well. One actor, Okieriete Onaodowan, was particularly vocal about the need to tell these stories, pitching numerous ideas to Donovan including that his character (Dean Miller) be shot or that the team respond to a shooting, but the producers identified an alternate approach to depicting "first responders on the front lines of the racism epidemic" because "first responders have to go out and save lives of racist assholes," Donovan said.

Vernoff and her team grappled with how to address systemic racism and policing through their firefighter series. George recounts how "it kept coming out wrong and became this really frustrating point for a lot of the people involved, from showrunner to actors."[41] The actors were ready to go to Vernoff to discuss their concerns when Vernoff called a meeting in which she beat them to the punch, expressing her own concerns that she and the writers were "screwing this up" and asking for their help: "We had this very open, very frank conversation, and by the end of it this idea was forming in [Vernoff's] mind, and it became one of my favorite episodes of television I've ever been involved with." George states that he'll be forever grateful to Vernoff for being "a white woman who was the showrunner having the humility to say, 'I don't think I'm getting this right. Help.' And for a real, open, honest conversation happening." In this, Vernoff illustrated an alternative to the ego George is more familiar with elsewhere in television, where showrunners have a set vision and demand it be followed, and instead recognized that "when you're having this conversation about race . . . maybe listen more, and . . . pull from people's real lives." In an unusually fast turnaround the episode was shot and broadcast just three or four weeks later.

The fourth season's twelfth episode, "Get Up, Stand Up," was anomalous to *Station 19*, as it comprises almost entirely conversations between individual firefighters and Diane Lewis (Tracie Thoms), a firefighter-turned-therapist who arrives at the station to help the team process the trauma of their experiences (see Figure 4.5). Donovan explains that this episode happened because, as Vernoff pointed out, "this isn't a typical season in any way . . . so let's all get involved," and Donovan herself found it to be a "fun creative challenge" that required a delicate balance because "art as commerce is sometimes an existential challenge." To craft this episode, Vernoff invited writers, actors, and producers to write their thoughts out and craft a monologue for whichever character they related to the most. Vernoff wanted them all to express how these characters would feel in this moment because they had arrived at work on May 25, mere hours after George Floyd's murder, without any idea what to say or do.

Interviews with writers and actors demonstrate a deep appreciation for Vernoff's handling of the cultural crisis they were all enduring. Angela Harvey, a writer and producer, recalls that "sometimes it's difficult for writers in the room to keep pushing a topic" because "you can raise the concern that you want, but you can only say it in so many different ways."[42] Here, however, Vernoff disrupted the status quo with her inclusive approach. There is then the concern that "the actor will probably not want to say" something in the script, which often leads to script adjustments; when asked who the actors are who tend to take issue with dialogue, Harvey responded, "Generally people of color. That's a really—I never thought about that. . . . Usually an actor of color that might push back on something that's culturally incorrect or specific." Echoing this, George describes actors as stewards of their characters, and that his job in playing Ben Warren is to consider what in the script does and does not make sense to him, meaning he occasionally needs explanations from writers to help him understand how they got to where they are; this exchange of ideas between writers and actors sometimes means that "the story gets deeper, gets, richer."[43] Notably, George says, "Whether you have the ability to do that is set up by what kind of norms are established in the rooms," recalling scripts that have "AWMF" ("as written, motherf——") scrawled on them and are not to be questioned or changed by actors. In those kinds of writers' rooms, actors must be concerned that their job is at risk if they challenge writers and producers about the stories being told, forcing them to wonder, "Is that gonna blow back on me and my job and my ability to play this character, which is the little bit of representation that happens in this world?" By contrast, rooms in Shondaland seem to "feel like it's a safe space to say, hey, why aren't we going deeper into this or why aren't we

FIG. 4.5. Diane listens to a firefighter after the 2020 protests on the "Get Up, Stand Up" episode of *Station 19* (2021).

exploring this aspect? . . . and that's happening more and more, those open rooms."

In the case of this episode, many actors submitted drafts, some of which made it onto the screen, and all of which helped inform a multifaceted episode. For example, Italian actress Stefania Stampinato (Dr. Carina DeLuca) helped writers to craft a discussion about U.S. policing from an outside perspective by questioning the "bad apple" language that has been used to dismiss bad police officers as anomalies in an otherwise fantastic institution.[44] Though the Writers Guild of America has rules about writer credits that prohibit all the actors from getting writing credits, the episode ends with a final card thanking twenty-six writers, actors, and others whose "experiences and perspectives . . . informed and enriched this episode." Director Daryn Okada describes this episode as "lots of mini films to get through to a general viewer," with each "mini film" focusing on a different character and their authentic, individualized experience of processing national events.[45] Okada remembers extended discussions about how "to make it personal—we wanted that whole story, that whole episode, to be something that was personal to each character." For example, the mini film for Dean Miller has no music and almost no dialogue; he simply enters the therapist's temporary office, and they stare at each other and silently shed a few tears until he draws himself back up and leaves with a simple "thanks." Okada notes, "If we've earned the viewers' attention and interest in the subject, at that point, I felt that that would be more powerful, just to see these two characters, and [Dean] honestly where he was." Though they tried it a few different ways, Okada felt it was more interesting for Diane to see the internal fight, the sadness, and humility play out on Dean's face and still having to put on a brave face and function in the world. "We were just very lucky that it all played and that the producers allowed us to do that; nothing was said, and we got it all." Okada knew that this kind of episode was not a guaranteed slam dunk, that it could do more harm than good, and he felt a personal responsibility to make sure it was done right.

Having worked on *Grey's* for years, Donovan had heard many times from fans that *Grey's* had helped them, for example, to accept gay people into their lives because of the gay characters found in their favorite medical drama; she hoped, therefore, that *Station 19* might get through to viewers who had never before heard a Black person's perspective on what it is like to be a Black person in America in the context of BLM, delivered from a beloved television firefighter rather than through "a line of angry tweets that don't sink in for someone who's not exposed to other cultures." They did not want to lecture the audience but to depict these firefighters as exhausted by this world, starting with a physical and mental breaking point in the opening scene and followed by weighty conversations. Okada notes that it is difficult to tell these stories because you have forty-two minutes to tell both sides and let the audience decide for itself: "I think society is trained to have good guys and bad guys . . . and you always want to try to guess who's the bad guy." Though the character of Jack—a cis-hetero white man—might have become the de facto "bad guy" in the firehouse, Jason George describes Jack as "very useful" in, he says jokingly, "weaponizing the show for good, to have . . . broader conversations" because Jack allows for "an innovative way to get into that conversation." For example, after the two Black firefighters are arrested, Jack functioned as "a window into someone who wants to be an ally but doesn't quite—'I don't get this. . . . This is not my personal experience, so I don't quite know when I'm screwing up or when I'm doing it right—so help me out,'" thus echoing a conversation occurring throughout the country and assuredly among *Station 19*'s viewers. Rather than "talking down to people [or] being pedantic, patronizing," Ben and Jack model a conversation that George suggests "every person of color has had."[46]

George recognizes the gift of being able to do this, as Shondaland series "create that safe space for and encourage the fans and people who watch" to have such conversations. "When you come into somebody's house every week, you become their friend in their mind, and so we become their friends, saying, 'Let's have this conversation.'" The conversation, George hopes, isn't too awkward for the viewer but instead a frank conversation where viewers can get answers that illuminate points on which they are genuinely confused. Through a show like *Station 19*, creators take viewers' intentions as positive and demonstrate how certain behaviors are problematic. Television writers will typically provide content to take viewers' minds off of what's happening in the world around them, "but then sometimes stuff—Black Lives Matter, MeToo—come up that are so powerful and so important that . . . we gotta talk." This kind of emotional labor surely doesn't appeal to all writers and producers, but George thinks "more and more shows are starting to realize that there's real interesting and nuanced TV that can come out of having that as a part of the regular conversation, you know, that you don't need to shy away from it" and that "there's a way to do it that isn't preachy . . . that is still interesting and good TV and fascinating and, surprise, surprise, relatable to a lot more people than just the kind of people who look like the person who's dealing with it on the show."

Because *Station 19* tries to speak and appeal to a broad audience, Okada explains, they try to use that to their advantage and to use their exposure "by being creative and ingenious in ways that are engaging to tell stories that will make someone stop there rather than going to a streaming network." Moreover, Donovan acknowledged a feeling of responsibility that comes with producing one of the few television shows that regularly brings in ten million viewers. This episode was unique because they were trying to quell an emotional fire rather than an actual one. This included not just Black characters expressing their heartbreak, but Korean American Travis questioning whether he has any right to complain about anti-Asian race crimes when Black Americans have it so much worse, and Jack trying to figure out how to support his Black friends when he, as a white man, will never fully understand what they are going through. It was important to them all that the station is not monolithic, that each individual did not come at the issue from the same position and perspective, because diversity of perspective is present among any population. It was therefore important that the white firefighters not be these perfectly understanding allies, rather, that they grapple with discussions of systemic racism and realize that their Black colleagues "have had to shut up and act like everything's fine" for years.[47]

In crafting this episode, there were also numerous tricky conversations to be had about actors' dialogue where some actors were concerned their characters would say something ignorant and be pinned as racist. Donovan recalls that they were a bit scared to do an episode where the cast sits around discussing their feelings on racism and wondered whether the network would even allow it, and they kept expecting more pushback from network executives. Instead, the network supported them fully, and the resulting episode garnered an encouraging response from the public that reassured the team that they were contributing to the greater good, helping people to see themselves, feel seen, and know that they matter. The only major concern for the network—specifically Standards & Practices—was that statistics incorporated into dialogue be factually sound. For example, when Victoria shares information about the rates at which Black girls are sexually trafficked, S&P ensured that the numbers she provides are accurate but had no qualms about including this information and did not ask producers to shy away from conversations surrounding BLM or police brutality. There was also the minor trick of creating police uniforms that merely said "police" rather than "Seattle PD" so as to avoid potential lawsuits.

Though *Station 19* depicted numerous police officers behaving badly, Donovan never heard from police officers, and it seems police did not take issue with *Station 19*'s approach of showing some of these "bad apples" or discussing the bigger institutional problems plaguing the United States. From her perspective, "bad apples" in policing are typically framed as patrolmen with implicit bias or corrupt commissioners and the like, but *Station 19* recognizes that these structures reinforce each other, with patrolling officers spoiling the bunch through the protections extended to them. If there are no consequences for using unnecessary force or violating civil liberties, they will not learn, and so season four started to tackle this while setting up the fifth season to explore what the next step is after defunding the police. As they were in production, cities around the country were hearing the call to do something about their flawed systems and broken institutions, if only to avoid the public shame that is brought by constant protests. Donovan noted that *Station 19* was figuring out what to do simultaneously with the real world, developing a storyline about a crisis intervention alternative to policing at the same time that Seattle was developing such a program. In exploring ways to tackle this historical moment, the writers learned of a group in Eugene, Oregon, called Crisis Assistance Helping Out on the Streets (CAHOOTS) that sends a mobile team of trained first responders such as EMTs and firefighters, rather than police, to assist with nonviolent crises. The writers created their own version of CAHOOTS, led by Dean Miller. This was part of a push to not just represent tragedy, but to indicate potential paths forward.

Having shown why there is such a need for protests and reform, the next question was how to show what next steps might actually look like in a world where the police have been defunded—not dismantled, but not given a seemingly endless budget and a mandate to address all crises among the citizenry. Seattle police and fire announced soon thereafter that they too were working to develop something along these lines. *Station 19*'s approach shows the public that defunding the police doesn't just mean getting rid of them, rather, pushing through the growing pains that come with any change and finding a better way to do things. Donovan muses, "Digging into that in great detail to show what that looks like . . . will be interesting to see how people respond." In expanding their characters' mandate beyond firefighting and sending firefighters on mental health calls in lieu of armed police officers, "the firefighters are doing the work of de-escalation along with trained civilians," and it is a challenge with a substantial learning curve, but Vernoff's team was dedicated to "getting it right."

The investment in crisis intervention provided an ongoing entry point to conversations about policing that would last beyond the fourth season. Season four ends with Dean settling a lawsuit with the city for the police's handling of events in the fifth episode, but Donovan points out that while this is realistic, it couldn't be the end of their engagement with the issues of police brutality and systemic racism. "The reality would probably be . . . they just settle these lawsuits and then move on, and nothing happens," but Donovan described this as "f-g depressing. And . . . that can't just be all it is . . . that can't be the payoff of this whole season . . . that . . . we're just going to go back to how it was." Donovan describes the repeated conversations about going back and showing more reasons for the need to protest, versus the recognition that they didn't need to show more of "why it's bad that police shoot Black people." Instead, Donovan articulates a "need to show the alternative" and how much better things could be, from a more macro perspective. "We're trying to show it's both taking those people with guns who are maybe racist or just ill-informed off the force . . . but then also addressing it from a higher level of institutionally making them understand what the need is." When we spoke in August of 2021, Donovan admitted she was "still processing how it all went and . . . what could have gone better" but that she was also "really proud because there were times [she] had to really fight and push to keep doing it," and that the responses from fans, critics, and even academics "has been personally selfishly validating."

Conclusion

Through overviews and case studies, this chapter outlines the breadth and depth of the Black Lives Matter movement's cultural forum on broadcast television. Across comedies and dramas, the amount of diversity within writers' rooms and casts proves consequential for the kinds of stories those programs will tell and, just as importantly, will ignore. Operating outside of the cop genre, sitcoms and television's doctors, lawyers, and firefighters are able to challenge the status quo of copaganda and the tendency to valorize police regardless of their behaviors. If cop shows can't see the forest for the trees—or the rotten orchard for the bad apples—sitcoms and other subgenres of drama are able to do this and invite viewers to do so as well.

In my final chapter, I consider the ultimate implications of the BLM movement for the broadcast entertainment television industry following the calming of national sentiments. The BLM movement helped to bring about some industrial changes both on- and off-screen, but some of those changes proved short-lived. In many cases, networks and studios' promises of progress have been exposed as little more than well-meaning but incompetent pledges at best and public relations stunts at worst. Still, while the moratorium on new cop shows effectively mandated by the events of the summer of 2020 ended quickly thereafter, the new cop shows did not return to the pre-BLM status quo of copaganda. This conclusion demonstrates the tensions that exist between those who promote media activism and those who stand in the way of progress.

5

Beyond 2020

Or, Back to Business as Usual?

If the Black Lives Matter movement can be understood to have started quietly with the first #BlackLivesMatter tweet on July 13, 2013—the day Trayvon Martin's murderer was acquitted—then the ten-year anniversary of the BLM movement passed quietly as Hollywood writers and actors protested outside of the studios that dominate broadcast airwaves; their signs proclaimed not that Black Lives Matter, but that they deserve dignity and respect from a system that benefits from exploiting them. Still, their picketing for increased transparency and protections against artificial intelligence was not wholly divorced from the same systemic inequalities that motivated the creation of a Black Lives Matter movement. Themed pickets brought groups together to highlight their value and their contributions to society and to cultural storytelling practices. Latinas Acting Up, formed by a group of Latina writers and actresses, blasted salsa music and danced outside Disney's gates. Think Tank for Inclusion & Equity (TTIE) advocated for BIPOC writers who would have the hardest time finding work once "business as usual" resumed. Drew Carey spent tens of thousands of dollars feeding people who were out of work, and a popular talking point on the line was how few working actors work enough to qualify for insurance. Writers and actors were joined by other unions, including nurses, teachers, and teamsters. Police could occasionally be found, for example, preventing people from parking on Keystone Street (just outside of Disney) for no apparent reason other than that Disney wanted to further inconvenience the very protestors they were already antagonizing by refusing to negotiate.

This vignette speaks to the tensions that exist within media industries comprising individuals whose personal and professional interests are varied and do not always align. It illustrates the limits of corporate investment in doing the right thing if those at the top of the corporate ladder suspect that doing the wrong thing will make them more money. It also highlights the sometimes arbitrary nature of policing in the United States, in which cops do not always have to account for their actions, be they real officers in Hollywood or fictional officers on television. Ultimately, *Black and Blue TV* contributes to scholarly and industry discourses by providing a framework for examining the relationship between studios and networks, writers and actors, activists and officers, and challenging the limited inclusion of BIPOC people in the industry and BIPOC characters and themes on screen.

My reliance on interviews provides a wealth of information but is not without its limitations. Some people granted interviews after I convinced their managers or agents that their contributions would be valuable in an exploration of broadcast television's engagement with the Black Lives Matter movement, but even more did not respond, and the LAPD's Media Relations Division was "unable to accommodate" my request. A few of my interview subjects are friends of friends, and others were friends of people I'd already interviewed who passed along contact information with an endorsement of my project. Others still were people I happened to meet while picketing alongside writers and actors during the 2023 strikes, who were careful not to violate strike rules in discussing previous years' work with me. Most people who spoke with me communicated a genuine desire to be part of making the world a better place through their creative work, but a few seemed defensive at the suggestion that they should have any such intention or that they had any kind of moral duty as a content creator on what has long been our most powerful and far-reaching medium. All this is to say that the people who stand as the biggest roadblocks to expanding Black Lives Matter's cultural forum on broadcast television—the people who depict BLM as anti-white reverse-racism and who troll Black writers with racist comments in the writers' room—did not make themselves available for comment. The picture I'm able to provide is therefore incomplete, but not without value.

Additional limitations are due to the necessary constraints of a book-length research project. I defined my scope as the finite terrain of scripted reality-based, live-action prime-time broadcast content. While I look forward to future research that expands BLM's cultural forum to cable and streaming originals, I feared that trying to account for the entirety of the televisual landscape would prove untenable. I similarly made gestures to discussions of casting, talent agencies, advertisers, and other elements that influence the cultural forum, but I primarily focused my attention on the above-the-line creatives who write, produce, direct, and star in content, and the people—the writers and activists—who try to move the needle and disrupt the status quo of hiring and storytelling practices.

In this concluding chapter, I consider the ultimate implications of the first decade of the BLM movement for broadcast television, including the end of the moratorium on cop shows and backlash against diversity, equity, and inclusion (DEI) initiatives. I start with an exploration of two post-moratorium cop shows to emerge: the color-washed *Will Trent* (ABC, 2023–present) that replaced many white characters from the source material with BIPOC actors, and the wildly diverse *East New York* (CBS, 2022–2023) that did not survive its freshman season. The next section looks at the ways studios and networks, despite the progressive discourses fueling *Will Trent*, are reversing course on many of the promises made in 2020 that would promote diversity among industry creatives. I close with thoughts from industry professionals who consider the responsibilities inherent in storytelling through the broadcast medium and reflect on shifts in industry practices over time.

After 2020: The Return of the Force

In *Normalizing Injustice*, Color of Change states, "We need new standards to be socialized and implemented across the industry. Those standards must be backed up by meaningful incentives that reward responsible storytelling, as well as by real consequences that hold executives accountable when they enable (or even encourage) demonstrably harmful stereotypes and inaccuracies to go unchecked."[1] Though Color of Change has not published an updated report that accounts for the newest additions to the genre, *Will Trent* and *East New York* certainly take a more responsible approach to depicting police and their interactions with the people they have sworn to protect.

No new police shows premiered in the fall of 2020, though *Walker* premiered in January 2021 after being announced in October of 2019,[2] and *Law & Order: Organized Crime* premiered in April 2021 after being announced in March of 2020.[3] Several people I spoke with acknowledged a moratorium on new cop shows, but it did not last long; *East New York* was picked up in May of 2022 and premiered in October of 2022,[4] though it was canceled after one season in May of 2023.[5] *Will Trent* was then ordered to series in August of 2022 and premiered the following January, and is still airing as I write this.[6] It is worth noting that neither of these series aligns with the traditional approach to cop shows that proved so problematic for the BLM movement.

East New York was created by Billy Finkelstein and Mike Flynn. Finkelstein was a writer and producer whose previous credits include *NYPD Blue*, *Law & Order*, and *L.A. Law*, and who had created *Brooklyn South* and the infamous short-lived cop musical *Cop Rock*. Flynn had written and produced for *Queen Sugar* on the Oprah Winfrey Network and *Raising Kanan*, a spin-off of the Black-cast drama *Power* on Starz. When Finkelstein pitched the series, a man named Tom Sherman was running dramas at CBS and Sherman wanted to do a cop show that might be a successor to *NYPD Blue*; Finkelstein and Sherman had previously worked on a pilot for another racialized cop show for CBS, but whereas that series "ended up not getting made," the seed of the idea developed into *East New York*. Both Finkelstein and Flynn wanted to highlight the role of race in policing and present alternatives to the status quo of cop shows. Finkelstein specifically wanted to create a series that would "view police, the police hierarchy, factoring in race," and Flynn was inspired by a news story about police officers who were living in housing projects to better integrate them into the community rather than presenting as an occupying army that drives into the city every day from Long Island or the suburbs. Finkelstein tells me, "The two of us joined forces and created *East New York*."[7] The result was a series that critic Angie Han says "tries to have it both ways" by grappling "gingerly . . . with thorny issues like the inequality of criminal justice in America and the deeply damaged relationship between civilians and law enforcement," even as it replicates the very comforts of the cop genre it presumes to tackle.[8]

East New York follows deputy inspector Regina Haywood (Amanda Warren), a Black woman precinct commander in East New York, an area that Finkelstein describes as "in the gentrifying of Brooklyn—it's where that stops" (see Figure 5.1).[9] The population there is poor and largely Black and Hispanic, and crime rates are high. Finkelstein focused on race "as a component in the hierarchies of the department—also, in the way cops did their job," as with policing housing projects. A naturalistic approach to a police series in East New York would require frequent engagement with race in ways cop shows have typically avoided. Like *S.W.A.T.*, this series was able to explore the ways "a Black cop has more in common in some ways with a white cop than he does with a Black noncop; the job dictates certain realities in your life" including a certain level of risk while also being "scrutinized much more closely than cops ever were in the past." Finkelstein used this heightened emphasis on race to explore, for example, how the murders of two men whose bodies are found in East New York—a white hedge fund manager from Manhattan and a Black man in the housing projects—are

FIG. 5.1. Regina gives her detectives orders on the *East New York* episode "Misdemeanor Homicide" (2022).

treated in a pecking order. Finkelstein points out that "the disparity with which those two events are treated in the priorities of a police department that has major crimes committed every day" might go unnoticed in other cop shows, but DI Haywood brings attention to and challenges these procedural inequalities.

While *East New York* emphasizes the role of race in policing, Finkelstein shares, "I don't feel as though my principal obligation is to serve any organization particularly; it's just to write the best things I can write" in the context of the characters and environment he has created. At the same time, he does not rely solely on police as technical advisors. "I think anybody who has put in any time as a writer ought to have a variety of people that they talk to," be it a formal or an informal arrangement, and "to be influenced by events, by significant, relevant events of which the newspapers are full." Finkelstein suggests it is important that writers keep their eyes open and be available to inspiration from different places "and fill up the well" of ideas for storytelling in broadcast television. "Some of those stories are going to be sympathetic to cops, and some of those stories are going to be antagonistic to cops," Finkelstein notes. For example, *East New York*'s depiction of a police union official "was not a particularly sympathetic portrayal of what a police union does and results in," but an honest portrayal will allow writers to "avoid a too-easy characterization of being on one side or the other." The character was therefore not a monster but rather a politician, as is often the case for those who run police unions.

It is not entirely clear why *East New York* was canceled after just one season. Finkelstein reports that feedback and network notes from CBS varied by episode, typically seeking clarity on plot points and expressing concerns about the show's accessibility to an audience; there was not concern about the race-focused approach *East New York* took to depicting and challenging policing. While "some of it was financial at the higher corporate levels at CBS," Finkelstein theorizes it was more a matter of fit with the network. "I think we were messy. . . . [*East New York*] was nuanced in a way that a lot of very successful cop shows" are not. Cop shows are built on the idea of catching the bad guy every week, as is done in *Law & Order* and *NCIS*. "And there's a satisfaction to viewing shows like that. There's a big audience for those shows. They like it. . . . That was not *East New York*." Rather, *East New York* was a character-driven series that had procedural elements but with added layers and nuance compared to the norm. The characters "were not all good, they were not all bad. . . . There was a human dimension to them. They were not plot tropes. And that ultimately did not serve us . . . within the network that we were on." Indeed, *East New York* ultimately suggests an insurmountable limitation on what a cop show can accomplish when the goal is examining policing institutions, because implicit throughout is the idea that Haywood and a few other good apples can save the NYPD from rot better than defunding the police or an institutional overhaul can. Finkelstein thinks *East New York* was "maybe unnecessarily complicated" in that way, leading *East New York* to be "unceremoniously dumped after a season" despite having attracted an audience.

Will Trent, based on the book series by Karin Slaughter, found more success on ABC despite also diverging from traditional police storytelling. The titular character of Will Trent is a Georgia Bureau of Investigation (GBI) officer in Atlanta, and the cast comprises other GBI officers as well as Atlanta PD, with whom GBI shares an office building. Trent was found in an alley as a baby and raised in foster care with no idea of who he was, and cocreator Daniel Thomsen describes Trent as "kind of raised by the city of Atlanta."[10] Thomsen was curious "what that lack of identity would look like on somebody whose job it was to be law enforcement and how to overcome trauma . . . I felt like I hadn't seen a character like that." After the brief moratorium on cop shows, "ABC really wanted a show that had an episodic crime-solving franchise," having failed to reboot *NYPD Blue*. "So they were seeking to fill that hole in their schedule" and wanted an episodic cop show "that they could put on the air and air reruns, and then give to Hulu as well." Thomsen is clear, though, that he does not want *Will Trent* to be just another police procedural. "I hope that we are making a show that people don't watch because they want to feel the security of law and order in the same way that people watch a show like *Blue Bloods* or *SVU*. I hope that what we're making is a show that is using law enforcement as . . . a storytelling paradigm for morality tales, and these character journeys of really f-d up people." The goal in creating *Will Trent*, Thomsen explains, "was not to be as much of a police procedural as a lot of other shows," and the amount of time dedicated to cases in any given episode is "a lot less than *Law & Order* and all the CBS shows. . . . We're trying to do [an] operatic show" in which race is frequently a central issue.

Will Trent is set up to offer numerous avenues for engagement with themes and issues highlighted by the BLM movement, including its diverse writers and cast, character-driven approach, setting, and use of consultants. Though the source material consists largely of white characters and is written by a white woman, Thomsen and his cocreator Liz Heldens "decided to cast more with an eye towards the actual makeup of the area" in addition to hiring numerous Black and Latino people to work as writers and producers; Thomsen notes that ABC monitors diversity among staff and sets standards, and that *Will Trent* exceeds expectations organically rather than for the purpose of checking boxes as so many other series have seemingly done in the past decade. In terms of casting, Slaughter's Will Trent is tall, slim, and sandy-haired, where "his height along with this suit is kind of the defining trait of him as this outsider" among the GBI.[11] Thomsen and Heldens did not want to be limited to a talent pool that fit such a small portion of actors. Puerto Rican actor Ramón Rodriguez was suggested by the studio, which had worked with him on a failed pilot and believed in his potential star quality, and the cocreators happily pursued the lead, having enjoyed both Rodriguez's work as a performer and their in-person interactions with him. "Fantastic actor—really dedicated—and it gave us an opportunity to add some more specificity" to a character that is fundamentally "a man without an identity."[12] Vaguely understanding by his appearance that he is Latino, Trent eventually has the opportunity to go undercover with a Latino crime family and "kind of explore that in a hypothetical sense" before ultimately unearthing information about his mother and connecting with extended family.[13] Casting also deviated from the book by casting Black actresses as Trent's partner, Faith Mitchell (Iantha Richardson), and supervisor, Amanda Wagner (*The Wire*'s Sonja Sohn). This cast allows for greater discussion of systemic racism in policing than would be found in a white-led cast, as Thomsen

FIG. 5.2. Will, Faith, and Amanda discuss a case on the *Will Trent* episode "Don't Let It Happen Again" (2023).

notes that "when we're adding those stories, it's being driven by our casting" (see Figure 5.2).

Thomsen and his cocreator relied on technical assistants from the GBI in the form of consultants who, as is typically the case, helped to ensure characters follow procedures correctly and explained the chain of command. However, these consultants did not promote a propagandic depiction of law enforcement as police consultants are suspected of doing. Thomsen explains, "I think that they understand that it's . . . a soap opera, and it's heightened reality. So even when the story paints the GBI in not the 'proper' light, they're like, 'OK.'" The GBI's primary representation is through the racially diverse characters of Trent, Mitchell, and Wagner, who have weighed in on the depiction of BIPOC people. Though Trent is Latino, he does not know it until he learns who his mother was, and so the first time *Will Trent* shows a Latino community, it is because Trent is undercover to infiltrate a crime family. As Thomsen reports, "It was a bummer but also we talked about it with Ramón and . . . our writers, and . . . we're gonna do more in season two because we're going to get into . . . Trent's family." Thomsen led discussions with writers and Rodríguez to workshop ways to avoid the typical one-dimensional vilification of Latinos by carefully crafting a backstory, thus providing layers so that *Will Trent*, which has "opted into crime as our storytelling world," could respectfully include more BIPOC actors in episodic roles. For her part, Richardson has also contributed through research into law enforcement's policies regarding Black women's hairstyles, helping to ensure that her character's hair is presented authentically.

As an example of *Will Trent*'s narrative engagement with race, the third episode draws on the history of Lake Lanier in Georgia. Lake Lanier, a reservoir that feeds Atlanta, was created by flooding primarily Black-owned farmland in the 1950s. The episode focuses on the area's history of racially motivated attacks and explores the reality of policing as a Black person. This "was an enormously successful episode" that "got great responses" from viewers as well as the network and studio, Thomsen said. He seems somewhat surprised in sharing that there were no network notes asking him, "Can we make this more about . . . the killer and less about [race]?" Thomsen's approach in representing his law enforcement officers is meant not to act as a public service announcement or to "put these characters out there who are just too supernaturally good" but to model good behavior, part of which includes disallowing bad apples to spoil the bunch. His officers, be they APD or GBI, "are very conflicted" and "have their own weaknesses and . . . insecurities . . . but have lines that other cops don't, that other cop shows don't." One APD character, Michael Wormwood, functions as a reexamination of the antihero, a military veteran "who grew up watching cop shows and became a cop because . . . he wants to be one of those TV cops—and it's gonna go in a dark direction." Acknowledging that he is uninterested in stories that make viewers wonder what they would do and how far they would go to save their loved ones, or "indulging in the fantasy of being special enough to break every rule," Thomsen is instead invested in showing cops haunted by the mistakes they have made and "dispelling the fantasy that cops can do whatever they want."

Faced with the reality that another Floyd-level BLM movement might occur during the run of *Will Trent*, Thomsen predicts he would "want to find a way to address that feeling in a way that felt like it was part of the show." Recalling *The West Wing*'s 9/11 episode "Isaac and Ishmael," which was written, filmed, and broadcast in three weeks, Thomsen asserts, "I would not do that." Thomsen considered whether *West Wing* creator Aaron Sorkin felt an obligation to create that episode, which aired independently of the ongoing narrative, and decided that perhaps given where *The West Wing* was "in the zeitgeist, and the fact that it was a show that opened with the fluttering American flag . . . maybe they felt like it had more of a responsibility or even just an opportunity . . . to weigh in on it." A cop series featuring two Black women officers in prominent roles would certainly have numerous organic and authentic ways to incorporate BLM themes, as the series already highlights issues of institutionalized racism in U.S. policing.

Post-Floyd police procedurals show progressive potential on screen, but what about the experiences of BIPOC writers and others working behind the scenes? It seems the inclusion of BIPOC people in various writers' rooms and executive suites was not handled as deftly by networks and studios as it was in and on *Will Trent*, and that many of the numerous promises made by networks and studios in 2020 have been forgotten or ignored. For example, TTIE's Barb Friend describes the call for stories about underrepresented groups following George Floyd's murder and the enthusiasm with which studios and networks wanted to meet with BIPOC storytellers, but says that as BLM faded from headlines, these same companies reverted to a preference for whitewashed content with "broad appeal."[14] TTIE member Angela Harvey echoed this sentiment when asked about whether she has seen changes in broadcasting. Harvey began by addressing 2020, "when there were so many projects that were picked up by writers of color and put into development," but looking ahead to a few short years, finds that "it started to become clear that those shows weren't turning up on the airwaves. And so I think the writing's been on the wall for a minute."[15] Addressing the industry in 2023, Harvey notes that "all of those shows have either died or are just stuck in the cycle of development, and then it became clear that the studios intended to starve out the writers from January—they stopped buying from everyone" leading up to the strike.

Some of the failed pledges made in 2020 related to the growth of and support for DEI programs and departments. Numerous news and trade articles in 2023 highlighted reverses in course toward a more diverse industry, most notably with the exodus of DEI executives. In June of 2023, six Black women in senior leadership posts left their jobs at companies like Disney and Warner Bros. Discovery, purportedly prompted by a lack of support and the "overwhelming cultural exhaustion that has plagued Black leaders."[16] Echoing concerns raised elsewhere, part of the reason for this downturn is that "Hollywood's institutions have thus far failed to make inclusion part of the industry's DNA," essentially creating a system in which DEI executives are tasked with effecting structural consequences without making structural changes.[17] In other words, networks and studios are interested in looking progressive and equitable but will not allow the kinds of industry changes required to produce equity in a meaningful way. This illustrates the danger that comes with ineffectual media activism and the failure to "operationalize inclusion"; as DEI consultant Kristen Marston states, "It's OK to lean into those moments in powerful ways, but it's not OK to use those moments as leverage for PR."[18] One thing Harvey was unhappily confident about in 2023 was that "they're making changes to who's in charge of diversity and definitely keeping it away from the hands of execs who know how to develop quality content and putting it in the hands of HR professionals. It's a big step backwards." In this way, studios and networks can boast an increase in numbers of BIPOC executives but appoint them to positions in which they have no substantive input in the kinds of content being told and the range of voices empowered to contribute to television's cultural forum. Just one studio—NBCUniversal—has "appeared to successfully maintain a focus on inclusion" because they have structured DEI positions to work closely with and directly report to creatives and executives rather than being held at a distance. This helps to position them to effect change in content.

In addition to these poorly executed pushes for progress, Harvey expressed concern regarding legal backlash. One month after the Supreme Court ruling, Harvey points out that "if the Supreme Court's going to overturn affirmative action . . . and the Republicans have DEI in their sights next, it's not hard to connect the dots." Notably, the conservative group America First Legal Foundation has filed a host of complaints against Fortune 500 companies, claiming that corporate diversity and hiring practices violate civil rights law—effectively claiming "reverse discrimination" against white people.[19] America First has attempted to intervene in media as well, backing *SEAL Team*'s Brian Beneker in his reverse-racism suit against CBS following his failure to be promoted.[20] Coming on the heels of the Supreme Court's decision to end race-conscious admissions that "were permitted, in part, based on the idea that there are educational benefits to having a diverse student body," the legal attacks on promoting diversity instead promote a color-blind approach that does not tend to work out well for BIPOC people.[21] This fosters an environment where studios and networks have an excuse to revert to a system that disproportionately serves white creators, granted a certain degree of cover due to the fact that they must make choices that will avoid further lawsuits. For those with a genuine interest in helping to level the playing field for systemically underprivileged communities, the specter of lawsuits lurks. Programs like Shonda Rhimes's Ladder program, which creates a pipeline to below-the-line positions, and her Producers Inclusion Initiative, which gives aspiring producers on-set experience in a studio system, are under threat.[22]

However, there is a case to be made—as CBS has done in the case of the *SEAL Team* lawsuit—that their hiring practices are protected by the First Amendment.[23] Because the people who are hired to create content are the ones who then decide what that content looks like, as *Black and Blue TV* has made clear, CBS affirms their right to hire who they like, including the right to prioritize qualified BIPOC candidates. Limiting a network (or studio or showrunner) in its ability to choose writers, as Beneker and other disgruntled white people might hope to do, unconstitutionally impairs the network's ability to shape the messages it broadcasts. Moreover, recent case law outside of media suggests that the government cannot force a private company to hire applicants who will express views with which the company disagrees. These legal battles are unlikely to be resolved quickly as antidiversity groups continue in their efforts to return American culture to the pre–civil rights era. Still, the success of CBS and similar cases, in tandem with clear pushes for antiracist progress, allows for a few possibilities. Not only could a network like CBS defend its right to require diversity, but brave executives and showrunners could clean house by weeding out writers and others who espouse racist perspectives. Industry changes are challenging and slow-moving, certainly, but as *Black and Blue TV* has illustrated, a few people with power and integrity can start a movement, be it through a Twitter hashtag that leads to global protests or a progressive showrunner who destabilizes a genre and expands television's cultural forum.

Official DEI initiatives are, of course, not the only component in increasing diversity or improving access and representation, and mere numbers are insufficient for tracking trends and demonstrating improvements in the broadcast industry. *S.W.A.T.* creator Aaron Rahsaan Thomas is skeptical of some of the ways progress is claimed but remains generally optimistic about progress, blending a critique of misleading data with qualitative insight into changes in writers' rooms. As Thomas understands it, gross numbers of Black creators have increased, but this is misleading, as it coincides with an era of peak TV in which the gross number of programs is also growing; in this same period, Thomas believes that the percentage of BIPOC showrunners is generally holding steady such that their impact on the business of television is not growing. "What I will say," Thomas continues, "is that I do think the environment, the way we have these conversations, has changed . . . now you can openly discuss any of these elements within our business regarding the importance of those diversity."[24] Whereas calls for diversity might once have come from "that one person in a room [who] feels strongly . . . and feels like an outsider and feels alone," who might then drop the subject in order to survive the industry, it is now a common enough concern that people are more comfortable speaking candidly about issues of diversity and representation. Thomas attributes this to generational shifts, suggesting that Gen Z discusses it far more frequently than previous generations. "I don't think that's going away; I don't think all of a sudden Gen Z is going to decide, 'No, we kind of like the way baby boomers did—screw it.'" Thomas concludes, "I don't think this is going anywhere. All the trends indicate that these will be conversations that will stick around and these will be things that you can't sweep back under the rug."

In September of 2024, *The Hollywood Reporter* published their annual Forces of Change power list to spotlight "industry leaders who actively use their clout and platform to create opportunities in the business for those who are historically excluded—even and especially when it is not in their job description to do so."[25] They note that this last criterion is all the more critical now; four years after Floyd's murder spurred companies to loudly proclaim the value of diversity and pledge millions of dollars to improve media industries, many companies have "shed their DEI-designated employees en masse," as it is no longer "in vogue" to open doors to underrepresented groups. The suggestion here is that improvements in DEI can come from a variety of sources and positions, not merely those ostensibly designed for that purpose, and that there is a large and growing population in media—including broadcast television—that is not done trying to effect change.

Not Quite Business as Usual

In our two-hour discussion of Black Lives Matter, *Station 19*, and the state of race relations in Hollywood, Jason George shared an analogy about a person who is physically attacked. George's analogy provided a typology for four different kinds of people: the victim who is attacked, the villain who attacks, the outsider who witnesses the attack and intervenes to help the victim, and the outsider who witnesses the attack and does not intervene.[26] To this we might add a fifth type—the outsider who joins the attacker in the violence—but George's point is that if you do not help the victim, then you are enabling the villain. As a decade of BLM-era television demonstrates, television shows function similarly. Programs that feature cops who police based on racial biases and are championed for violating civil liberties are a problem when they reinforce popular discourses that BIPOC people are inherently criminal and that cops are "the good guys." Showrunners and other creatives who do not overtly spew racism can still contribute to the problem if they do not actively work to combat racism—if they see the (symbolic) violence of their genre and walk away, dismissing it as somebody else's problem. After years of research and dozens of interviews, it is my conclusion that there is a growing population of broadcast creatives who understand the power they hold to make the world a better place and who are interested in being part of a solution; they have seen the beating, and they want to stop it. They create inclusive writers' rooms and bring in expert consultants from numerous fields, and their diverse casts perform dialogue that invites audiences to consider pathways toward progress. They expand the cultural forum of one of the largest social movements in U.S. history.

Part of expanding the forum is changing the business-as-usual approach to television production. One possible change that George promotes, and which he suggests has expanded since 2020, is open rooms in which writers engage actors in developing scripts. Prior to post-Floyd seasons of *Station 19*, for example, the writers and producers would Zoom with each cast member "and literally just find out what's going on in your life, what's resonating for you, and they'll see if that can factor into their things," including "cultural stuff" like issues relating to race. George suggests things worked similarly for the cable series *Good Trouble* (Freeform, 2019–2024), which also has a diverse cast that was invested in ongoing engagement with BLM. Writers' and producers' conversations with actors helped to fuel conversations that spanned multiple seasons, and building on actors' experiences "is crucial to making it feel like that work . . . feels authentic." By contrast, George suggests, business-as-usual procedurals "often get a little closer to 'AWMF' unless . . . part of your point [as with series like *S.W.A.T.*] was to have some of that conversation."

The people I spoke with understand 2020 not as the end of racism in America, much less television, but as a moment in a cycle. Speaking in 2023, *Station 19* writer/producer Angela Harvey recalled that in 2020 "there was some very dramatic hand wringing, yeah. And now there's a reset that's turning into, I think, a bit of a backlash. Same as the country. . . . Hollywood's not that different from America at large."[27] This speaks to the ebbs and flows surrounding any trauma; actor Jason George similarly raised the issue of culture's cyclical engagement with issues, noting that "in trying to have these conversations and trying to do something that moves the needle . . . events happen, and then it's done. The event that spurs something, and then people go out and do something, they rally, and then that . . . event that is part of the solution happens, and you're done. And of course you're not done. The key is building up systems out of those events, but that's a much, much harder thing to do." *Black and Blue TV* traces the trauma of police brutality against BIPOC citizens, but other scholars could just as easily trace sexual violence and the #MeToo movement or gun violence and the endless stream of school shootings. The difference now, as George perceives it, is that "we have, especially with . . . social media, this democratization of media—this conversation stays simmering in a way that it didn't before, in the larger community."

Unlike the "very special episodes" of *The Jeffersons* and *Good Times*, today's engagement is more likely to bleed into multiepisode or even season-long arcs or become part of the background of the show.

Fred Berner has more than two decades of experience directing and producing cop shows, and he is able to offer a more historical perspective on television production practices than many of the younger writers and showrunners I interviewed. Speaking to the relationship with networks and advertisers, Berner shares, "I never felt a harness in terms of the stories that we wanted to tell," even in a broadcast medium beholden to advertisers. Networks might have concerns about how graphic a depiction was, but generally "there's no issue that's off the table."[28] While the network has long functioned as "the gatekeeper for something that might offend a sponsor," Berner perceives it to work in reverse in recent years. For example, Berner suggests that if the sponsor is "a pillowman sponsor, someone that the networks don't want anything to do with" or "a super uber Christian racist franchise, we don't really want your advertising dollars," whereas once there would have been a concerted effort not to offend the sponsor. Berner also recognizes a "quantum shift after the George Floyd incident, to just rectify the wrong and tell the other story"—in other words, to expand the cultural forum. Reflecting *Law & Order: SVU*'s 2013 episode "American Tragedy," Berner feels it "might have equivocated back in the day and tried to overcomplicate and not be pedantic about it in the best tradition of *Law & Order*" in ways they would not in the future. At the same time, Berner is concerned that "we could all do well by not having made progress quite so fast because progress on some level creates a whiplash or a backlash" and that it would have been better to achieve "deeper understandings that would have taken place over a slightly longer period of time."

While some shows have the impulse to expand the cultural forum baked into their DNA, most do not. Post-Floyd episodes of *SVU* had attempted "to shed light on the fact that, even as good as your intentions, cops can be blind when they've already unconsciously decided if a suspect could have [committed the crime] or not based on class or race or gender," which Barba notes earned them "some flack . . . for being too woke."[29] The series was attempting to be "part of the history and the moment" in which it was produced, to show "where are we in terms of the police and civilians' relationship, where we are in terms of the bigger picture of police work and protecting civilians and calling for accountability." This included an episode that called out qualified immunity, which protects officers from being sued for using excessive force or violating civil liberties. While *Law & Order: SVU* might not be able to claim the progressive potential of shows like *The Rookie* and

S.W.A.T., it nevertheless demonstrates the possibility of evolving to expand the cultural forum—to be less racist, and occasionally antiracist, and to improve their standing with Color of Change.

As Lori Lopez points out, "Media provides both a rallying point for activism and a means for shifting the conversation to what really matters," specifically the place of marginalized communities in American society.[30] This is not a simple process but one that requires diligence, dedication, and the confidence to invest in a different kind of storytelling. The Black Lives Matter movement has been and will continue to be mediated by the broadcast television industry; it has proved effective in rallying antiracist stories and prodiversity employment practices, though not without hurdles and missteps. By learning from and amplifying the voices of writers, producers, directors, showrunners, and activists whose work embraces the interconnectedness of social movements and entertainment media, we see how individuals experience their roles and understand their responsibilities. While it is often a matter of taking two steps forward only to be pushed one step back, social movements' pressure points occasionally facilitate a few more steps in the right direction.

Acknowledgments

I am so incredibly grateful to everyone who helped me find my voice as a media scholar. To Tim Havens, my doctoral advisor and permanent mentor, for the thousand and one moments of wisdom and guidance he has provided me, and for not giving it a second thought when I would stage sit-ins in his office. To Rita Zajacz and Gigi Durham for making my doctoral defense such a fun experience that I wanted to do it all over again. And to my reviewers, who might have broken me of my imposter syndrome at long last.

I'm also grateful to the many, many people who contributed to this book. I wrote my first article on the relationship between television and the Black Lives Matter movement after seeing it addressed in some of my favorite shows in 2015, and another after I was blown away by *Station 19*'s powerful engagement with George Floyd's murder, but my esteemed editor Nicole Solano gave me the confidence to tackle the subject with a book. I was lucky to have a dear friend, Neil Landau, who had industry friends willing to speak with me about their work. I count myself blessed to have been in Los Angeles in 2023, where I could join writers and actors on the picket line and learn about their experiences creating BLM-era content. Special thanks to Kiley Donovan, Jason George, Alexi Hawley, Fredrick Kotto, Niceole Levy, Tery Lopez, Shawn Ryan, and Aaron Rahsaan Thomas for being exceptionally helpful in developing my understanding of the complexities that have plagued the television industry in the past thirty years.

And finally, my most heartfelt thanks to those who have taken care of me, body and soul. My mother, Dr. Elizabeth Nelson, who showed me what it is like to let your inquisitive mind chart your career path, and who did not notice when her occasional attempts to limit my TV time proved unsuccessful because I could hear the TV from the dining room and see its reflection on the windows of our den. Dr. Jennifer Turchi, my occasional coauthor and forever sister, who knows me better than anyone (and I am a better person for it). Sarah Faruqui, who has only ever shown warmth and love to those she holds dear. And to Sammy, the best bear a girl could ask for.

Notes

Introduction

1. Black Lives Matter, "About," n/d, accessed August 10, 2023, https://blacklivesmatter.com/about/.
2. Steven Aoun, "Bearing Witness: Black Lives Matter Protests as Media, and Mediated, Event," *Metro Magazine* 207 (2021): 103.
3. Armed Conflict Location & Event Data Project (ACLED), "Demonstrations and Political Violence in America: New Data for Summer 2020," September 3, 2020, https://acleddata.com/2020/09/03/demonstrations-political-violence-in-america-new-data-for-summer-2020/.
4. ACLED.
5. Dave Collins, "146 NYC Police Committed Misconduct in 2020 Protests: Report," *AP News*, February 6, 2023, https://apnews.com/article/politics-protests-and-demonstrations-george-floyd-new-york-city-505491e2bf8657df2448fcc99520ba6e.
6. Rick Porter, "TV Long View: How Much Network TV Depends on Cop Shows," *The Hollywood Reporter*, June 20, 2020, https://www.hollywoodreporter.com/tv/tv-news/heres-how-network-tv-depends-cop-shows-1299504/.
7. Kathleen M. Donovan and Charles F. Klahm IV, "The Role of Entertainment Media in Perceptions of Police Use of Force," *Criminal Justice & Behavior* 42, no. 12 (2015): 1262; Porter, n.p.; Nielsen, "Top 10," 2023, https://www.nielsen.com/top-ten/.
8. Rob C. Mawby, "Completing the 'Half-Formed Picture'? Media Images of Policing," in *Criminal Visions: Media Representations of Crime and Justice*, ed. Paul Mason (Willan Publishing, 2003), 214–237; Robert Reiner, "Romantic Realism: Policing and the Media," in *Core Issues in Policing*, 2nd ed., ed. Frank Leishman, Barry Loveday, and Stephen P. Savage (Longman, 2000): 52–66; Wesley Skogan and Kathleen Frydl, *Fairness and Effectiveness in Policing: The Evidence* (National Academies Press, 2004).

9. Color of Change, *Normalizing Injustice: The Dangerous Misrepresentations That Define Television's Scripted Crime Genre* (The USC Annenberg Norman Lear Center, 2020).
10. Mapping Police Violence, 2022, https://mappingpoliceviolence.org/?utm_campaign=launch&utm_source=google&utm_medium=ad&utm_term=mapping%20police%20violence&gad_source=1&gclid=CjwKCAjwreW2BhBhEiwAavLwfJVRVtVFf3xnDnIgNNwNu9fgqef5mMVZ5UGDmSfqOa8g9x-wyBXsdMBoCoPYQAvD_BwE.
11. Constance Grady, "How 70 Years of Cop Shows Taught Us to Valorize the Police," *Vox*, April 12, 2021, https://www.vox.com/culture/22375412/police-show-procedurals-hollywood-history-dragnet-keystone-cops-brooklyn-nine-nine-wire-blue-bloods; Tatiana Siegel, "Can Hollywood Really Quit the Force?" *The Hollywood Reporter*, July 1, 2020, 38.
12. Benjamin Bowling, Robert Reiner, and James Sheptycki, *The Politics of the Police*, 5th ed. (Oxford University Press, 2019), 218.
13. Bowling et al., 218.
14. Porter, n.p.; Will Thorne, "Cop Shows Under the Microscope," *Variety*, June 16, 2020, 18.
15. Elaine Low and Angelique Jackson, "The Reckoning over Representation," *Variety*, June 30, 2020, 33.
16. Matt Donnelly, "Blue and Gold: Hollywood's Ties to Law Enforcement," *Variety*, June 16, 2020, 13–14.
17. Thorne, 18.
18. Michael Arntfield, "TVPD: The Generational Diegetics of the Police Procedural on American Television," *Canadian Review of American Studies* 41, no. 1 (2011): 76.
19. Aoun, 104.
20. Steven D. Stark, "Perry Mason Meets Sonny Crockett: The History of Lawyers and the Police as Television Heroes," *University of Miami Law Review* 42, no. 1 (1988): 280; David Garland, *The Culture of Control* (Oxford University Press, 2001), 61.
21. Bowling et al., 217; Todd Gitlin, *Inside Prime Time* (University of California Press, 2000), 279.
22. Bowling et al., 216–217.
23. Robert Reiner, *The Politics of the Police*, 4th ed. (Oxford University Press, 2010), 178.
24. André Brock, "From the Blackhand Side: Twitter as a Cultural Conversation," *Journal of Broadcasting & Electronic Media* 56, no. 4 (2012): 538.
25. José Van Dijck, *The Culture of Connectivity: A Critical History of Social Media* (Oxford University Press, 2013), 69.

26. Deen Freelon, Charlton D. McIlwain, and Meredith D. Clark, "Beyond the Hashtag" (Center for Media & Social Impact, 2016), 9.
27. Elizabeth Day, "#BlackLivesMatter: The Birth of a New Civil Rights Movement," *The Guardian*, July 19, 2015, https://www.theguardian.com/world/2015/jul/19/blacklivesmatter-birth-civil-rights-movement.
28. Rachel L. Bailey, Glenna L. Read, YaoJun Harry Yan, Jiawei Liu, David A. Makin, and Dale Willits, "Camera Point-of-View Exacerbates Racial Bias in Viewers of Police Use of Force Videos," *Journal of Communication* 71, no. 2 (2021): 247; Mary Angela Bock, "Film the Police! Cop-Watching and Its Embodied Narratives," *Journal of Communication* 66, no. 1 (2016): 14; Sarah J. Jackson and Brooke Foucault Welles, "Hijacking #MYNYPD: Social Media Dissent and Networked Counterpublics," *Journal of Communication* 65, no. 6 (2015): 932.
29. Aoun, 104.
30. Bailey et al., 246.
31. Franklin Zimring, *When Police Kill* (Harvard University Press, 2017), 36.
32. Zimring, 204–206.
33. Dominic Bearfield, Robert Maranto, and Patrick J. Wolf, "Making Violence Transparent: Ranking Police Departments in Major U.S. Cities to Make Black Lives Matter," *Public Integrity* 23 (2021): 173.
34. Day, n.p.
35. Bearfield et al., 173.
36. Bearfield et al., 164.
37. Bearfield et al., 164–165; Vanessa Williamson, Kris-Stella Trump, and Katherine Levine Einstein, "Black Lives Matter: Evidence That Police-Caused Deaths Predict Protest Activity," *Perspectives on Politics* 16, no. 2 (2018): 405.
38. Astrid Dirikx, Jan Van den Bulck, and Stephan Parmentier, "The Police as Societal Moral Agents: 'Procedural Justice' and the Analysis of Police Fiction," *Journal of Broadcasting & Electronic Media* 56, no. 1 (2012): 39.
39. Arntfield, 92.
40. Roger Sabin, *Cop Shows: A Critical History of Police Dramas on Television* (McFarland & Company, 2015), 1.
41. John Corner, *Critical Ideas in Television Studies* (Clarendon Press, 1999), 5; Shelley Manis, "'These Are [Our] Stories': Engaging Cultural Debate and Performing Contradictions in *Law & Order*," *Quarterly Review of Film & Video* 26, no. 3 (2009): 194.
42. Brooks Robards, "The Police Show," in *TV Genres: A Handbook and Reference Guide*, ed. Brian Geoffrey Rose (Greenwood Press, 1985), 11.
43. Jonathan Nichols-Pethick, *TV Cops: The Contemporary American Television Police Drama* (Routledge, 2012), 49.

44. James M. Carlson, *Prime Time Law Enforcement: Crime Show Viewing and Attitudes Toward the Criminal Justice System* (Praeger, 1985), 2; Mawby; Robert Reiner, *The Politics of the Police*, 3rd ed. (Oxford University Press, 2000), 139.
45. Bowling et al., 215; Gitlin, 254; David Shaw, "Chief Parker Molded LAPD Image—Then Came the '60s," *Los Angeles Times*, May 25, 1992, https://www.latimes.com/archives/la-xpm-1992-05-25-mn-236-story.html; Sue Turnbull, *TV Crime Drama* (Edinburgh University Press, 2014), 80.
46. Sydney Head, "Content Analysis of Television Drama Programs," *Quarterly of Film, Radio and Television* 9 (1954): 182.
47. Alyssa Rosenberg, "How Police Censorship Shaped Hollywood," *Washington Post*, October 24, 2016, https://www.washingtonpost.com/sf/opinions/2016/10/24/how-police-censorship-shaped-hollywood/.
48. Rosenberg, "Police Censorship."
49. Alyssa Rosenberg, "In Pop Culture, There Are No Bad Police Shootings," *Washington Post*, October 26, 2016, https://www.washingtonpost.com/sf/opinions/2016/10/26/in-pop-culture-there-are-no-bad-police-shootings/.
50. Rosenberg, "Pop Culture."
51. George Gerbner, "The Television World of Violence," in *Mass Media and Violence*, ed. David Lange, Robert Baker, and Sandra Balls (U.S. Government Printing Office, 1969), 338.
52. Joseph R. Dominick, "Crime and Law Enforcement on Prime-Time Television," *Public Opinion Quarterly* 37, no. 2 (1973): 247.
53. Jessica Allen, Sonia Livingstone, and Robert Reiner, "True Lies: Changing Images of Crime in British Postwar Cinema," *European Journal of Communication* 13, no. 1 (1998): 67; Robert S. Lichter, Linda S. Lichter, and Daniel Amundson, *Images of Government in TV Entertainment* (Partnership for Trust in Government, 1999), 96. Robert S. Lichter, Linda S. Lichter, and Daniel Amundson. *Images of Government in TV Entertainment 1998–2001* (Partnership for Trust in Government, 2002), 15; Shaw, 215.
54. Allen et al., 84; Marianne Colbran, *Media Representations of Police and Crime: Shaping the Police Television Drama* (Palgrave Macmillan, 2014), 10; Reiner, "Romantic Realism"; Robert Reiner, *Law and Order: An Honest Citizen's Guide to Crime and Control* (Polity Press, 2007), 142.
55. Bowling et al., 215.
56. Jason Mittell, *Genre & Television: From Cop Shows to Cartoons in American Culture* (Routledge, 2004), 123; Reiner, "*Law & Order*," 62.
57. Bowling et al., 215; Robert Reiner, Sonia Livingstone, and Jessica Allen, "No More Happy Endings? The Media and Popular Concern About Crime Since the Second World War," in *Crime, Risk and Insecurity*, ed. Tim Hope and Richard Sparks (Routledge, 2000), 119; Robert Reiner, Sonia Livingstone, and Jessica

Allen, "From Law and Order to Lynch Mobs: Crime News Since the Second World War," in *Criminal Visions*, ed. Paul Mason (Routledge, 2003), 19.

58. Bowling et al., 216; John Dennington and John Tulloch, "Cops, Consensus, and Ideology," *Screen Edition* 20 (1976): 39.
59. Richard Sparks, *Television & the Drama of Crime: Moral Tales and the Place of Crime in Public Life* (Open University Press, 1992), 131.
60. Arntfield, 83; Sue Thornham and Tony Purvis, *Television Drama: Theories & Identities* (Palgrave Macmillan, 2005), 46.
61. Nichols-Pethick, 3.
62. Nichols-Pethick, 7.
63. Lichter et al., *Images of Government in TV Entertainment*, 84; Nichols-Pethick, 162.
64. Reiner, "Romantic Realism," 62.
65. Nichols-Pethick, 8.
66. Mike Chopra-Gant, "The Law of the Father, the Law of the Land: Power, Gender and Race in *The Shield*," *Journal of American Studies* 41, no. 3 (2007): 665.
67. Nichols-Pethick, 7.
68. Nichols-Pethick, 104; Marc Ouellette, "'It'll Pass': *NYPD Blue*'s Sipowicz and Mundane Masculinity," *Universitas* 2, no. 2 (2006): 1.
69. Chopra-Gant, 671; Michael L. Wayne, "Ambivalent Anti-Heroes and Racist Rednecks on Basic Cable: Post-Race Ideology and White Masculinity on FX," *Journal of Popular Television* 2, no. 2 (2014): 212.
70. David Simon, "Introduction," in *The Wire: Truth Be Told*, ed. Rafael Alvarez (Cannondale Books, 2009), 33.
71. Alex Edwards, "*Brooklyn Nine-Nine* as Copaganda: A Critical Analysis," *Medium*, August 27, 2020, https://medium.com/@ohgodscrewthis/brooklyn-nine-nine-as-copaganda-a-critical-analysis-6cca54cae7f8.
72. Ray Surette, *Media, Crime, & Criminal Justice: Images, Realities, & Policies* (Wadsworth, Cengage Learning, 2011), 98.
73. Sarah Eschholz, Matthew Mallard, and Stacey Flynn, "Images of Prime Time Justice: A Content Analysis of *NYPD Blue* and *Law & Order*," *Journal of Criminal Justice and Popular Culture* 10, no. 3 (2004): 173; Surette, *Media, Crime, and Criminal Justice*, 97; Jan Van den Bulck, "Fictional Cops: Who Are They, and What Are They Teaching Us?" in *Law Enforcement, Communication and Community*, ed. Howard Giles (John Benjamins Publishing, 2002), 110.
74. Color of Change, 32.
75. Bowling et al., 217.
76. Roland Zullo, "Should More Law Enforcement Be the Answer to Crime?" in *Policing and Race in America: Economic, Political, and Social Dynamics*, ed. James D. Ward (Lexington Books, 2018), 123.

77. Color of Change, 32.
78. Donnelly, 13; Alan Jenkins, "It's Time for a 'Bigotry Pass' on Scripts," *The Hollywood Reporter*, June 10, 2020, 8; Thorne, 18.
79. Anita Lam, *Making Crime Television: Producing Entertaining Representations of Crime for Television Broadcast* (Routledge, 2014), 31.
80. Donnelly, 14; Siegel, 39.
81. Donnelly, 13.
82. Color of Change, 55.
83. Robert Reiner, *Crime: The Mystery of the Common-Sense Concept* (Polity Press, 2016), 133; Richard V. Ericson, "Patrolling the Facts: Secrecy and Publicity in Police Work," *British Journal of Sociology* 40, no. 2 (1989): 224.
84. Jenkins, 8.
85. Dawn Chmielewski, "How *Law & Order*'s Dick Wolf Is Reimagining His Shows in the Wake of the BLM Protests, *Forbes*, July 24, 2020, https://www.forbes.com/sites/dawnchmielewski/2020/07/24/how-law-orders-dick-wolf-is-reimagining-his-shows-in-the-wake-of-the-blm-protests/?sh=33e278e156a7.
86. Grady, n.p.; Steven Zeitchik, "CBS Is Remaking Its Police Shows for the Black Lives Matter Era," *Washington Post*, October 13, 2020, https://www.washingtonpost.com/business/2020/10/14/cbs-police-shows-black-lives-matter/.
87. Horace Newcomb and Paul M. Hirsch, "Television as a Cultural Forum," *Quarterly Review of Film Studies* 8, no. 3 (1983): 49.
88. Amanda D. Lotz, "Using 'Network' Theory in the Post-Network Era: Fictional 9/11 U.S. Television Discourses as a 'Cultural Forum,'" *Screen* 45, no. 4 (2004): 424; Nichols-Pethick, 184.
89. Newcomb and Hirsch, 49.
90. Lotz, 432; Nichols-Pethick, 11.
91. Laurena Bernabo, "Copaganda and Post-Floyd TVPD: Broadcast Television's Response to Policing in 2020," *Journal of Communication* 72, no. 4 (2022): 488.
92. Julie D'Acci, "Cultural Studies, Television Studies, and the Crisis in the Humanities," in *Television After TV: Essays on a Medium in Transition*, ed. Lynn Spigel and Jan Olsson (Duke University Press, 2004), 431.
93. D'Acci, 434.
94. Stuart Hall, "Encoding/Decoding," *Culture* (1980): 125; Richard Johnson, "The Story So Far: And Further Transformations?" in *Introduction to Contemporary Cultural Studies*, ed. David Punter (Longman, 1986), 280; Elana Levine, "Toward a Paradigm for Media Production Research: Behind the Scenes at *General Hospital*," *Critical Studies in Media Communication* 18, no. 1 (2001): 67.
95. Levine, 81.
96. Mittell, 349.
97. Joseph Turow, *Media Industries* (Longman, 1984), 161.

98. Aniko Bodroghkozy, *Equal Time: Television and the Civil Rights Movement* (University of Illinois Press, 2012), 3.
99. Bodroghkozy, 156.
100. Sasha Torres, *Black, White, and In Color: Television and Black Civil Rights* (Princeton University Press, 2003), 48.
101. Jade Petermon and Leland G. Spencer, "Black Queer Womanhood Matters: Searching for the Queer Herstory of Black Lives Matter in Television Dramas," *Critical Studies in Media Communication* 35, no. 4 (2019): 340.
102. Brandy Monk-Payton, "From 'Relevance' to 'Reckoning' or, Channeling Black Lives Matter on TV—Part One," *Flow*, October 18, 2021, https://www.flowjournal.org/2021/10/from-relevance-to-reckoning-part-one/.
103. Morgan Genevieve Blue, "Accidental Deaths: The Violence of Representing Childhood in *Law & Order: Special Victims Unit*," *Red Feather Journal: An International Journal of Children in Popular Culture* 2, no. 2 (2011): 3.
104. Allen et al.; Katherine Beckett and Theodore Sasson, *The Politics of Injustice: Crime and Punishment in America* (Fine Forge Press, 2000); Donovan and Klahm; James Garofalo, "Crime and the Mass Media: A Selective Review of Research," *Journal of Research in Crime and Delinquency* 18, no. 2 (1981): 325; Robert S. Lichter, Linda S. Lichter, and Stanley Rothman, *Prime Time: How TV Portrays American Culture* (Regnery Publishing, 1994); Paul Mason, *Reading the Bill: An Analysis of the Thames Television Police Drama* (Bristol Centre for Criminal Justice, 1992); Reiner, "*Law & Order*"; Reiner et al., "No More Happy Endings?"; Robert Reiner, Sonia Livingstone, and Jessica Allen, "Casino Culture: Media and Crime in a Winner-Loser Society," in *Crime, Risk and Justice: The Politics of Crime Control in Liberal Democracies*, ed. Kevin Stetson and Robert R. Sullivan (Willan, 2001), 175–193; Reiner et al., "From Law and Order to Lynch Mobs"; Sparks.
105. John Thornton Caldwell, "Cultures of Production: Studying Industry's Deep Texts, Reflexive Rituals, and Managed Self-Disclosures," in *Media Industries: History, Theory, and Method*, ed. Alisa Perren and Jennifer Holt (Wiley, 2011), 199–212. Timothy Havens, Amanda D. Lotz, and Serra Tinic, "Critical Media Industry Studies: A Research Approach," *Communication, Culture & Critique* 2, no. 2 (2009): 234–253.
106. Havens et al., 237.
107. Caldwell, 200.
108. Daniel Herbert, Amanda D. Lotz, and Aswin Punathambekar, *Media Industry Studies* (Polity, 2020): 50.
109. Monk-Payton, n.p.
110. Todd Gitlin, "Prime Time Ideology: The Hegemonic Process in Television Entertainment," *Social Problems* 26, no. 3 (1979): 254.

Chapter 1 BLM and DEI

1. Writers Guild of America West, *2015 TV Staffing Brief* (WGAW, 2015), 14.
2. Darnell Hunt, Ana-Christina Ramón, and Zachary Price, *2014 Hollywood Diversity Report: Making Sense of the Disconnect* (UCLA, 2014), 5.
3. Aaron Rahsaan Thomas in discussion with the author, July 2022.
4. Hunt et al., *2014*, 5. See also: Robert M. Entman and Andrew Rojecki, *The Black Image in the White Mind* (University of Chicago Press, 2000) and Darnell Hunt, "Black Content, White Control," in *Channeling Blackness: Studies on Television and Race in America*, ed. Darnell Hunt (Oxford University Press, 2005), 267–302.
5. Rebecca Sun, "Opinion: It's Time to Retire the Phrase 'Diversity Is Good for Business,'" *The Hollywood Reporter*, December 28, 2018, https://www.hollywoodreporter.com/lifestyle/lifestyle-news/time-retire-phrase-diversity-is-good-business-1171920/.
6. Rosy Cordero, "UCLA's Hollywood Diversity Report Reveals TV Content from Diverse Writers and with Diverse Casts Resonated with Pandemic Audiences," *Deadline*, October 26, 2021, https://deadline.com/2021/10/ucla-hollywood-diversity-report-tv-representation-inclusion-1234862431/; Darnell Hunt and Ana-Christina Ramón, "TV Viewers Favor Shows with Diverse Casts and Authentic Storylines," *Forbes*, November 9, 2023, https://www.forbes.com/sites/drdarnellhuntanddranachristinaramon/2023/11/09/tv-viewers-favor-shows-with-diverse-casts-and-authentic-storylines/.
7. Hunt and Ramón.
8. Sun.
9. Charna Flam, "Asian and Black Actors Saw Representation Gains in 2022 Movies and TV, According to Study," *Variety*, April 17, 2023, https://variety.com/2023/film/news/film-tv-representation-diversity-2022-1235583955/; Dave McNary, "Hollywood Diversity Shows Some Gains, but Falls Short in Most Areas (Study)," *Variety*, February 27, 2018, https://variety.com/2018/film/news/hollywood-diversity-falls-short-ucla-report-1202711370/; Christy Piña, "After Years of Increased Latin Presence in TV, Film, New Study Finds Representation Is Declining," *The Hollywood Reporter*, September 27, 2023, https://www.hollywoodreporter.com/tv/tv-news/latinos-in-media-report-2023-decrease-representation-1235598748/; Christy Piña, "Study: Diversity in TV Casting Increasing, More Lead Roles for Women," *The Hollywood Reporter*, October 27, 2022, https://www.hollywoodreporter.com/tv/tv-news/ucla-hollywood-diversity-report-tv-2022-1235249634/; David Robb, "UCLA TV Diversity Report Finds 'Progress' for Women and Minorities, but Latinos Still Lag Far Behind; White

Male Show Creators Tend to Get Bigger Budgets," *Deadline*, October 27, 2022, https://deadline.com/2022/10/2022-hollywood-tv-diversity-report-ucla-results-1235155191/; Bryn Sandberg, "Diversity Improves Among TV Actors But Execs Still Largely White and Male, Study Finds," *The Hollywood Reporter*, October 22, 2020, https://www.hollywoodreporter.com/tv/tv-news/diversity-improves-among-tv-actors-but-execs-still-largely-white-and-male-study-finds-4080967/; Rebecca Sun, "People of the Global Majority Finally Overindexed on Broadcast Scripted Series in 2019–20: Study," *The Hollywood Reporter*, October 26, 2021, https://www.hollywoodreporter.com/tv/tv-news/hollywood-diversity-report-2021-broadcast-tv-scripted-1235036855/; Rebecca Sun, "Study Finds Racial Disparity in Writers' Compensation and Showrunner Opportunities," *The Hollywood Reporter*, May 24, 2022, https://www.hollywoodreporter.com/tv/tv-news/tv-writers-diversity-study-1235152849/.

10. Courtney Brannon Donoghue, *The Value Gap: Female-Driven Films from Pitch to Premiere* (University of Texas Press, 2023), 28.
11. Lori Kido Lopez, *Asian American Media Activism: Fighting for Cultural Citizenship* (New York University Press, 2016), 7.
12. Lopez, 22–23.
13. Lopez, 14.
14. Writers Guild of America West, *The 2005 Hollywood Writers Report: Catching Up with a Changing America?* (WGAW, 2005), 3.
15. Writers Guild of America West, *The 2007 Hollywood Writers Report: Whose Stories Are WE Telling?* (WGAW, 2007), 9.
16. Writers Guild of America West, *The 2009 Hollywood Writers Report: Re-Writing An All-Too-Familiar Story?* (WGAW, 2009), 15.
17. Writers Guild of America West, *The 2011 Hollywood Writers Report: Recession And Regression* (WGAW, 2011), 5.
18. Writers Guild of America West, *The 2012 Hollywood Writers Report: Recession And Regression* (WGAW, 2012), 26.
19. Writers Guild of America West, *The 2014 Hollywood Writers Report: Turning Missed Opportunities Into Realized Ones* (WGAW, 2014), 20.
20. Writers Guild of America West, *2013 TV Staffing Brief* (WGAW, 2013), 2.
21. WGAW, *2013*, 5.
22. WGAW, *2015*, 2.
23. WGAW, *2015*, 8.
24. Writers Guild of America West, *The 2016 Hollywood Writers Report: Renaissance in Reverse?* (UCLA, 2016), 22.
25. WGAW, *2016*, 15.
26. Writers Guild of America West, *WGAW Inclusion Report Card: 2017-2018 TV Staffing Season* (WGAW, 2018), 1.

27. Writers Guild of America West, *WGAW Inclusion Report Card: Update On 2019 TV Season Staffing Season* (WGAW, 2019), 1; Writers Guild of America West, *WGAW Inclusion Report 2020* (WGAW, 2020), 1.
28. WGAW, *2020*, 13.
29. WGAW, *2020*, 14.
30. Writers Guild of America West, *Inclusion & Equity Report 2022* (WGAW, 2022), 5.
31. WGAW, *2022*, 5–6.
32. Amity Paye in discussion with the author, September 2022.
33. WGAW, *2013*, 9.
34. WGAW, *2022*, 3.
35. Niceole Levy in discussion with the author, July 2023.
36. Amanda Green in discussion with the author, August 2021.
37. Kiley Donovan in discussion with the author, August 2021.
38. Color of Change, *Race in the Writers' Room: How Hollywood Whitewashes the Stories That Shape America* (Color of Change, 2017), 17.
39. Color of Change, 44.
40. Talicia Raggs in discussion with the author, July 2022.
41. Alexi Hawley in discussion with the author, April 2023.
42. Angela Harvey in discussion with the author, July 2023.
43. Think Tank for Inclusion and Equity, *Behind the Scenes: The State of Inclusion and Equity in TV Writers' Rooms* (TTIE, 2019), 4.
44. TTIE, 18–39.
45. Darnell Hunt, Ana-Christina Ramón, Michael Tran, Amberia Sargent, and Debanjan Roychoudhury, *Hollywood Diversity Report 2018: Five Years of Progress and Missed Opportunities* (UCLA, 2018), 6.
46. Darnell Hunt and Ana-Christina Ramón, *2015 Hollywood Diversity Report: Flipping the Script* (Los Angeles: UCLA, 2015), 2.
47. Hunt et al., *2014*, 12.
48. Hunt et al., *2014*, 13.
49. Ana-Christina Ramón, Michael Tran, and Darnell Hunt, *Hollywood Diversity Report 2023: Exclusivity in Progress* (UCLA, 2023), 17.
50. Ramón et al., *2023*, 29.
51. Hunt et al., *2014*, 20.
52. Michael Brandt in discussion with the author, July 2023.
53. William Lee, "Black Firefighters Still Make Up Only 15% of the Chicago Fire Department," *Chicago Tribune*, April 17, 2022, https://www.chicagotribune.com/2022/04/17/black-firefighters-still-make-up-only-15-of-the-chicago-fire-department-i-dont-want-to-talk-about-racism-what-are-we-going-to-do-to-change-it/.
54. Maha Chehlaoui in discussion with the author, January 2024.

55. Color of Change, *Normalizing Injustice: The Dangerous Misrepresentations That Define Television's Scripted Crime Drama* (Color of Change, 2020), 33.
56. Color of Change, *Normalizing Injustice*, 11.
57. Jason George in discussion with the author, September 2023.
58. Jenny Jue in discussion with the author, July 2023.
59. The Nielsen Company, *The Global Black Audience: Shaping the Future of Media* (The Nielsen Company, 2024), 6.
60. Writers Guild of America West, *The 2007 Hollywood Writers Report: Whose Stories Are We Telling?* (WGAW, 2007), 16.
61. Lopez, 24.
62. Darnell M. Hunt, *The State of Career Advancement for Diverse Hollywood Writers: Surveying Pitfalls and Best Practices* (WGAW, 2019), 11–12.
63. Think Tank For Inclusion & Equity, Behind the Scenes: The State Of Inclusion And Equity In TV Writers Rooms (TTIE, 2019), 17.
64. Hunt, *The State of Career Advancement*, 16.
65. Christie D'Zurilla, "CBS Announces Diversity Overhaul of Writers Rooms and Script-Development Program," *Los Angeles Times*, July 13, 2020, https://www.latimes.com/entertainment-arts/tv/story/2020-07-13/cbs-racial-diversity-effort-writers-development-bipoc.
66. Shawn Ryan in discussion with the author, May 2023.
67. Gene Maddaus, "CBS Defends Diversity Hiring on *SEAL Team* from 'Anti-White Discrimination' Suit," *Variety*, May 23, 2024, https://variety.com/2024/tv/news/cbs-seal-team-diversity-hiring-brian-beneker-lawsuit-1236015143/.
68. Lynette Rice, "Altered Reality," *Entertainment Weekly*, February 2, 2022, https://ew.com/tv/cbs-diversity-survivor-big-brother/.
69. Fred Berner in discussion with the author, July 2022.
70. Shireen Razack in discussion with the author, January 2024.
71. Fredrick Kotto in discussion with the author, August 2024.
72. Thomas.
73. Lesley Goldberg, "*Grey's Anatomy* Showrunner Krista Vernoff Inks ABC Studios Overall Deal," *The Hollywood Reporter*, January 22, 2019, https://www.hollywoodreporter.com/tv/tv-news/greys-anatomy-showrunner-krista-vernoff-inks-abc-studios-deal-1178067/.
74. Joe Otterson, "*Grey's Anatomy, Station 19* Showrunner Krista Vernoff Renews Overall Deal with ABC Signature," *Variety*, March 25, 2021, https://variety.com/2021/tv/news/krista-vernoff-overall-deal-abc-signature-1234938174/.
75. Raggs.
76. Razack.
77. WGAW, *2013*, 10.

78. Kira VandenBrande in discussion with the author, February 2024.
79. Lopez, 41.
80. Lopez, 52.
81. Kristen Schilt, "AM/FM Activism: Taking National Media Tools to a Local Level," *Journal of Gay and Lesbian Social Services* 16, no. 3 (2003): 184.
82. Mikey O'Connell, "How One Writers Room Is Rethinking Policing on TV," *The Hollywood Reporter*, December 7, 2020, https://www.hollywoodreporter.com/tv/tv-news/how-one-writers-room-is-rethinking-policing-on-tv-4101100/.
83. O'Connell.
84. Barb Friend in discussion with the author, January 2024.
85. Green.
86. "About Us," Geena Davis Institute, accessed July 1, 2024, https://geenadavisinstitute.org/about-us/.
87. Elizabeth Kilpatrick in discussion with the author, January 2024.
88. Hunt, *2005*, 5.
89. Evan Allgood, "Diary of a Patient Suffering from the Woke-Mind Virus," *New Yorker*, May 5, 2023, https://www.newyorker.com/humor/daily-shouts/diary-of-a-patient-suffering-from-the-woke-mind-virus; Kathryn Cramer Brownell, "Hollywood Has Always Been Political. And It Hasn't Always Been Liberal," *Washington Post*, March 2, 2018, https://www.washingtonpost.com/outlook/hollywood-has-always-been-political-and-it-hasnt-always-been-liberal/2018/03/02/5e8456c2-1d8e-11e8-9de1-147dd2df3829_story.html.

Chapter 2 Early BLM Cop Shows (2013-2020)

1. Todd Gitlin, *Inside Prime Time* (University of California Press, 2000), 254; Sue Turnbull, *TV Crime Drama* (Edinburgh University Press, 2014), 80.
2. Laurena Bernabo, "Copaganda and Post-Floyd TVPD: Broadcast Television's Response to Policing in 2020," *Journal of Communication* 72, no. 4 (2022): 489; Jonathan Nichols-Pethick, *TV Cops: The Contemporary American Television Police Drama* (Routledge, 2012), 17.
3. Rob C. Mawby, "Completing the 'Half-Formed Picture?' Media Images of Policing," in *Criminal Visions: Media Representations of Crime and Justice*, ed. Paul Mason (Willam Publishing, 2003), 220; Nichols-Pethick, 112.
4. Robert Reiner, "Romantic Realism: Policing and the Media," in *Core Issues in Policing* (2nd ed.), ed. Frank Leishman, Barry Loveday, and Stephen Savage (Longman, 2000), 62.
5. David Simon, "Letter to HBO," introduction to *The Wire: Truth Be Told*, ed. Rafael Alvarez (Canongate Books, 2009), 36.

6. Rick Porter, "TV Long View: How Much Network TV Depends on Cop Shows," *The Hollywood Reporter*, June 20, 2020, https://www.hollywoodreporter.com/tv/tv-news/heres-how-network-tv-depends-cop-shows-1299504/; Will Thorne, "Cop Shows Under the Microscope," *Variety*, June 16, 2020, 18.
7. Scott Frank, "Reel Reality: Science Consultants in Hollywood," *Science as Culture* 12, no. 4 (2003): 440.
8. Frank, 428.
9. Jessica L. Davis, Gianna Savoie, and Nancy Longnecker, "Science, Fiction, and Santa Claus: Hollywood Creator and Consultant Perceptions of Fictional Science in Film and Television," *Frontiers in Communication* 8 (2023): 11.
10. Davis et al., 11.
11. Fredrick Kotto in discussion with the author, August 2024.
12. Alex Edwards, "*Brooklyn Nine-Nine* as Copaganda: A Critical Analysis," *Medium*, August 27, 2020, https://medium.com/@ohgodscrewthis/brooklyn-nine-nine-as-copaganda-a-critical-analysis-6cca54cae7f8; Constance Grady, "How 70 Years of Cop Shows Taught Us to Valorize the Police," *Vox*, April 12, 2021, https://www.vox.com/culture/22375412/police-show-procedurals-hollywood-history-dragnet-keystone-cops-brooklyn-nine-nine-wire-blue-bloods; Tatiana Siegel, "Can Hollywood Really Quit the Force?" *The Hollywood Reporter*, July 1, 2020, 38.
13. Frank, 448; Amanda Green in discussion with the author, August 2021.
14. Frank, 448.
15. Michael Brandt in discussion with the author, July 2023.
16. Frank, 443.
17. Green.
18. Brandt.
19. Kotto.
20. Alexi Hawley in discussion with the author, April 2023.
21. Philip J. Lane, "The Existential Condition of Television Crime Drama," *Journal of Popular Culture* 34, no. 4 (2001): 137.
22. John Sumser, *Morality and Social Order in Television Crime Drama* (McFarland, 1996), 155.
23. Lane, 139.
24. Nichols-Pethick, 75.
25. Billy Finkelstein in discussion with the author, July 2023.
26. Concepción Cascajosa Virino, "The Derivation of a Television Crime Drama," in *Interrogating The Shield*, ed. Nicholas Ray (Syracuse University Press, 2012), 18.
27. Nichols-Pethick, 104.
28. E. Deirdre Pribram, "Viewer Discretion Advised: Moral and Emotional Codes in *NYPD Blue*," *Creative Screenwriting* 4, no. 4 (1997): 104.

29. Rovin R. Means Coleman and Jasmine Nicole Cobb, "*Training Day* and *The Shield*: Evil Cops and the Taint of Blackness," in *The Changing Face of Evil in Film and Television*, ed. Martin F. Norden (Brill, 2007), 102.
30. David Milch and Bill Clark, *True Blue: The Real Stories Behind "NYPD Blue"* (Willliam Morrow and Company, Inc., 1995), 55.
31. Kotto.
32. Laura Schiff, "Maestro in Blue," *Creative Screenwriting* (1997): 5.
33. Nichols-Pethick, 110.
34. Milch and Clark, 184.
35. Marc Ouellette, "'It'll Pass': *NYPD Blue*'s Sipowicz and Mundane Masculinity," *Universitas* 2, no. 2 (2006): 1.
36. Niceole Levy in discussion with the author, July 2023.
37. Jason P. Vest, *The Wire, Deadwood, Homicide, and NYPD Blue: Violence Is Power* (Santa Praeger, 2010), 77.
38. Vest, 78.
39. David Simon, "The Reporter 1: Cops Killers and Crispy Critters," *The Audacity of Despair: Collected Prose, Links and Occasional Venting from David Simon*, November 1, 1992, https://davidsimon.com/the-reporter-i-cops-killers-and-crispy-critters/.
40. Vest, 79.
41. Vest, 84.
42. Vest, 83.
43. Vest, 84; Nichols-Pethick, 76.
44. Nichols-Pethick, 76.
45. Vest, 82.
46. Douglas L. Howard, "*The Shield*: Family Meeting," in *Television Finales: From "Howdy Doody" to "Girls"*, ed. Douglas L. Howard and David Bianculllo (Syracuse University Press, 2018), 324; Nicholas Ray, "Introduction: Trees Falling," in *Interrogating "The Shield"*, 6.
47. Howard, 326, 325.
48. Shawn Ryan in discussion with the author, May 2023.
49. Color of Change, *Normalizing Injustice: The Dangerous Misrepresentations That Define Television's Scripted Crime Genre* (The USC Annenberg Norman Lear Center, 2020), 35.
50. Kieran Fisher, "Why *Blue Bloods* is 'Copaganda' According to YouTube and Reddit," *Looper*, August 18, 2023, https://www.looper.com/1370144/bluebloods-copaganda-youtube-reddit/.
51. Laura Hudson, "Breath Easily, White America," *Slate*, December 30, 2014, https://slate.com/culture/2014/12/blue-bloods-starring-tom-selleck-the-nypd-white-viewers-and-black-new-yorkers.html.

52. Hudson.
53. Hudson.
54. Green.
55. Fred Berner in discussion with the author, July 2022.
56. Norberto Barba in discussion with the author, July 2022.
57. Neil Landau, *The TV Showrunner's Roadmap* (2nd ed.) (Routledge, 2022), xix; Michael Newman and Elana Levine, *Legitimating Television: Media Convergence and Cultural Status* (Routledge, 2012), 39.
58. Newman and Levine, 57.
59. Muriel Cantor, *The Hollywood TV Producer: His Work and His Audience* (Basic Books, 1971), 49.
60. Horace Newcomb and Robert Alley, *The Producer's Medium: Conversations with Creators of American TV* (Oxford University Press, 1983), xii.
61. Pierre Bourdieu, *Distinction* (Harvard University Press, 1979), 325.
62. Daniel Herbert, Amanda Lotz, and Aswin Punathambekar, *Media Industry Studies* (Polity, 2020), 48.
63. Mark Banks, "Moral Economy and Cultural Work," *Sociology* 40, no. 3 (2006): 456.
64. Aaron Rahsaan Thomas in discussion with the author, July 2022.
65. Hawley.
66. Thomas.
67. Hawley.
68. Ryan.
69. Brandt.
70. Thomas.
71. Ryan.
72. Hawley.
73. Brandt.
74. Alyssa Rosenberg, "In Pop Culture, There Are No Bad Police Shootings," *Washington Post*, October 26, 2016, https://www.washingtonpost.com/sf/opinions/2016/10/26/in-pop-culture-there-are-no-bad-police-shootings/.
75. Hawley.
76. Newman and Levine, 48.
77. Color of Change.
78. Hawley.

Chapter 3 Post-Floyd TVPD

1. Alexi Hawley in discussion with the author, April 2023.
2. "About Color of Change," Color of Change, accessed August 4, 2023, https://colorofchange.org/about/.

3. Color of Change, 8.
4. Amity Paye in discussion with the author, September 2022.
5. Color of Change, 32.
6. Color of Change, 11.
7. Talicia Raggs in discussion with the author, September 2022.
8. Color of Change, 32.
9. Color of Change, 8.
10. John Behring in discussion with the author, August 2022.
11. Fred Berner in discussion with the author, July 2022.
12. Jann Turner in discussion with the author, September 2022.
13. Dominic Patten, "*Blue Bloods* EP Kevin Wade on Tonight's Season 11 Debut, Whoopi Goldberg, Police Brutality, & Pandemic Production," *Deadline*, December 4, 2020, https://deadline.com/2020/12/blue-bloods-spoilers-recap-coronavirus-whoopi-goldberg-season-debut-kevin-wade-interview-police-cbs-1234649887/.
14. Hawley.
15. Shawn Ryan in discussion with the author, May 2023.
16. Aaron Rahsaan Thomas in discussion with the author, July 2022.
17. Norberto Barba in discussion with the author, September 2022.
18. Raggs.
19. Thomas.
20. Hawley.
21. Patten.
22. Patten.
23. Benjamin Bowling, Robert Reiner, and James Sheptycki, *The Politics of the Police*, 5th ed. (Oxford University Press, 2019); Simon Holdaway, *Black Police Associations: An Analysis of Race and Ethnicity within Constabularies* (Oxford University Press, 2009), 176.
24. Bowling et al., 178; Janet Foster, Tim Newburn, and Anna Souhami, *Assessing the Impact of the Stephen Lawrence Inquiry* (Home Office, 2005), 37; Coretta Phillips and Ben Bowling, "Ethnicities, Racism, Crime and Criminal Justice," in *The Oxford Handbook of Criminology*, ed. Alison Liebling, Shadd Maruna, and Lesley McAra (Oxford University Press, 2017), 206; Wesley G. Skogan and Kathleen Frydl, *Fairness and Effectiveness in Policing: The Evidence* (National Academies Press, 2004), 312.
25. Bethan Loftus, *Police Culture in a Changing World* (Oxford University Press, 2009), 28.
26. Loftus, 33; Janet Foster, "'It Might Have Been Incompetent, But It Wasn't Racist': Murder Detectives' Perceptions of the Lawrence Inquiry and Its Impact on Homicide Investigation in London," *Policing and Society* 18, no. 2 (2008): 110.

27. Arjay Smith in discussion with the author, October 2023.
28. Thomas.
29. L. Scott Silverii, *Cop Culture: Why Good Cops Go Bad* (CRC Press, 2014), 6.
30. Bowling et al., 174.
31. Bowling et al., 174.
32. Maurice Punch, "Rotten Orchards: 'Pestilence,' Police Misconduct and System Failure" *Policing and Society* 13, no. 2 (2003): 172.
33. John P. Crank, *Understanding Police Culture*, 2nd ed. (Anderson Publishing, 2004), 258; Skogan and Frydl, 312.
34. Foster et al., 37.
35. Loftus, 33; Foster, 110.
36. Jonathan Nichols-Pethick, *TV Cops: The Contemporary American Television Police Drama* (Routledge, 2012), 112.
37. Horace Newcomb and Paul M. Hirsch, "Television as a Cultural Forum," *Quarterly Review of Film Studies* 8 (1983): 49.
38. Todd Gitlin, "Prime Time Ideology: The Hegemonic Process in Television Entertainment," *Social Problems* 26, no. 3 (1979): 254.
39. Amanda D. Lotz, "Using 'Network' Theory in the Post-Network Era: Fictional 9/11 US Television Discourse as a 'Cultural Forum,'" *Screen* 45, no. 4 (2004): 429.
40. Alex Edwards, "*Brooklyn Nine-Nine* as Copaganda: A Critical Analysis," Medium, August 27, 2020, https://medium.com/@ohgodscrewthis/brooklyn-nine-nine-as-copaganda-a-critical-analysis-6cca54cae7f8.
41. Ana-Christina Ramón, Michael Tran, and Darnell Hunt, *Hollywood Diversity Report 2022: A New, Post-Pandemic Normal?* (UCLA, 2022), 15; Ramón, Michael Tran, and Darnell Hunt, *Hollywood Diversity Report 2023: Exclusivity in Progress* (UCLA, 2023), 17.

Chapter 4 Beyond the Police Procedural

1. Brandy Monk-Payton, "From 'Relevance' to 'Reckoning' or, Channeling Black Lives Matter on TV—Part One," *Flow*, October 18, 2021, https://www.flowjournal.org/2021/10/from-relevance-to-reckoning-part-one/.
2. Caroline Framke, "*The Carmichael Show* Revives, Challenges, and Reenergizes the Very Special Episode," *Vox*, March 9, 2016, https://www.vox.com/2015/9/9/9297113/carmichael-show-nbc-review.
3. Monk-Payton.
4. Katie Storey, "*New Girl*'s Lamorne Morris Praises Show Writers for Addressing Police Brutality After He Started to Feel 'Weird' About Winston Being a Cop," *Metro*, June 3, 2020, https://metro.co.uk/2020/06/03/new-girl-lamorne-morris-felt-weird-winston-cop-praises-writers-address-police-brutality-12799987/.

5. Megan Angelo, "*New Girl* Star Lamorne Morris on Writing This Week's Story Line About Race and the Police," *New York Times*, April 7, 2015, https://archive.nytimes.com/artsbeat.blogs.nytimes.com/2015/04/07/new-girl-interview-winston-lamorne-morris-race/?_r=0.
6. Angelo.
7. Framke.
8. Daniel Fienberg, "*Black-ish* Boss on Tackling Police Brutality: 'I Didn't Want to Politicize the Show,'" *The Hollywood Reporter*, February 24, 2016, https://www.hollywoodreporter.com/tv/tv-news/black-ish-boss-police-brutality-869397/.
9. Daniel Feinberg, "'black-ish' Boss on Tackling Police Brutallity: 'I Didn't Want to Politicize the Show,'" *The Hollywood Reporter,* February 24, 2016, https://www.hollywoodreporter.com/tv/tv-news/black-ish-boss-police-brutality-869397/.
10. Michael Schur in discussion with the author, June 2023.
11. Alyssa Rosenberg, "*Brooklyn Nine-Nine*'s Dan Goor on Cop Comedy, Community Policing and NYPD History," *Washington Post*, October 24, 2016, https://www.washingtonpost.com/news/act-four/wp/2016/10/24/brooklyn-nine-nines-dan-goor-on-cop-comedy-community-policing-and-nypd-history/.
12. Rosenberg, "*Brooklyn Nine-Nine*."
13. Rosenberg. "*Brooklyn Nine-Nine*."
14. Erin Banco, Spencer Ackerman, and Asawin Suebsaeng, "'Uncomfortable Mission': Pentagon Tries to Retreat from Trump's Call to 'Dominate' Protests," *The Daily Beast*, June 4, 2020, https://www.thedailybeast.com/pentagon-tries-to-retreat-from-trumps-call-to-dominate-protests.
15. Alyssa Rosenberg, "Showrunner Dan Goor on the *Brooklyn Nine-Nine* Stop-and-Frisk Episode and the Talk," *Washington Post,* May 3, 2017, https://www.washingtonpost.com/news/act-four/wp/2017/05/03/showrunner-dan-goor-on-the-brooklyn-nine-nine-stop-and-frisk-episode-and-the-talk/.
16. Alex Edwards, "*Brooklyn Nine-Nine* as Copaganda: A Critical Analysis," Medium, August 27, 2020, https://medium.com/@ohgodscrewthis/brooklyn-nine-nine-as-copaganda-a-critical-analysis-6cca54cae7f8.
17. Edwards.
18. Vivian Kane, "*Brooklyn Nine-Nine* Threw Out 4 Episodes and Will Reportedly Rework Its Whole Direction in the Wake of Police Protests," *The Mary Sue*, June 24, 2020, https://www.themarysue.com/brooklyn-nine-nine-changing-directions/.
19. "Terry Crews Says *Brooklyn Nine-Nine* New Episodes Are Scrapped: 'We Have to Start Over,'" *AccessOnline*, June 23, 2020, https://www.accessonline.com/articles/terry-crews-says-brooklyn-nine-nine-new-episodes-are-scrapped-we-have-to-start-over.

20. Maria Elena Fernandez, "Why Did *Magnum P.I.*'s Showrunner Think He Didn't Hire a Latinx Writer?" *Vulture*, August 28, 2018, https://www.vulture.com/2018/08/magnum-pi-peter-lenkov-latinx-writer.html; Javier Grillo-Marxuach, "A Latino TV Writer Calls B.S. on Hollywood's Diversity Excuses," *The Hollywood Reporter*, August 16, 2018, https://www.hollywoodreporter.com/news/general-news/latino-producer-responds-magnum-pi-flap-stop-avoiding-diversity-1134562/.
21. Fernandez; Grillo-Marxuach.
22. Nicole Sperling, "Writers Mutiny at *All Rise*, the Rare CBS Show with a Black Female Lead," *New York Times*, August 20, 2020, https://www.nytimes.com/2020/08/20/business/media/all-rise-cbs-writers.html.
23. Vlada Gelman, "*New Amsterdam* Preview: Max Takes on Systemic Racism at the Hospital," *TVLine*, April 5, 2021, https://tvline.com/interviews/new-amsterdam-spoilers-season-3-episode-6-systemic-racism-1234657160/.
24. Kristen J. Warner, *The Cultural Politics of Colorblind TV Casting* (Routledge, 2015), 69.
25. Warner, *Colorblind TV Casting*, 13.
26. Kiley Donovan in discussion with the author, August 2021.
27. Kristen J. Warner, "The Racial Logic of *Grey's Anatomy*: Shonda Rhimes and Her 'Post-Civil Rights, Post-Feminist' Series," *Television & New Media* 16, no. 17 (2015): 636.
28. Jann Turner in discussion with the author, September 2022.
29. Lesley Goldberg, "Why *Grey's Anatomy* Just Overtly Tackled Unconscious Bias," *The Hollywood Reporter*, January 18, 2018, https://www.hollywoodreporter.com/tv/tv-news/why-greys-anatomy-just-overtly-tackled-unconscious-bias-1078509/.
30. Samantha Highfill, "*All American* Boss Discusses Powerful Black Lives Matter Episode," *Entertainment Weekly*, April 26, 2021, https://ew.com/tv/all-american-black-lives-matter-episode-nkechi-okoro-carroll/.
31. Sperling.
32. Nellie Andreeva, "*All Rise* Creator/EP Greg Spottiswood Fired by Warner Bros. TV Over Misconduct Allegations, Dropped by APA." *Deadline*, March 24, 2021, https://deadline.com/2021/03/all-rise-creator-executive-producer-greg-spottiswood-fired-misconduct-allegations-offensive-comments-writers-room-1234721403/; Sperling.
33. Sperling.
34. Sperling.
35. Andreeva; Sperling.
36. Andreeva.
37. Laurena Bernabo, "Expanding Television's Cultural Forum in the Digital Era: Prime Time Television, Twitter, and Black Lives Matter," *Journal of Broadcasting & Electronic Media* 63, no. 1 (2019): 85.

38. Donovan.
39. Jason George in discussion with the author, September 2023.
40. Donovan.
41. George.
42. Angela Harvey in discussion with the author, July 2023.
43. George.
44. Donovan.
45. Daryn Okada in discussion with the author, August 2022.
46. George.
47. Donovan.

Chapter 5 Beyond 2020

1. Color of Change, *Normalizing Injustice: The Dangerous Misrepresentations That Define Television's Scripted Crime Genre* (The USC Annenberg Norman Lear Center, 2020), 49.
2. Nellie Andreeva, "*Walker, Texas Ranger* Reboot Starring Jared Padalecki Lands at the CW," *Deadline*, October 11, 2019, https://deadline.com/2019/10/walker-texas-ranger-reboot-starring-jared-padalecki-the-cw-reimagening-chuck-norris-1202758080/.
3. Nellie Andreeva, "Christopher Miloni as *SVU* Character Elliot Stabler to Headline New Dick Wolf Drama Series for NBC," *Deadline*, March 31, 2020, https://deadline.com/2020/03/christopher-meloni-returns-new-dick-wolf-series-elliot-stabler-nbc-law-order-svu-1202896323/.
4. Rick Porter, "Cops, Firefighters, Lawyers Score CBS Series Pickups," *The Hollywood Reporter*, May 12, 2022, https://www.hollywoodreporter.com/tv/tv-news/cbs-picks-up-dramas-east-new-york-fire-country-so-help-me-todd-1235145735/.
5. Nellie Andreeva, "*East New York* Canceled by CBS After One Season," *Deadline*, May 8, 2023, https://deadline.com/2023/05/east-new-york-canceled-cbs-one-season-1235357988/.
6. Joe Otterson, "*Will Trent* Ordered to Series at ABC for Midseason 2022–2023," *Variety*, August 8, 2022, https://variety.com/2022/tv/news/will-trent-abc-series-1235335901/.
7. Billy Finkelstein in discussion with the author, July 2023.
8. Angie Han, "*East New York* Review: CBS Series Illustrates the Limits of Network Police Procedurals," *The Hollywood Reporter*, October 2, 2022, https://www.hollywoodreporter.com/tv/tv-reviews/east-new-york-cbs-1235230345/.
9. Finkelstein.
10. Daniel Thomsen in discussion with the author, July 2023.

11. Thomsen.
12. Thomsen.
13. Thomsen.
14. Barb Friend in discussion with the author, January 2024.
15. Angela Harvey in discussion with the author, July 2023.
16. Clayton Davis, "Black Women Executives Are Exiting Studio Leadership Posts and Hollywood's Doing Nothing About It," *Variety*, July 5, 2023, https://variety.com/2023/film/columns/black-women-hollywood-diversity-dei-executives-leaving-1235660463/.
17. Raquel Harris and Sharon Knolle, "Hollywood's Diversity Exec Exodus Eposes Industry-Wide Dysfunction—What Is the Path Forward?" *The Wrap*, July 17, 2023, https://www.thewrap.com/hollywood-dei-executives/.
18. Harris and Knolle.
19. Winston Cho, "Hollywood Diversity Initiatives May Be Challenged After Supreme Court Affirmative Action Ruling," *The Hollywood Reporter*, July 14, 2023, https://www.hollywoodreporter.com/business/business-news/dei-supreme-court-affirmative-action-hollywood-1235532273/.
20. Gene Maddaus, "CBS Defends Diversity Hiring on *SEAL Team* from 'Anti-White Discrimination' Suit," *Variety*, May 23, 2024, https://variety.com/2024/tv/news/cbs-seal-team-diversity-hiring-brian-beneker-lawsuit-1236015143/.
21. Cho.
22. Malcolm Venable, "How Shondaland's Inclusion Initiatives Are Changing Hollywood and Lives," *Shondaland*, June 14, 2023, https://www.shondaland.com/inspire/a44120586/how-shondalands-inclusion-initiatives-are-changing-hollywood-and-lives/.
23. Maddaus.
24. Aaron Rahsaan Thomas in discussion with the author, July 2022.
25. Rebecca Sun, "DEI Departments May Be Closing, But These 40 Hollywood Heavyweights Are Still Agitating for Change," *The Hollywood Reporter*, September 11, 2024, https://www.hollywoodreporter.com/lists/hollywood-top-forces-for-change-2024/.
26. Jason George in discussion with the author, September 2023.
27. Harvey.
28. Fred Berner in discussion with the author, July 2022.
29. Norberto Barba in discussion with the author, July 2022.
30. Lori Lopez, *Asian American Media Activism: Fighting for Cultural Citizenship* (New York University Press, 2016), 183.

Index

Note: Page numbers in italics refer to figures.

About the Author

LAURENA BERNABO is an assistant professor of entertainment and media studies at the University of Georgia. She earned her PhD and MA from the University of Iowa in communication studies with an emphasis in media history and culture, and her BA from the University of Illinois. She is thrilled to have made a career out of watching and reading, thinking, talking, and writing about television.